Memories of
Lac du Flambeau Elders

Edited by Elizabeth M. Tornes

A Brief History of Waaswaagoning Ojibweg
by Leon Valliere, Jr.

Photographs by Greg Gent

Center for the Study of Upper Midwestern Cultures
901 University Bay Dr.
Madison, Wisconsin 53705

Printed in the United States of America

Memories of the Lac du Flambeau Elders / edited by Elizabeth M. Tornes.
With an introduction by Leon Valliere, Jr.
Photographs by Greg Gent.
ISBN 0-924119-21-7

This book is dedicated with love to my family.

Acknowledgments

This book would not have been completed without the generous assistance of many people, whom it gives me pleasure to thank. First of all, I am very thankful to all the elders who opened their lives and hearts to me: Agnes Archdale, Liza Brown, Gib Chapman, Reva Chapman, Celia Defoe, Billi Mae Chosa, Joe Chosa, Ben Chosa, Josephine Doud, Wanda Brown Hunt, Georgian Kinstedt, Marie Spruce, Delia Smith, Grace Artishon, and Rose Ann Fee. Ningichi-apiitenamaag agow gete chaaya' aag. I have such great respect for these elders. By their word and example, they taught me to appreciate the gift of life.

I would also like to thank all the interviewers, who spoke well and listened carefully: Mildred "Tinker" Schuman, Donnie Carufel, Marilyn Conto, Barb Chosa, Phyllis White, and Verdaine Farmilant. Thanks also to the family members of the elders, who clarified many details in the interviews and provided useful information and at times, photos: Phyllis White, Loretta "Wause" St. Germaine, Leon Valliere, Sr., Susie Poupart, Thurman Bear, Jr., Rose Scott, Jackie Beson, and Gladys Williams. Thanks to Bill Ackley for lending me photos from his collection to use in the book. Thanks to David Grignon, Menominee Historic Preservation Director, for instructing us on oral history, and to Alan Moore, Sr., editor of the *Lac du Flambeau News*, for editing the newspaper series. Thanks, too, to Pat Hrabik-Sebby, Kelly Jackson, Melinda Young, and Cindy Stiles of the Lac du Flambeau Historic Preservation Office for historical information. Thanks especially to my co-workers on the book, Leon (Boycee) Valliere for his excellent historical introduction, and Greg Gent for the beautiful portraits of the elders.

I would like to acknowledge the Wisconsin Humanities Council for the original grant for the Lac du Flambeau Oral History project and Beloit College for a Keefer grant that extended it. I would also like to thank the Lac du Flambeau Cultural and Historical Society for grant support that allowed Leon, Greg, and me to complete the work on the book.

I am very grateful to Joe Chosa for his friendship through the years, his teaching, and all his generous help with the Ojibwe language, in the book and in life. I am also grateful to Joe Salmons of the Center for Upper Midwestern Cultural Studies for all his editorial assistance, and to Mark Louden, Eric Platt, and Kimberly Miller for their hard work on preparing the manuscript for publication. Thanks also to Patty Leow, who read the manuscript early on and gave us some valuable input. Thanks also to Dave Myler for scanning and editing many photos for the book, and to Chris Anthony and Nina Isham at the George W. Brown, Jr. Museum and Cultural Center for help with the historical photos.

Finally, I would like to thank Elisa Farmilant, Peter Hanson, Anne Jones, and Rand Valentine who helped in many ways with the manuscript and were a constant support during the preparation of the book. Thank you for your friendship and kindness. Miigwich to all those who have helped and supported me in the creation of this book.

Contents

Editor's Introduction
by Elizabeth Tornes

"Apane waaswaaganing anishinaabeg ogii-manaaji'aawaan gete anishinaabeg. Gete anishinaabeg apane ogii-gikinoo'amaawaan oshki'ayaa'aag gaye oniijaanisiiwaan ge-izhi-bimaadiziiwaad niigaan gakeya. Gete anishinaabeg apane ogii-wiikwajitoonaawaa da gikinoo'amaawaad agiw epichi apiitendaagwak gwayak mino anishinaabe bimaadiziwin."

"The Lac du Flambeau people have always respected their elders. The elders have always taught young people and children how to live their lives in the future. The elders have always tried to instruct them to highly value the good Anishinaabe way of life."

—Ozaawaabik (Joe Chosa), interviewed in this collection

The Lac du Flambeau Ojibwe people have always treasured their elders. They are the keepers of the wisdom of the Anishinaabeg, the language, customs, values, religious beliefs, and way of life that have been handed down for generations. The Ojibwe say that the elders have walked down a long road and gathered a great deal of knowledge on their journey, and for this reason we should always respect them.

I feel lucky to have gotten to know these elders through my work on the Lac du Flambeau Oral History Project, where this collection originated, and grateful to have the opportunity to preserve some of their words. This project took me personally down a long path that has ended in Lac du Flambeau, where I live today. In the early 1990s I was teaching at Beloit College, coming up to the reservation to visit friends. I loved the area and its hauntingly beautiful woods and lakes, and eventually I bought a house here, spending summers and vacation times. I learned that Ojibwe language classes were being taught at the Niijii Center, formerly the boys' dormitory of the Bureau of Indian Affairs boarding school. (*Niijii* means 'friend' in Ojibwe.) The class was an important component of the Family Circles Program, a curriculum designed to strengthen families by bringing back traditional ways of parenting and emphasizing traditional values. I began attending these classes, offered every Monday and Wednesday evening, and it was there that I met three remarkable elders: Reva Chapman, Joe Chosa, and Cecilia Defoe.

Joe, Reva, and Celia taught the Ojibwe language and also told many stories—about life in "the old days," hunting and fishing, picking berries, making rice and maple sugar, and about animals and the earth. Stories about growing up with the Ojibwe language and the traditional way of life that was so much a part of their lives, it seemed to be as much a part of them as the air they breathed. They also talked about more painful topics: the boarding school, the loss of land, the loss of the Ojibwe language and traditional ways, and persecution by non-Indians. These were stories of loss but also stories of hope for the future. Their teaching was part of a larger movement to bring back Anishinaabe customs, beliefs, and values, and to restore cultural identity in Lac du Flambeau.

There was a great deal of verbal artistry in their stories and much humor, which fascinated me, as it did the rest of the class. I had been reading a good deal of oral history at Beloit, teaching it as part of my Native American literature class, and was interested in putting these ideas to practical application. Listening to these elders' stories, which were an integral part of their teaching, I felt inspired to preserve them and the stories of other elders as well.

Language and communication have always been among the recorded strengths of the Ojibwe people: transcripts of speeches, treaty negotiations, and other documents have shown a centuries-old lineage of highly skilled Ojibwe orators. The oral tradition has always been the primary method of passing on knowledge among Native peoples of North America. Since time immemorial, stories have served the Ojibwe people as educational tools, to instruct young people about traditional culture, values, and beliefs, and also as historical records, preserving family and tribal history. In the Lac du Flambeau Oral History Project I hoped to tap those oral traditions to create a living history that might otherwise be lost. I received a grant from the Wisconsin Humanities Council in 1995 to support the project, and was released from teaching for the spring semester 1996 to carry it out. The project had three main objectives: first, to train tribal members to interview elders, recording the interviews on audio cassettes; second, to transcribe the tapes and publish the edited transcriptions, along with photographs of the elders, as a series in the tribal newspaper, the *Lac du Flambeau News*; and finally, to publish the elders' interviews and photos as a book collection. This publication realizes the final dream of the project.

The first step involved training tribal members to interview elders. The project was designed this way so that the relatives or friends of an elder could help him or her feel more relaxed in the interview, as well as allow elders to talk about things important to them that might not be communicated to someone they did not know. On January 6, 1996, we held the interview-training workshop in the basement of the Lac du Flambeau Museum. It was twenty-five degrees below zero, a bone chilling but sunny morning, and despite the frigid temperatures ten people turned out for the workshop. David Grignon, historic preservation director for the Menominee Tribe, presented us with a list of the questions (included in the appendix) that had been used for the Menominee oral history project and served as a model for ours. He gave us much helpful guidance on conducting interviews with elders. Dick Brooks, then program director for WOJB-FM on the Lac Courte Oreilles reservation, also instructed us in interviewing techniques, and in the use of the audio recording equipment. We also considered producing the interviews as a series of radio programs, but for various reasons this did not materialize. The Lac du Flambeau Elders Resource Council—Joe, Celia, and Reva—suggested adding, "What advice would you give to a young person who wants to live a good life?" at the end of the questions: This was an excellent suggestion, which yielded gems of wisdom from the elders interviewed.

The next step was to conduct "pre-interviews." Each interviewer and I (who served as sound engineer, doing the recording) met with the elder, presented him or her with a tobacco offering and a gift—a traditional way of requesting an elder's assistance—and explained the scope and purpose of the interview. We reviewed the questions and discussed other topics the elder might like to talk about in the interview. Finally, we conducted the interview at the elder's home. The interviewers were very good at making the elders feel comfortable. They were respectful and sensitive, following the elder's cues in their questions and paying attention to their need to take breaks or end the session.

The main goal of the interviewing method was to allow the interviewers and interviewees the flexibility to diverge from the list of questions and branch off into any topic either one of them felt to be of interest, thus allowing tribal members to produce those stories that most interested them. In this way I hoped that the oral histories would reflect an Ojibwe perspective, not that of an outsider. At times elders requested another interview, as did the interviewer. As a result, some elder interviews went on for a total of two or three hours. Two sets of sisters, Liza Brown and Agnes Archdale, and Grace Artishon and Delia Smith, chose to be interviewed together (in this case I indicate the name before each response, to identify who is speaking). The elders talked in great detail about many things: life at the boarding school, the Depression, the CCC camp, World War II, resorts, the railroad, dances, tourism, downtown Flambeau, religious ceremonies, medicine men, trapping, guiding, hunting, fishing, gathering berries, making wild rice and maple sugar. Interviewers took notes when a story or topic that interested them came up, sometimes returning to them later.

The first few questions asked for biographical information: questions about the elder's Indian name and clan and about names of family members, schooling, influential people, and childhood memories. Questions then shifted to more general ones such as "How did people make their living?" and "What changes have you seen in your lifetime on the reservation?" The question "What celebrations or ceremonies do you remember?" elicited memories of Indian dances and religious ceremonies as well as memories of going door-to-door to shake hands and visit with neighbors on New Year's Day. Questions about schooling brought forth many painful memories of the BIA boarding school era in Lac du Flambeau. During this period, from 1895 to 1934, Indian children were essentially kidnapped from their homes, separated from their families, and forced to live at school where they ate, worked, and marched in a military-style regimen, sleeping in unheated dormitories that were locked at night to prevent escape. As Celia Defoe remarked, "They stole our childhood, you might as well say." Children were forbidden to wear traditional clothing and moccasins and instead had to wear European uniforms and shoes and to cut their hair short. They were severely punished for practicing their traditional religion and customs or for speaking their native language. Beatings, hair pulling, strapping, and other forms of corporal punishment were not uncommon. The painful stories about this period are abundant in this collection, yet they illustrate a chapter in American history that one rarely finds in history books.

"What do you remember about the Depression years?" elicited a wide range of responses. In some cases elders recalled the difficult poverty of that period, while others believed Lac du Flambeau families were less affected than others by the Depression. Responses ranged from Wanda Hunt's "I just remember being so poor. Seemed like one time all we lived on was potatoes, and meat when we could get it," to Celia Defoe's "I didn't even know (when the Depression was). I asked Reva, 'I don't either,' she said. 'We were never hungry. Because we lived off the land.'"

"During the Depression years, we used to have to skimp," said Josephine Doud. "It was hard to get food. Really hard. But they managed to feed us. My daddy always planted a garden." Ben Chosa recalled, "It was a tough time around here. Although I think we fared better than a lot of the surrounding communities because of the fishing. Like I said, there were fifty guides here, and they were being paid top wages. And it seemed it was the best guiding in the thirties and forties. I don't know why that is, but there was a lot of money people around here."

Liza Brown said she did not feel poor during the Depression: "We never thought of being poor, because we always had something to eat, and the love and care of our folks." Gib Chapman, the oldest person interviewed, responded with a story: "No work, nothing. The government give us sheep and flour and stuff. I must have been six, seven years old when they sent them up here. Molasses, tea, sugar, salt pork, then they come up with them sheep. God, them sheep must have been killed or froze to death out west. Whole sheep . . . I got one of them, I stuck it out there and a dog come along, a couple dogs . . . looked at it, started barking, turn around and run back! (laughs) Yeah, there was hardly no meat on them!"

The final question was, "What advice would you give to young people who want to live a good life?" Responses ranged from advice on being true to yourself and being proud to be Indian to admonitions to stay away from alcohol and drugs, to keep busy, respect elders, and return to traditional Indian ways. Rose Ann Fee advised, "Tell them to do as the old saying goes, 'Don't follow the other person, just follow yourself.'" Georgian Kinstedt urged young people, "Listen to your parents! They're only trying to steer you in the right direction, to enhance your life someday. You learn from that." Joe Chosa asserted, "I think, being an Indian person, that people should be proud of their culture, be proud of their heritage, be proud of the fact that they are Indian people. And I think that there's no reason in the world why a person shouldn't be holding their head up high and show people that." Josephine Doud remarked, "Nowadays some people smoke pot, go out drinking. They need to do something. I'd tell them to get out, keep your mind busy! Just keep busy, I say." In a similar vein Wanda Hunt said, "I think the best thing for young people is to stay in school, stay off drugs, drinks. Because they can always succeed in life if they put their mind to it." Agnes Archdale advised, "Get all the education you can possibly get."

One can see in just these two questions the range and diversity of elders' responses. While there is overlap in the elders' backgrounds and experiences, each response is highly individualized, both in content and style. Throughout this collection, one gets a vivid sense of a strong voice and a dynamic personality behind each narrative. This is one characteristic of Ojibwe elders that has always struck me: their amazing vitality. Some of the elderly ladies interviewed here participated in healing ceremonies that lasted long into the night; some of the elderly men still pole a canoe and knock rice all day long in the fall or go spearing through the ice in the bitter cold of midwinter. Another striking quality is their sense of humor, as Gib Chapman's quote illustrates: It is a quality that has helped them, perhaps, to survive against great odds, along with the knowledge of how to live in balance with all things and an enduring faith.

Originally the project called for interviewing twenty-five elders in their seventies and eighties, going from the oldest to the youngest, using a list provided by the Lac du Flambeau Enrollment Department. Some elders did not wish to be interviewed, and we respected their wishes. The reality of interviewing elders was that it took much more time than we had expected. It often took several weeks to arrange for a meeting date and time that would be convenient for the elder and interviewer, and it often required two or three visits to go through the list of questions and talk about other areas of interest. Elders, being of more fragile health generally, sometimes became ill, and the interview would have to be postponed. As a result, the whole project, from interviews to transcription, editing to publication, lasted months longer than we had planned, and we interviewed a total of fifteen elders. Occasionally I myself conducted an interview, when a family member was not available, and if the elder knew me and felt comfortable with me. Whenever an interview took place, it always seemed as if the sky had opened up. So much knowledge, so much history, so many vivid memories came from these elders—it seemed that they had been storing it all up for years in their minds and in their hearts to share. They were extremely generous with what they told us and gracious in allowing us to record them, and ultimately, to have the interviews published. Elders' families were also very helpful in arranging the interviews as well as in providing additional biographical information for this publication.

After recording each interview, I transcribed it and took it back to the elder to review it and, if they wished, to edit out any material they did not want published. Once these changes were made, the interview was passed on to the newspaper editors, Alan Moore, Sr., and later Cappy Landin, who edited them for length. Finally, each elder's interview was published in the *Lac du Flambeau News*, along with a photo of the elder taken at the time of the interview. The first interview, Reva Chapman's, appeared in the February 1996 edition and every month thereafter until all fifteen elders' interviews were published.

The Lac du Flambeau community seemed very interested in reading the interviews and getting a glimpse of life on the reservation long ago. Some readers, tribal members living outside of Lac du Flambeau, wrote to the editor and said the interview series was their favorite feature in the paper. People in the community, especially elders, discussed the stories among themselves, comparing them with their own memories of the past. Non-Native people in surrounding communities sometimes approached elders and told them how much they had enjoyed reading a given interview. Reva Chapman told me that someone she had not seen for years approached her in a store in Minocqua, the neighboring town, and praised her interview. The original goals of the project—to preserve tribal history and stimulate its discussion among tribal members as well as to promote understanding of the Lac du Flambeau Ojibwe among outsiders—seemed everywhere in evidence.

Coincidentally, at the time these interviews took place, a sacred site on the reservation, Strawberry Island, was being threatened by development, and the community mobilized to protect it. David Grignon had encouraged us to include questions about places with cultural, spiritual, or historical significance, as they had done in the Menominee oral history project, in order to use information gleaned from the elders to both recognize and preserve those places. We did as he suggested, and many elders told stories about the history and beliefs surrounding Strawberry Island and other sites. These stories and others like them can be used, if necessary, in support of the cultural importance of such places and hopefully to protect them if they are threatened. Such places play an important role in the spiritual, cultural, and historical legacy of the Lac du Flambeau Ojibwe, and the elders' stories make this very clear.

It might be helpful at this point to say something about the transcription process. Oral storytelling is a performative act, and transferring that performance to the written page inevitably flattens it, renders it into a different medium by removing the visual, auditory, and physical dynamics of the speaker/audience interaction that occurs in storytelling. I tried to overcome this in part by capturing the storytelling as much as possible in transcribing the tapes: describing the elder's tone of voice, gestures, sighs, or laughter in parentheses, and using punctuation to give a sense of the tempo of the elder's speech, showing where the elder paused, and for how long. I also included any interjections like "geez," "enit?" or "hina?" (from "ina," an Ojibwe word indicating a question and often carried over into English) and vocalizations, when they occurred. The interviews were transcribed verbatim. Only the questions and comments of the interviewer were omitted in order to create a more flowing narrative and to keep the focus on the elder. I began a new paragraph when the topic shifted and inserted an asterisk to indicate a new section of the interview, usually prompted by a question. When an elder spoke in the Ojibwe language, I transcribed it in the commonly accepted double vowel system of orthography, using the elder's own translation into English whenever possible. When necessary, I consulted with fluent elder Joe Chosa, director of the Ojibwe Language Program, on translating Ojibwe names and phrases into English. If there was uncertainty about the meaning of an Ojibwe name, I left it untranslated rather than risk translating it incorrectly.

It is my hope that these stories and photographs will help preserve a period in the rich history of the people of Lac du Flambeau, as told in their own words, for future generations. I hope that those who read these stories will have a better knowledge and appreciation of how the people of Lac du Flambeau lived through the many changes of the twentieth century: their enduring way of life, beliefs, customs, and ceremonies; their struggles and their triumphs; and especially, their spirit of resilience. I also hope readers will gain a deeper understanding of, and respect for, the Lac du Flambeau Ojibwe people and their way of life. It gives me great pleasure to share the stories of these *gete anishinaabeg* I feel so honored to have known. Above all it is the humanity of these elders that touched me deeply, and I hope we can learn from the life lessons they share with us.

A Brief History of the Waaswaaganing Ojibweg
Lac du Flambeau Chippewa Indians
Gaa-izhiwebak ishkweyaang
by Leon Valliere, Jr.

In 1995 Beth Tornes received a grant from the Wisconsin Humanities Council to capture oral histories from elders residing on the Lac du Flambeau Chippewa Indian Reservation, here in northern Wisconsin. The fifteen stories provided by the elders have an immeasurable value because they:

- represent reflections from a Lac du Flambeau Native Elder point of view;

- provide reservation perspectives on key historical events;

- describe the continuity of Native culture, despite an ever-changing world;

- preserve these unique perspectives for future generations.

To a reader versed in the history of the Wisconsin Chippewa the stories are easily interpreted, but for a reader unfamiliar with this history, some difficulty may arise with specific historical aspects of the Lac du Flambeau Band of Lake Superior Chippewa Indians. A common mistake made by non-Ojibwe language speakers, is the use of "Chippewa."

Those unfamiliar with Ojibwe language mistakenly translated the name of our tribe long ago. *Ojibweg* is the plural form. *Anishinaabeg* is another common term the Ojibweg use to define themselves and other Native people. Often, throughout the Historical Introduction, "the Ojibwe" is used as a collective term.

Within this Historical Introduction I have attempted to organize the vast span of information and time and describe things commonly known to locals. This will allow the reader to understand who was involved, when these events happened, what occurred, where, and some discussion of why. Additionally, a large number of Ojibwe terms and phrases will be featured. A page describing Ojibwe sounds has been provided to assist readers in accurate pronunciation.

Let us begin by identifying a time line and where on the time line these narratives occur. I distinguish four time periods, which include the Pre-European Contact Era, Fur-Trade Era, Treaty-Making Era, and Reservation-Life Era, as they apply to the Lac du Flambeau Ojibwe of Wisconsin.

A time line follows which shows the beginning of these time periods.

←——Pre Contact—Fur Trade—Treaty Making——Reservation Life——Today——→
                1634   1837   1854   2003

It is the Reservation period that is primarily represented in the Lac du Flambeau elder narratives. Within the Reservation-Life Era, key episodes discussed will include: logging, boarding school, the Great Depression, resorts and tourism, and modern times. Recurring themes within each of these episodes include transportation, sustenance, religion, locations, occupations, and leisure. A logical question may be, "If it is merely the Reservation-Life Era discussed in the narratives, why all the other history?" In reply, today's events are based upon the past, and previous episodes in our history continue to have effects today.

It is important for readers to have a larger understanding of historical events prior to the Reservation-Life Era in order to understand the attitudes carried by the contributing elders. Just as the larger society has undergone change over time so has the Lac du Flambeau Reservation.

The list that follows represents merely some key dates in the history of the Lac du Flambeau people. Following each of these key dates, I will explain the historical event marked by that date. These explanations should assist the readers in understanding how these events affected the lives of the contributing elders.

Precontact Era

1492   Columbus arrives after visits from Vikings

Fur-Trade Era

1634   Frenchman Jean Nicolet arrives in what is now called Wisconsin
1680   Ojibwe continue westward to Chequamagon from Sault Ste. Marie
1745   Kiishkiman establishes Waaswaaganing Village later known as Lac du Flambeau
1760   British defeat French at Montreal
1776   Revolutionary War begins as colonists seek independence from British
1812   Americans fight British in War of 1812

Treaty-Making Era

1825   Ojibwe sign treaty with U.S. Government at Prairie Du Chien
1826   Ojibwe sign treaty with U.S. Government at Fond du Lac
1836   Wisconsin becomes a federally recognized territory

1837	Ojibwe sign pine treaty with U.S. Government at Ft. Snelling
1842	Ojibwe sign mineral treaty with U.S. Government at LaPointe
1848	Wisconsin becomes a state
1849	Ojibwe leaders travel to Washington, DC, to oppose removal
1850	Removal Order results in Sandy Lake Episode in Minnesota
1852	Ojibwe leaders travel to Washington, DC, to urge the president to rescind the Removal Order
1854	Ojibwe sign treaty with U.S. Government at LaPointe

Reservation-Life Era

1866	Civil Rights Bill is passed, providing equal rights for all except Native Americans
1874–1877	Government suggests Lac du Flambeau band members make allotment selections
1883	Allotment of reservation land to individuals begins logging
1886	Logging begins within Lac du Flambeau reservation
1887	Congress passes Dawes Act also known as General Allotment Act
1888	Logging operations suspended on-reservation by federal government
1891	Dawes Act amended to allow leasing and contract logging
1892	Logging operations resume within Lac du Flambeau Reservation
1894	Sawmill built at Lac du Flambeau
1895	Boarding school established at Lac du Flambeau
1903–1934	Dawes Act impacts allotments on Lac du Flambeau Reservation
1906	Burke Act allows Indian agents to define competency of allottees
1914–1918	Lac du Flambeau Band members volunteer and aid in the World War I effort
1922	Lumber mill at Lac du Flambeau closes
1922	Popularity of northwoods resorts increases with train and automobile travelers
1924	All Native Americans including Ojibwe become United States citizens
1930	Great Depression begins in United States following stock market crash
1934	Federal day school begins in Lac du Flambeau
1934	Lac du Flambeau Tribe ratifies new tribal constitution under the Indian Reorganization Act
1936	First tribal council established at Lac du Flambeau
1939–1945	Lac du Flambeau Band members volunteer and aid in the World War II effort
1946	Simpson Electric Meter Company begins operations at Lac du Flambeau
1948	Flambeau School District No. 1 begins, thus ending federal school
1952	Indian Relocation Services begins

1953	Congress approves Public Law 280 giving Wisconsin jurisdiction on Indian lands including the Lac du Flambeau Reservation
1968	Indian Civil Rights Act is passed
1978	Federal Judge James Doyle rules Ojibwe treaty rights were extinguished
1983	U.S. Court of Appeals reverses Doyle decision and issues Voigt Decision
1985	Lac du Flambeau begins spring off-reservation spear fishing
1989	Tribe members vote "No" to proposed lease of off reservation fishing rights to the State of Wisconsin
1989	Lac du Flambeau Museum and Cultural Center opens
1990	Federal Judge Crabb rules Ojibwe are not entitled to any past damages from the State of Wisconsin for prohibiting exercise of treaty rights
1991	Federal Judge Crabb rules against Ojibwe timber rights claim
1993	Newly constructed K–8 Lac du Flambeau public school opens
1996	Newly constructed Lake of the Torches Casino opens at Lac du Flambeau

The following paragraphs provide a brief description of the key dates listed above as well as additional reading for those wanting to gain a broader understanding.

Pre-Contact Era

1492   Columbus arrives after visits from Vikings (See *Who's the Savage?* by David Wrone.)

North America already had a long history before Columbus arrived with diverse peoples that possessed diverse languages, cultures, and governments. Oral history of the Ojibwe, as in other world cultures is also diverse. It has commonly been related that long ago our ancestors were once on the coast of the North Atlantic. Ojibwe prophets predicted the coming of the Europeans. These prophets told of a place where food would grow on water (wild rice), which would be the new homeland of the Ojibwe. The Ojibwe, accompanied by their allied tribes the Ottawa and Potawatomi, began the western trek in search of the new homeland. This alliance came to be known as the Three Fires Confederacy. The three tribal groups with a common language moved westward, establishing a number of key villages along the St. Lawrence River before eventually arriving at their current homelands. It is important to realize that these Anishinaabeg, the Ojibwe, Odaawaa, and Boodewaadomiig are distinct tribes.

During the migration small groups or bands of these respective tribes purposefully separated from the larger group and moved north, west, and south. The Ojibwe groups divided into northern and southern groups. The northern group expanded westward across what would become Canada, while the southern group moved primarily across today's Michigan, Wisconsin, and Minnesota.

Fur-Trade Era

The Fur-Trade Era began before Jean Nicolet arrived in what is now called Wisconsin. The Huron were considered to be the middlemen of trade, as they accepted the risk of moving goods for trade into the dangerous regions the French and British refused to enter. Most often fur pelts were traded for tools, weapons, foods, and clothing. Eventually, as fur trade became accepted by the interior tribes, the French and British sent their traders and established trading posts. Over a period of 150 years of intense trading, the French, British, Americans, and numerous tribes would continually reshape the economic, political, and social patterns of the North American continent. The demand for profit would result in the loss of life for many, as numerous skirmishes, battles, and wars were waged between tribes and nations.

1634   Frenchman Jean Nicolet arrives in what is now called Wisconsin

Elevated interest in the resources of this region by France resulted in a visit by Jean Nicolet. The Ottawa and Ojibwe had already established trade relationships with the French, but the French had not yet established any trading posts in the region. The Ottawa requested French intervention regarding trade problems with the people named Winnebago by the Ojibwe. The Ottawa reported to the French that their envoys had been killed and eaten by the *Winnebago* warriors. Known to themselves as Ho-Chunk, this tribal group was already in what is now Wisconsin. Nicolet's visit was an attempt to settle the differences between the Ho-Chunk and others wishing to trade pelts for French goods.

1680   Ojibwe continue westward to Chequamagon from Sault Ste. Marie

Oral history provided by some Ojibwe elders state that "small, but fierce groups of Ojibwe were already on Madeline Island long prior to 1620." By 1680 the French had established trade relations with the Ojibwe, and the available resources were insufficient at Sault Ste. Marie. Diminishing resources and attacks from the east by the Iroquois contributed to the decision by leaders to move greater numbers of Ojibwe westward. The expansion of territory also allowed the Ojibwe to expand their trading relationship with others.

Upon arriving at Chequamagon Bay, close to the modern-day city of Ashland, Wisconsin, the Ojibwe met resistance from members of the Dakota (Sioux) Tribe. The Ojibwe named the Sioux people Bwaanag. The Ojibwe lived on Moniingwanekaaning (Madeline Island) off the coast, as a safety measure against attacking Sioux war parties. War between these two tribes would continue until approximately 1825. A provision within the treaty signed at Prairie du Chien stated the Ojibwe would agree to cease fighting with other tribes. Eventually, following many years of warfare with the Ojibwe, the majority of Sioux ceased woodland hunting and trapping and moved westward in search of buffalo, adapting the horse and plains culture.

Chequamagon is a derivation of the Ojibwe word *zhakaa'amikong*, which refers to a cultural legend whereby a dam was constructed to stop a large beaver from crossing. The beaver was not stopped due to the softness of the dam, hence the name meaning "the place of the beaver where it is soft." The broken dam is the stretch of land and small islands between the bay on the Wisconsin mainland that stretches toward what is now known as Madeline Island on Lake Superior.

1745   Kiishkiman establishes Waaswaaganing Village later known as Lac du Flambeau

Following a long presence on Madeline Island, the Ojibwe began establishing villages inland. The villages were established after Ojibwe took control of interior lands previously controlled by the Sioux and the Sac and Fox Tribes. In establishing the Lac du Flambeau village the Ojibwe left Madeline Island and moved inland. In approximately 1745 Azhedewish (Bad Pelican), Chief of the Crane Clan led his band to the headwaters of the Wisconsin River, near Gete-Gitigaaning (Lac Vieux Desert). Bad Pelican passed away, leaving his hereditary chieftainship to his son, whose name over time has come to be known as Kiishkiman. Historians have translated his name as "Sharpened Stone," which may be a version of the Ojibwe word for an object that is cut sharp. Prior to trade items being available to Ojibwe, knives were fashioned of both stone and bone.

Kiishkiman succeeded in removing the other tribes and led his band into the interior of Wisconsin. The primary village was established and named Waaswaaganing, or Place of the Torch. This name references the use of the torch by Ojibwe while spear fishing the lakes of the region. Members of this band created subvillages in a large radius around the central village.

Following trade relationships with other tribes, trading began with the Wemitigooshiig (French). Trading with the North West Company of France was centered on furs provided by the tribe in exchange for metal and cloth goods including guns, traps, kettles, knives, axes, blankets, clothing, and beads. Intermarriage began between French traders and Ojibwe women. French missionaries attempted unsuccessfully to convert the Ojibwe to Christianity.

1760   British defeat French at Montreal

The Zhaaganaashag (British) also sought to increase their influence and control the resources of the interior. A very complicated number of events, including attempts by the British to monopolize trade, resulted in war with the French. Prior to the war some Ojibwe were trading with the British as some goods were cheaper in trade and the quality was said to be superior. Eventually, both the British and French enlisted various tribes of the region to aid in the war for control of trade. French-controlled Moonii'aang (Montreal) fell to the British, thus ending the war and the

French grip on trade control. The British immediately moved into previously held French forts and trading posts. The Ojibwe were dependent upon trade goods, and were thus forced to continue trading with the British. The number of furs now necessary to gain English goods was raised, creating disagreements and animosities.

1776   Revolutionary War begins as Colonists seek independence from British

The colonists waged a successful war of independence from British control. The United States was born, but only on the eastern Atlantic coast. In the interior of what is now the United States, it was still tribal country. The British continued to trade with the Ojibwe and other tribes even after the war, but the leadership of the newly formed United States determined that British affairs with the tribes must cease. This decision was one of the factors leading to the War of 1812 between the British and the United States.

1812   Americans fight British in War of 1812

The War of 1812 not only involved the Americans and British, but also various tribes. The Lac du Flambeau Ojibwe under the order of Kiishkiman remained neutral during the war. Despite the American victory, British continue to have trade arrangements with the Ojibwe up to 1815.

The ages of trade between the Ojibwe with first the Wemitigooshiig (French) and then the Zhaaganaashag (English) ended during this period. Those called Gichi-Mookomaanag (Long Knives) were the next group the Ojibwe were forced to deal with. Ojibwe called the Americans "Long Knives" in reference to the long sabers carried by the soldiers. By 1830 the tribes east of the Ohio River were either forcibly removed or conquered by the United States.

Treaty-Making Era

The Americans defeated a group of tribes that made war against them in 1794 at the Battle of Fallen Timbers. The British had urged the tribes to fight the Americans because they were concerned with the potential loss of fur trade opportunities, as the ever-expanding colonists continued to clear land for farming. As land was cleared, animals were displaced and fewer opportunities existed for tribes attempting to trap or hunt animals. The furs were exchanged for trade goods. As a result of the violence, a treaty was drawn up whereby the tribes agreed to give up land. This treaty was the first one signed by the Ojibwe. It was called the Greenville Treaty, as it was signed in Greenville, Ohio, in 1795. This was the first of over forty that would be signed by the Ojibwe with the Americans.

Treaties represent formal agreements between two or more nations. The Americans used treaties as a means to gain access to land and resources. Agreements for land cession promised payments to tribes in the form of cash, goods, and services. The trade economy had already started its demise by 1815. This demise coupled with ever-growing poverty led the Ojibwe to enter into treaty arrangements as a means to provide for both their present population and future generations. Prior to the signing of treaties the Ojibwe considered themselves to be the owners of the territory. Afterward the Ojibwe understood that hunting, fishing and gathering rights had been retained. Additionally, language in the treaties stated that the United States would provide specific quantities of cash, goods, and services. Tribal leaders continue to urge the United States to fulfill these promises.

The following dates provide a summary of primary treaties signed by the Ojibwe with the Americans as well as descriptions of some key historical events during the Treaty-Making Era.

1825   Ojibwe sign treaty with U.S. Government at Prairie Du Chien

Representatives of various tribes were called together by the United States government to delineate their lands. The Ojibwe understood that they were to define their territories, so the divisions of their respective lands would be regarded as permanent. They also understood that they were to bury their war clubs deeply. By doing so, they agreed not to wage war with others, including the Americans. In return they would be compensated.

The territories defined by those attending were controversial, thus the Ojibwe requested that the United States meet with them to explain the original treaty. This meeting was held at Fond du Lac, and as a result the Treaty of 1826 was signed. With regard to the Treaty signed at Prairie du Chien, the Ojibwe later noted to the Americans, "We have no knowledge of any presents to have been made either in Money or Goods. True, coats were given to the Chiefs and occasionally a glass of whiskey, also occasionally a beef to make soup of." (See *Statement Made by the Indians, A Bilingual Petition of the Chippewa of Lake Superior 1864*, edited by John Nichols.)

1826   Ojibwe sign treaty with U.S. Government at Fond du Lac

The treaty council held in 1826 is where American officials asserted that "the whole Chippewa tribe" had assented to the principles and policies as outlined in the Treaty of Prairie du Chien. The treaty stated Ojibwe would allow *miskwaabik* (copper) to be removed from their lands. This agreement did not involve any land cessions. The discovery of large deposits of copper ore along the shores of Lake Superior increased the desire by profiteers to remove the Ojibwe from their homelands and begin the process of commercial mining, lumbering, and fishing.

1836   Wisconsin becomes a federally recognized territory

The previously named Northwest Territory had been divided up, and Wisconsin was recognized as a territory by the American Government. By 1836 many more Europeans had entered the United States and begun moving westward. Most tribes to the east had succumbed to the military superiority of the American forces. The then named Wisconsin Territory was home to the Ojibwe, Menominee, and Winnebago (Ho-Chunk) Tribes. The first residents of Wisconsin were primarily farmers, who were later followed by miners and timbermen.

1837   Ojibwe sign pine treaty with U.S. Government at Ft. Snelling

This treaty was known as both "The Lumberman's Treaty" and the St. Peters Treaty. It resulted in the Ojibwe relinquishing property rights on portions of their previously defined territories. In exchange the United States government promised cash payments, goods, and services. The Ojibwe retained hunting, fishing, and gathering rights during this exchange. One item that worried the Ojibwe immensely was the possibility of complete removal from their territory, which was a treaty provision at the discretion of the president, albeit not agreed upon by the Ojibwe. Historians have noted Ojibwe lands were poor farming soils, and the interest in mining was diminishing during this period. The cession of Ojibwe lands started the "legal" access to logging areas in the region.

1842   Ojibwe sign mineral treaty with U.S. Government at LaPointe

The Miner's Treaty also known as the LaPointe Treaty with the Chippewa was signed in 1842. The Chippewa who signed the treaty agreed to cede ten million acres of their homelands in northern Wisconsin and the western part of Michigan's Upper Peninsula. The Ojibwe expected that the federal government in return would provide them cash, goods, and services over a twenty-five-year annuity schedule. The Ojibwe leaders would again retain the right to hunt, fish, and gather within the lands ceded.

1848   Wisconsin becomes a state

On May 29, 1848, President Polk signed a bill that created the State of Wisconsin from the previously named territory.

1849   Ojibwe leaders travel to Washington, DC, to oppose removal

Chippewa leaders present a pictographic petition to the President James P. Polk, asking the president to guarantee the Ojibwe a permanent home in Wisconsin.

1850   Removal Order results in Sandy Lake Episode at Minnesota

The United States had hopes that the Ojibwe of Wisconsin could be removed into Minnesota. In 1850 President Zachary Taylor signed the presidential Removal Order. It ordered all Ojibwe of Wisconsin to be removed to a reservation at Sandy Lake, Minnesota. Annuity payments had previously been made at LaPointe on Madeline Island. The government then ordered that the annuity payment site would be moved to Sandy Lake. The payment date was also changed from summer to late fall. While traveling and waiting for government officials to make annuity payments, four hundred Ojibwe died. This incident became known as the Wisconsin Death March. Following the incident, Wisconsin Ojibwe returned to their respective homelands even more determined to resist removal. Recently, Ojibwe Tribes have memorialized those that perished during this incident. Various monuments honoring these ancestors, have been constructed by the Ojibwe tribes in the Sandy Lake, Minnesota, area.

1852   Ojibwe leaders travel to Washington, DC, to urge the President to rescind Removal Order

Chief Buffalo and other Ojibwe, including those from Lac du Flambeau were able to convince President Millard Fillmore to rescind the removal order. The Ojibwe people were given approval of the president to remain in Wisconsin. The Ojibwe who were previously treated with respect and dignity were now forced to beg for their right to remain within the lands of their ancestors, despite having ceded millions of acres and countless resources.

1854   Ojibwe sign treaty with U.S. Government at LaPointe

In exchange for the cession of 7.16 million acres of land, the Ojibwe would receive $496,000 to be paid over a twenty-year period. Reservations were established in Wisconsin, Minnesota and Michigan for the Ojibwe as a result of the second treaty signed at LaPointe. The removal policy was officially abandoned. In Wisconsin the reservations of Lac du Flambeau, Red Cliff, Bad River, and Lac Courte Oreilles were created. Allotment of lands to individuals was cited within the treaty as a mechanism for individual land ownership within reservation boundaries.

Reservation-Life Era

Early reservation life was a time of transition. Before reservations were created the Ojibwe had been a highly mobile hunting and gathering society. This lifestyle led the Ojibwe throughout the north-central Wisconsin region in search of food. After establishing the reservation, the government expected Ojibwe people to stay within the reservation boundaries. Small groups continued to lead a nomadic lifestyle despite the outlawing of such ways.

Those who settled on the reservation were affected in many ways. Forced acculturation began to erode the Ojibwe language, lifestyle, and relationships to others. The Ojibwe became increasingly dependent on government assistance promised in treaties. Due to the lack of jobs, many families were very poor.

Over time various government policies designed to heighten American power over tribes were applied throughout the United States. The people of Lac du Flambeau were affected by Federal laws that:

- allowed access to timber within reservations,
- allotted lands to individual tribal members,
- established boarding schools,
- reorganized tribal government,
- gave civil and criminal jurisdiction on reservations to states.

The reservation land at Lac du Flambeau was once covered by an ancient forest. Profiteers systematically cut the majority of Wisconsin's forests with the exception of reservation lands. Initially, timber harvests on reservations were illegal. Profiteering strategies and policy effectively resulted in the demise of nearly all virgin timber within the reservation. The General Allotment Act and the Burke Act were key laws that allowed logging to occur on reservation lands.

Other federal polices were designed to detribalize the Ojibwe. By using this strategy government officials believed the Ojibwe would join the melting pot of America. They hoped that in time the Ojibwe would abandon their tribal identity.

The first effort was creation of tribal boarding schools. Their plan was to stop all younger Ojibwe from living the traditional lifestyle of their ancestors. The government thought by teaching new religions, language, and ways of living, this goal could be reached.

Other attempts at changing the Ojibwe people include the Citizenship Act, Indian Reorganization Act, Indian Relocation Services Plan and Public Law 280. The efforts did have effect, but failed to completely remake the Ojibwe people into mainstream Americans. Instead, the Ojibwe people maintained their tribal identify via traditional customs, language, and ceremonies at Lac du Flambeau and throughout Ojibwe country.

At a point when Ojibwe identity was again being challenged, a major issue surfaced in Wisconsin. The legal and physical battle to reaffirm off-reservation treaty rights began in the mid 1970s. The Supreme Court ruled that Ojibwe did have rights as outlined in treaties to hunt, fish, and gather outside reservation boundaries. The ruling created a very controversial period in Wisconsin's history. The complex issue was litigated over a nearly sixteen-year period and resulted in a stronger Ojibwe nation and greater protection for natural resources.

The economy of the reservation always reflected federal and state polices. Typically the unemployment rate on the reservation was very high. Many Ojibwe have lived in poverty for generations as few opportunities existed on the reservation. When casino gaming operations began, the revenue base increased at Lac du Flambeau. This resulted in improved living conditions and greater employment opportunities within the reservation.

Many more events than those described below have occurred during the reservation period at Lac du Flambeau. Historic events typically contain numerous associated tales and are often subject to varied interpretations. For these reasons, additional reading is highly recommended. The following dates will merely show some key events in the history of reservation life at Lac du Flambeau.

1866   Civil Rights Bill passed providing equal rights for all, except Native Americans

When the Civil Rights Bill passed into law, it further evidenced the attitude that tribal people and women were not equal to others residing in the United States.

1874–1877   Government suggests Lac du Flambeau band members make allotment selections

Allotments are defined as parcels of land within the reservation. The allotted land parcels were once owned by the tribe as a whole, but following allotment the land was considered to be conditionally the property of an individual tribal member. Conditions were attached to the individual receiving an allotment, primarily how long it would take to gain full ownership and under what conditions it could be sold.

The government's initial plan was to have individual tribal members select allotments from tribal reservation lands, make allotments to individuals, and then sell the remaining lands within the reservation. The plan called for funds generated from the sale of remaining reservations lands to be invested on behalf of the tribe. It failed because Lac du Flambeau Ojibwe elders strongly opposed it. The motivation for this plan was access to timber within the Lac du Flambeau reservation. Most timber in Wisconsin had been cut, with the exception of reservation lands where cutting was prohibited. Despite this failure, timber barons were still able to cut much of the Lac du Flambeau forest. Tribal members continually voiced their dissatisfaction to the deaf ears of officials. Much later in history, members of the Ojibwe tribe would argue unsuccessfully for reimbursement for lost timber revenues.

1883   Allotment of reservation land to individuals begins logging

As a provision of the 1854 Treaty, individual tribal members could be granted land allotments. As logging companies had high interest in reservation timber, they dialogued with government appointed Indian agents on the reservations. The agent would assign allotments and act as a middleman in the transactions. According to oral history, tribal people who received allotments were often either underpaid or not paid at all. No enforcement of where the loggers would cut was in place. Some oral histories relate total scams such as deceased persons being given allotments, and profits from timber sales going directly to unscrupulous Indian Agents.

1886   Logging begins within Lac du Flambeau reservation

Reservation lands that had been previously off limits to timber harvest were opened to logging companies. The limited number of allotments made somehow resulted in 9.6 million board feet of lumber being cut from within the reservation.

1887   Congress passes Dawes Act also known as General Allotment Act

A new policy was implemented that sought to disrupt the political infrastructure of the tribes. Indian agents and politicians believed that by breaking the reservation lands up, and allotting individuals parcels of land within the reservation tribe members would be more likely to act and think like other Wisconsin residents. In effect the aim was to lessen the authority of chiefs and detribalize the new land owners. Allottees would be required to care for the land for twenty-years, after which they would be deemed competent. Upon proving competency, they would gain full ownership of the allotted land, and also citizenship. Nationally, this Act, resulted in the reduction of native land holdings from over 140 million acres in 1886 to less than 50 million acres in 1934, when the policy was ended. Allotments had already began at Lac du Flambeau prior to the President's passage of the General Allotment Act pursuant to the 1854 Treaty.

1888   Logging operations suspended on-reservation by federal government

The widespread cutting by various loggers within the reservation led to a suspension of logging operations there. Federal officials understood, for the moment, that corruption was contributing to overharvesting of the Lac du Flambeau reservation.

1891   Dawes Act amended to allow leasing and contract logging

Succumbing to political pressures, Congress amended the Dawes Act to allow leasing and contract logging by non-band members. Logging companies operating in northern Wisconsin attempted to cut all the timber within the reservation.

1892   Logging operations resume within Lac du Flambeau Reservation

As a result of the Dawes Act, logging operation also resumed within the Lac du Flambeau reservation, as the Lac du Flambeau Lumber Company signed a twenty-year lease. Tribal members gained employment in different capacities with the logging industry.

1894   Sawmill built at Lac du Flambeau

Prior to 1894 many trees were floated out of northern Wisconsin via rivers and lakes. The logs had destinations in central Wisconsin, where large sawmills were already established. Trains were also used, following the construction of railroad tracks into remote areas. Cost and time constraints with transporting logs southward and the high quantity of timber on the reservation contributed to the decision to construct a sawmill at Lac du Flambeau.

The sawmill constructed at Lac du Flambeau was located in the area between Pokegama Lake and Long Lake, which is separated by the "hot pond." Today, the Indian Bowl and museum stand in this location. The sawmill provided jobs for many people at the expense of the forest. By the time of mill closed the majority of the reservation had been nearly deforested. Millions of board feet of lumber left the reservation during the operational period of the mill. Most nontribal mill employees left Lac du Flambeau in search of employment elsewhere. The majority of tribal people formerly employed at the mill returned to living off the land.

1895   Boarding school established at Lac du Flambeau

Federal policy regarding the education of Native children resulted in the establishment of residential boarding schools throughout the nation. Operation of residential boarding schools was often contracted out to Catholic or other Christian church groups. Thus in addition to education children were expected to participate in religious instruction as well. All children between the ages of four and eighteen were expected to attend the boarding school at Lac du Flambeau.

Many Ojibwe did not agree that their children required education at the boarding school. To assure children would attend, Indian agents and boarding school officials would travel around the reservation to pick up children for school. If the officials were told by a family that their children would not be attending, the officials would threaten the Ojibwe families with jail time and/or loss of government rights. Annuity and logging contracts were typically handled by the Indian agent, so these threats were taken very seriously by the parents and grandparents of Ojibwe children at Lac du Flambeau. Most would release their children to the Indian agent and school officials rather than risk loss of income or being jailed.

Some very young children were hidden, and some families moved to the remote areas of the reservation to avoid having their children taken from them. It was not uncommon for Indian agents to pick up a child that looked to be of school age and simply deliver him or her to the school with no notification to the family.

The boarding school operated year round and attempted to teach skills necessary for successful assimilation into mainstream society, including blacksmithing, farming, sewing, cooking, music, and general education. Most children did not understand English or any of the systems that were in place when they arrived. The children were forbidden to speak their native language or participate in any tribal customs. Offenders were beaten, marched, or forced to kneel or stand in place for hours. Children attempting to escape were also given additional punishments. Today's remaining elders who survived the boarding school experience are now talking about their experiences. Most acknowledge extreme mistreatment to themselves and others by boarding school officials. (See elder interviews.)

1903–1934   Dawes Act impacts allotments on Lac du Flambeau Reservation

The Lac du Flambeau Reservation was originally established as a result of the 1854 Treaty and resulted in twelve square miles of reservation. The Ojibwe word for reservation is *ishkonigan*, which translates to "that which is left over". Prior to and following the Burke Act, individual allotted lands were lost via sale to non-Indians. Oral history told by elders states the majority of allottees who sold land did not understand English, nor did they understand the concept of individual land ownership or sale. The traditional viewpoint on land was that it was the collective property of the Ojibwe Nation. This land was under the control of the chief who assisted his band in care taking of the lands. It was a normal process for the next generation of Ojibwe people to succeed them in the care-taking process.

Elders also stated that the extreme state of poverty on the reservation forced many individuals to sell land as a means to survive. During this period in Lac du Flambeau history, the majority of the frontage on the reservation's lakes previously owned by allottees was gained by non-Indians.

Today there are three types of land within the reservation: taxable (those lands lost in allotment sales), tribal (lands owned collectively by the band), and allotted (allotted lands that are now held in common ownership by the descendants of the original allottees). Recently, due to the multiplicity of competing interests, a plan has been initiated whereby the value of the land is appraised, a market value is attached, and the overall value is distributed equally to the multiple land owners. The land sold by multiple tribal land owners is now commonly owned by the tribe.

1906   Burke Act allows Indian agents to define competency of allottees.

Congress authorized the Burke Act in response to the growing Wisconsin population and high demand for access to tribal timber and mineral resources. As it was illegal for allottees to sell lands prior to holding them for twenty-five years, the public push for access to tribally held resources needed to be fast tracked. As a result of the Burke Act, Indian agents assigned to reservations were given the authority to decide whether an allottee was competent or not. Competent allottees could sell allotted land. Agents often schemed with speculators to determine desirable lands, declare the respective allottees competent, and then acquire it for themselves.

1914–1918   Lac du Flambeau Band members volunteer and aid in the World War I effort

Lac du Flambeau Ojibwe men enlisted in the armed forces when the United States entered World War I. Native people were not citizens, and were thus exempt from the draft. Ojibwe men participated in the war for the purposes of defending their homelands, continuing the Ojibwe tradition of warfare and monetary payment. Others moved to urban areas to contribute to war efforts. Following the war veterans and workers returning to the reservations found the state of poverty and illness had worsened and began to ask, "Why are our Ojibwe people in such a bad way?"

1922   Lumber mill at Lac du Flambeau closes

By this point the majority of forest lands that had been accessible had been harvested in northern Wisconsin. Memories of elders and photographs reveal a clear cut landscape. With the closing of the mill once plentiful jobs were now gone. Most mill employees left the area for other employment, and poverty conditions returned to Lac du Flambeau.

1922   Popularity of northwoods resorts increases with train and automobile travelers

The prosperity of the 1920s contributed to new development and jobs in northern Wisconsin, including Lac du Flambeau. Growth of industries and cities meant more people were working, and in need of a break. It also meant that people had the money to travel. Traveling vacationers either took the train or drove their own automobiles to the northwoods.

Developers in the northwoods started the resort economy. Resorts allowed vacationers to enjoy the peace and tranquility of the north, while taking part in recreational sport hunting, fishing, and boating. Ojibwe men gained employment as *giiwase/bima'ookiiwininiwag* (hunting/fishing guides) and groundsmen. Ojibwe women were employed as cooks, and housekeepers. The Ojibwe also created tourist shows, featuring live Native music and dancing for the price of admission. Ojibwe participants were paid for their efforts. The Ojibwe also produced craft work of beads, bark, and wood and sold these items to the visitors.

1924   All Native Americans including Ojibwe become United States citizens

All Native Americans became citizens of the United States in 1924. Prior to 1924 nearly half of the country's Ojibwe already had citizen status as a result of competency declarations by Indian agents. The efforts of tribal veterans during World War I contributed to congressional approval of this act. Native people also maintained sovereign status as members of their respective nations. There was no provision within this act that required Native people to relinquish tribal membership or identity.

Citizenship had little effect on the lives of Ojibwe. The Ojibwe continued to expect the government to uphold the agreements made during treaty signings. Citizenship did little to increase opportunity or create jobs within the impoverished reservation.

1930   Great Depression begins in United States following stock market crash

Following the crash of the stock market in 1929, the Great Depression hit the American economy. Since the logging operation and sawmill jobs had already largely ended at Lac du Flambeau, the crash of the stock market had relatively little impact compared to other areas.

The people continued to exist on hunting, fishing, and gathering, with limited gardening within the reservation boundaries. Prior to the signing of the 1854 Treaty establishing the reservation, the Ojibwe were able to maintain a nomadic hunting and gathering lifestyle. This way of life involved moving with the seasons and using the resources that sustained life. The original lifestyle had been changed by the establishment of reservations, forced acculturation, and dependancy. A depressed economy had already been in effect in Ojibwe country and would continue for many years into the future.

1934   Federal day school begins in Lac du Flambeau

The government begins closing its Indian boarding schools, likely due to cost factors. Federal day school began in Lac du Flambeau following the close of the boarding school. An important objective had been met by the boarding school approach. Following a thirty-six year run, the boarding school had effectively separated older Ojibwe from their children and grandchildren. Most survivors of the boarding school episode no longer spoke the Ojibwe language, attended Ojibwe ceremonies, or taught Ojibwe culture to their children. The following generations of Ojibwe were now expected to assimilate into a larger society.

1934   Lac du Flambeau Tribe ratifies new tribal constitution under the Indian Reorganization Act

In 1934 the Wheeler-Howard Act, which came to known as the Indian Reorganization Act (IRA), was initiated. The IRA established a national policy of tribal self-government through a tribal governing body, which would be an elected tribal council. This elected council would manage the affairs of its respective tribe.

Some Native Americans believe the Act was initially designed as a means to access resources within reservations. Hereditary chiefs and their councils made decisions regarding reservation lands within the United States. These chiefs and councils were often unwilling to cooperate with the government or developers who sought resources within their lands.

The power held by heredity chiefs and councils needed to be usurped to achieve specific development or resource access objectives. When old hereditary leadership objections were removed, resources sought were then obtained. For this reason some Native people believe the successful strategy of removing old leaders contributed to a nationwide policy of Indian Reorganization. The plan called for the election of newly formed tribal governments that would spread authority beyond an individual chief and his council.

Many tribes, including the Lac du Flambeau Tribe, were divided on the issue. Eventually an election was initiated by government officials which determined the Lac du Flambeau voters had indeed accepted Indian Reorganization. Despite guiding principles framed within IRA constitutions, some tribal people believe that United States government officials skillfully guided outcomes of early tribal government actions across the nations.

Those who supported the concept of Indian Reorganization noted that tribal sovereignty was actually strengthened, as the American government had officially agreed to recognize leadership defined by the respective tribes.

1936   First tribal council established at Lac du Flambeau.

In the first election to determine membership on the tribal council, eleven men and one woman were elected to two-year terms at Lac du Flambeau.

1939–1945   Lac du Flambeau Band members volunteer and aid in the World War II effort

Following the attack by the Japanese at Pearl Harbor, the Americans entered the war. Lac du Flambeau Ojibwe men and women enlisted in all branches of the military. Other Ojibwe people left Lac du Flambeau to support the war effort in factories and construction trades. Blackouts and rationing of goods were common at Lac du Flambeau and across the nation.

1946   Simpson Electric Meter Company begins operations at Lac du Flambeau

Ray Simpson opened the doors to the Simpson Electric Meter Company, thus providing jobs for many Lac du Flambeau residents. Simpson Electric became renowned for the quality of its test meters. Following many years of ownership by Simpson, the company was purchased by the Lac du Flambeau Tribe in 1986. The tribe continues to operate the company today.

1948　Flambeau School District No. 1 begins, thus ending federal school

By 1948 a larger number of non-Ojibwe were living within the reservation. Reservation land that had been purchased from allottees was classified as taxable property. The town of Lac du Flambeau had already been collecting property taxes for services prior to the establishment of the school. The federal government was still obligated to provide education to Ojibwe children as a result of treaties. A plan was initiated to create the Lac du Flambeau School District using local, state, and federal money to fund the operation of the school. All school age residents of Lac du Flambeau were eligible for public education.

1952　Indian Relocation Services begins

In the early 1950s some federal legislators drafted the "Termination Policy." The purpose of the policy was to try to lessen federal obligation to Native American tribes in the United States. The tribes on the other hand continued to remind the government of its treaty obligations. One component of the policy was termination of reservation status and subsequent loss of federal assistance. In Wisconsin the Menominee Tribe was terminated, with dreadful effects. The Menominee tribe later regained reservation status.

A major initiative known as the "Relocation Plan" was associated with federal termination policy. This plan was used to move tribal people off the reservations and into urban areas. The plan was marketed within the reservation via posters and recruitment presentations. Many half-truths were told to those Native people who enlisted. Promises of jobs and a better life led many Ojibwe away from the reservation. Upon arriving in the urban areas Native people found a new form of poverty and racism. Some did return home, yet many stayed. Those who stayed endured extreme hardships until the time of the Indian Civil Rights efforts in the 1960s.

Some elders believe the relocation effort was strategic in that many progressive tribal members would now be absent from the reservation. The absence of these band members greatly reduced opposition to the plan for state jurisdiction within the previously federally and tribally controlled reservation of Lac du Flambeau.

1953　Congress approves Public Law 280 giving Wisconsin jurisdiction on Indian lands including the Lac du Flambeau Reservation.

Prior to and after the signing of treaties, the Ojibwe have maintained a government-to-government relationship with the United States. The Ojibwe Nation is represented by a number of distinct bands. The Ojibwe of Lac du Flambeau have always considered themselves to be members of the Ojibwe nation, and by 1924 all accepted dual citizenship.

In 1953 a new experiment associated with the termination policy of the United States became Public Law 280. Five states including Wisconsin were selected to assist the federal government in this plan. Public Law 280 shifted some responsibility previously held by the federal government to the tribes and gave new authority to Wisconsin and other states. Congress originally intended to merely transfer its criminal jurisdiction to the states, but before being passed civil jurisdiction was also included in Public Law 280.

Initially non-Indian critics within the affected states were upset due to the lack of tax income and increased autonomy on the reservations. By 1968, however, when the first retrocession provisions were enacted, the five states, including Wisconsin, were very reluctant to give-up any jurisdictional power within the reservations.

A perceived positive effect of Public Law 280 was an increase in law enforcement within the reservations. Many non-Indians within and around reservations had long considered the reservations to be lawless.

Some tribal people believed that the government-to-government relationship was diminished, and treaty-based obligations were certain to be unmet by a third party, the state. They thus disagreed with Public Law 280.

As a result of the new law, tribal members who violated laws under its jurisdiction would now be prosecuted in state courts, as the traditional enforcement systems within the reservations were not recognized. The state now had the authority to impose its jurisdiction upon the tribe.

Following the passage of the Indian Civil Rights Act in 1968, federal assistance was provided to the tribes to develop civil and criminal codes within their respective reservations. As a result of these developments in tribal court systems, jurisdictional questions have arisen. State versus tribal authority in specific legal issues is continually being challenged and defined. The Lac du Flambeau Tribe is also a sovereign government, and does possess its own regulatory authority.

1968   Indian Civil Rights Act is passed

The Indian Civil Rights Act was passed in 1968, following period of civil unrest in the United States. Brave Ojibwe people fought for civil rights that would improve their treatment both on and off-reservation. Major reasons for the enactment of the Indian Civil Rights Act were documented racial attitudes and civil rights violations in and around reservations.

Lac du Flambeau Ojibwe also participated in Native American Civil Rights movement. Following relocation from the reservations many Ojibwe were subject to unfair housing laws and practices in cities. Native American community organizers in Chicago, Milwaukee, and the Twin Cities were joined by supporters in protests. During the sometimes-violent clashes with police, Ojibwe people were clubbed, punched, hit with water cannons, and teargassed.

Lac du Flambeau Ojibwe were also present at Winter Dam, the Novitiate Takeover, Nike Missile Base, Alcatraz, and Wounded Knee. Lac du Flambeau Ojibwe also testified at congressional hearings, including the National Indian Child Welfare Act.

The failed "Termination Policy" was replaced by a policy of "Self Determination for Tribes." This new policy assisted the tribes in accessing federal resources to develop needed infrastructures. Tribal housing, healthcare systems, education, law enforcement, and court systems were developed as a result of the self-determination policy.

1978   Federal Judge James Doyle rules off-reservation rights were extinguished

On March 8, 1974, brothers Fred and Mike Tribble, enrolled members at Lac Courte Oreilles Ojibwe reservation, were arrested by Wisconsin Department of Natural Resources wardens. The WDNR wardens cited the Tribble brothers for possession of a fish spear and for occupying a fish shanty off-reservation without proper identification attached. This incident took place on Chief Lake. The wardens acted on the assumption that the Ojibwe had no right to spear fish outside the boundaries of the reservation. The Tribble brothers did not agree. They and many other Ojibwe believed that hunting, fishing, and gathering rights were retained at the time of treaty signings.

On March 18, 1975, Lac Courte Oreilles Tribe filed a lawsuit against the State of Wisconsin. This lawsuit started an extremely controversial and sometimes violent period in Wisconsin's history. To resolve the treaty rights issue, a number of court rulings were required. The various phases of this legal issue spanned over a sixteen-year period. During the trials, the Ojibwe continually stated large land cessions were made during 1837 and 1842 treaty signings in exchange for cash, goods, and services. They also argued that the right to hunt, fish, and gather was retained. The Ojibwe firmly believed the State of Wisconsin had illegally prohibited off-reservation harvesting. They sued the State to stop them from enforcing state law against tribal members who were legally exercising reserved treaty rights. The Lac Courte Oreilles Tribe was joined by other Ojibwe tribes of Wisconsin including Lac du Flambeau in the lawsuit.

Following testimony and trial, Federal Judge James Doyle ruled that off-reservation rights for Ojibwe tribes associated with the treaties were nonexistent. Judge Doyle ruled that the Ojibwe had relinquished their rights when they accepted reservations as a condition of signing the 1854 Treaty. He also concluded that the 1850 Removal Order had withdrawn the rights in question. The Lac Courte Oreilles and other Ojibwe tribes appealed the decision.

1983   U.S. Court of Appeals reverses Doyle decision and issues Voigt decision

On January 25, 1983, the U.S. Court of Appeals, Seventh Circuit, reversed the 1978 Doyle ruling, thus reaffirming the rights of Ojibwe to hunt, fish, and gather within the ceded territories. With this major court victory the Ojibwe started a planning process to determining how off-reservation exercise of treaty rights would occur. The State of Wisconsin did appeal, but on October 3, 1983, the U.S. Supreme Court of Appeals refused to hear the appeal. This decision reaffirmed the treaty harvesting rights reserved by the Ojibwe people.

1985   Lac du Flambeau begins spring off-reservation spearfishing

In the spring of 1985 the Lac du Flambeau Ojibwe begin spearing walleye and musky in off-reservation lakes within the ceded territory. In response antitreaty groups organized to oppose the inherent rights of the Ojibwe. The most visible antitreaty groups included Stop Treaty Abuse–Wisconsin (STA–W) and Protect America's Rights and Resources (PARR). Lakes speared by Lac du Flambeau members were the site of chaotic, ugly, and sometimes violent protests. Over the next six years a limited number of protesters were arrested, both on and off water.

1989   Tribe members vote "No" to proposed lease of off-reservation fishing rights to the State of Wisconsin

In 1989 the State of Wisconsin proposed leasing the fishing rights of the Lac du Flambeau Band in exchange for $50 million in economic incentives over a ten-year period. The Lac du Flambeau tribal chairman and tribal council approved the tentative lease agreement, but a referendum vote of the tribal membership was necessary to approve the offer. When put to referendum vote among the tribal membership, the offer was rejected. The proposed leasing of treaty rights divided the Lac du Flambeau community.

1989   Lac du Flambeau Museum and Cultural Center opens

The Lac du Flambeau Museum and Cultural Center also opened its doors in 1989. Previously the Lac du Flambeau Public Library had exhibited a small number of tribal cultural items from earlier generations.

An increased interest in the past coincided with assertion of reserved treaty rights. Many community members donated items to supplement an already large collection of Lac du Flambeau Chippewa artifacts, cultural objects, and images. With financial support from federal sources and the Lac du Flambeau Tribe, the Lac du Flambeau Historical Society, led by Ben Guthrie, raised the additional dollars needed to complete the project.

Today, permanent exhibits within the museum depict the seasonal harvesting activities of the Lac du Flambeau tribe. Some examples of changing exhibits include various types of beadwork, basketry, spear-fishing decoys, canoe types, and fur trade items. Originally named the Lac du Flambeau Museum and Cultural Center, this facility was renamed the George W. Brown Jr. Museum and Cultural Center in honor of a Lac du Flambeau Band member. The museum continues to be a popular attraction today for tourists, school visitors, researchers, and tribal community members.

1990   Federal Judge Crabb rules Ojibwe are not entitled to any past damages from the State of Wisconsin for prohibiting exercise of Treaty rights

In 1990 the Ojibwe sued the State of Wisconsin for past damages related to their treaty rights. This lawsuit contended the Ojibwe were owed $300 million by the state for prohibiting them from exercising their off-reservation harvesting rights. Judge Crabb ruled that the state was protected by the Eleventh Amendment to the U.S. Constitution, and that it was therefore immune from prosecution. The tribes did not appeal the ruling.

1991   Federal Judge Crabb rules against Ojibwe timber rights claim

On February 22, 1991, Judge Crabb ruled on the timber phase of the trial. The Ojibwe argued that timber harvesting was an advanced form of tree cutting and thus should be included in their off-reservation harvesting rights. Judge Crabb disagreed with this argument. Her ruling stated that although the Ojibwe were using forest products at the time of treaty signings, they were not selling those forest products. The tribes did not appeal the ruling.

1993   Newly constructed K–8 Lac du Flambeau public school opens

The previous Lac du Flambeau Public School, which was located on the shores of Pokegama Lake, was rapidly deteriorating. Old construction materials, including asbestos, lead pipes, and paint were very evident. The students and staff population had outgrown the old facility. Administrator Richard Vought and school board members spearheaded plans to construct a new public school at Lac du Flambeau. The new construction was approved in a town referendum. The construction was completed, and the new school opened in 1993. It is located adjacent to Highway 47, east of the Lac du Flambeau Town Hall.

1996   Newly constructed Lake of the Torches Casino opens at Lac du Flambeau

In 1996 the new Lake of the Torches Casino and Convention Center opened its doors. Previously the tribe had operated a small casino in downtown Lac du Flambeau. The Lac du Flambeau Tribe generated new and greater revenues as a result of casino gaming and other entertainment. These revenues greatly benefited the Lac du Flambeau tribal membership in the form of services, programs, facilities, and per capita payments.

In the following paragraphs I describe locations mentioned by the elders in their interviews. Location descriptions include the Old Indian Village, Medicine Rock, Strawberry Island, the Round House, Bear River Pow-wow Grounds, and Woodmen's Hall.

Locations

Old Indian Village is the location of the first settlement on the Lac du Flambeau Reservation. It is located in the area of Flambeau Lake and Bear River juncture. This place, often referred to as simply "the Village" has undergone many changes since the Precontact Era. The Village was a separate location from the "New Town," as the town of Lac du Flambeau represented the site of the saw mill, stores, services, and non-Indians. The village also represented a new home for Ojibwe from other bands who moved into the area for work, school, or marriage. The language of Lac du Flambeau developed into two distinct dialects of Ojibwe language, the Old Indian Village dialect, and the Town dialect.

From the Precontact period to the Treaty-Making Era, the Village was likely most populated during the summer months. Families returned to the Village during summer months to renew family and clan ties, visit others, attend ceremonies, and for court. Tribal leaders met in council to discuss affairs affecting the tribe during the summer. During other seasons families moved to other locations in search of food and other resources necessary to sustain life.

The Village was a center for the Ojibwe of the immediate region. Other smaller camps and settlements were established in various locations within ten miles of the Village. Other Ojibwe also resided in the northern region of Wisconsin at Mercer, Turtle Lakes, Big Trout Lake, Wisconsin River, Pelican Lake, and Lac Vieux Desert. Fur trader Michael Cadotte had visited Lac du Flambeau for trading in 1782, thus establishing a trade center at Lac du Flambeau for the Ojibwe of the area. By 1792 the English Northwest Company had established a fur trading post here. Later the XY Company and American Fur Company would also have trading posts at Lac du Flambeau. (See James Bokern's unpublished master's thesis, "History and the Primary Canoe Routes of the Six Bands of Chippewa from the Lac du Flambeau District.")

Following the establishment of reservations, and the expansion of Wisconsin's population, the Old Indian Village underwent many changes. After the closure of the saw mill and the end of the logging era, traditional dwellings (*wiigiwaams* and other bark lodges) were gradually replaced by log and frame buildings.

The most notable aspect of the Old Indian Village was its representation as a stronghold of Ojibwe culture. The world around the people of the Old Indian Village was constantly changing. The people residing at the village tried to keep old traditions and culture alive. One of the traditional aspects of life at the Village was leadership. Originally, tribal councils included hereditary chiefs who were supported by headmen and a speaker. Following establishment of the reservation, new authorities appeared. Government-appointed Indian agents and boarding school officials wielded authority that was often despised, but seldom openly challenged by the Ojibwe.

Eventually, with acceptance of the Indian Reorganization Act and the establishment of the new tribal constitution, a new tribal council was voted into leadership. It marked the end of hereditary leadership and the old tribal council form of government at Lac du Flambeau.

Many people within the Village opposed the new form of government. Clear animosities existed between people residing in the New Town and Old Village. Those who opposed the new government and sought to hold onto Ojibwe traditions resided at or frequently visited the village at this point in history. In time as those with differences passed on, these animosities lessened.

Winds, fires, and time have claimed most of the original frame dwellings that once stood in the Old Indian Village, yet some still stand today and are inhabited. New housing development has occurred in the Village since the mid 1970s. Most band members now living throughout the reservation have relatives that once resided in the Village.

Medicine Rock: Looking east from the Old Indian Village, across the bay in Flambeau Lake on a point sits Gichi Mashkikii Asin (Big Medicine Rock). According to legend, our cultural hero, Wenaboozho, won this rock during the Makazin Ataagewin (Moccasin Game). During the contest the rock was small, but grew in size as Wenaboozho brought the rock closer to its final destination. At a certain point he was no longer able to carry the rock and began rolling him. As the rock was rolled, a path was cut into the ground. This path was filled by water and is now named Mako-ziibi or Makwa Ziibiing (Bear River). Wenaboozho decided to leave the Big Medicine Rock at the point described above, as he may have grown weary from rolling such a large rock. Our ancestors recognized the Big Medicine Rock as a spiritual location, and people today continue to show respect for this location.

Ode'minising (Strawberry Island) is located in Flambeau Lake. The island is also considered a sacred site by the Lac du Flambeau people. It is a known burial site for those who perished during a battle between Ojibwe and Sioux warriors. The exact date of the battle is unknown, but oral tradition relates that the battle did occur.

Two versions among many are commonly related in oral histories. In the first version, upon the arrival of Kiishkiman in 1745, the Ojibwe found Sioux on the island, fought them, and took control of the island and the area. In another version the Ojibwe had already taken control of the area, and a Bwaanag (Sioux) war party seeking revenge returned to Lac du Flambeau from the Bear River, but were defeated badly.

Today's elders continue to remind the younger generations to stay away or stay off the island completely. One reason they give is that both Ojibwe and Sioux warriors rest within the soil of the island. Ojibwe have great respect for the departed and encourage their youth to allow peaceful rest for all departed souls.

As a result of allotments, Strawberry Island was owned by an Ojibwe boy named Whitefeather. When a non-Ojibwe offered to purchase the land, the child was too young to enter into this transaction. The Indian agent at Lac du Flambeau helped the child's grandparents sell the approximately twenty-six-acre island to a non-Ojibwe in 1910. Oral history of the Ojibwe relates that Whitefeather did not live long after the sale of the island. During this period in Lac du Flambeau's history, many allotments were sold to non-Ojibwe people. Most premier lakeshore allotments at Lac du Flambeau were sold for minimal prices.

In 1976 the current owner, Walter Mills of Aspen, Colorado, was given permission to subdivide the island into sixteen parcels. The permits authorized for Mills created immediate concern at Lac du Flambeau. Efforts began to preserve Strawberry Island in its undeveloped state. In 1978 Strawberry Island appeared on the National Register of Historic Places. In 1994 Strawberry Island was added to the State of Wisconsin's Ten Most Endangered Historic Properties list.

In 1995 Walter Mills applied for permits to build a home and garage on one of the sixteen lots. The grave sites on the island combined with the sacred significance of the island created high concern among the Lac du Flambeau Ojibwe. Zoning regulations have halted any development to date. Attempts to negotiate a sale between the Lac du Flambeau Tribe and Mills have been unsuccessful thus far, as the tribe believes the asking price is inflated. In the summer of 2000 a tornado hit Strawberry Island. The island is marked by a visible path where trees were blown down by the winds.

The Round House is a log building in the Old Indian Village. The current Round House is an octagon-shaped structure made of white pine logs that was constructed in 1975. The Round House is a structure primarily used for ceremonial drum events. Other events include naming ceremonies, and feasts. An older structure, also known as the Round House, or the *niimi'idiiwigamig* (dance hall), was constructed following the arrival of Big Drums. It stood in the same vicinity but eventually succumbed to age and elements sometime in the 1950s. (See Thomas Vennum's *Ojibwa Dance Drum: Its History and Construction*.)

Bear River Pow-Wow Grounds, as it is known today, is another location within the Old Indian Village. It was also referred to as "the Pageant Grounds," "Indian Park," and simply "the Park." This site is a tract of land east and north of where the Bear River joins Flambeau Lake. Long ago, this was a campsite for people entering the Lac du Flambeau area from the northwest traveling by canoe on the Bear River. In the early reservation period ceremonial drum events were held at this location. As more non-tribal visitors came to the area, they found their way to the ceremonial grounds in Lac du Flambeau. The Ojibwe kindly welcomed visitors but also understood religious events could not be continually interrupted. Thus, special tourist shows were created. For the price of admission visitors could watch and participate in drumming and dancing. Performers were paid and other tribal people took advantage of the opportunity to sell arts, crafts, and foods. Eventually people from other tribal communities participated both as a means of income and as an opportunity to socialize with Lac du Flambeau people. It was not uncommon for families to camp throughout the summer at Bear River.

In 1982 Bear River Pow-Wow was started. The grounds, which had become overgrown following many years of disuse, were cleaned up and new structures were built. The site of an annual pow-wow since 1982, Bear River Pow-Wow serves as both a homecoming celebration for Lac du Flambeau people and a social dancing event for tribes from throughout the Great Lakes region. Most pow-wow dancers, from children to elders, proudly adorn themselves in ceremonial dress for this occasion.

Woodmen's Hall also known as "The Modern Woodmen Hall" was built around 1909. The building no longer stands. It was located in the vicinity of Simpson and Chicog Streets, on the east side of what is now known as Thunderbird Park. Elders state that after the sawmill was in operation, the structure was built for meetings, entertainment, and community functions for employees of the mill.

Most sawmill employees left Lac du Flambeau following the mill closure. Woodmen's Hall and homes previously occupied by the mill employees were abandoned. Tribal people immediately took up residence in the homes, and used Woodmen's Hall for ceremonial drum dances and other social affairs. The now-deceased elder James "Pipe" Mustache of Lac Courte Oreilles was a frequent visitor to Lac du Flambeau. He once related that he participated at a ceremonial drum dance in Woodmen's Hall in 1924 where drums used included a "town drum," drums from the Old Indian Village, and a visiting drum from Menominee Reservation. Other local elders state social dances involving band instruments were held in the Woodmen's Hall.

In this final section of the introduction, other topics related to the Reservation Period are also examined. Definitions and explanations related to topics discussed by the elders in their interviews will include: intertribal and interracial marriage, transportation, religion, medicine people and medicines, sports and leisure, language loss and revitalization, harvesting and sustenance, Wisconsin's restriction of tribal gathering rights, Ojibwe challenges to state authority to regulate off-reservation harvesting, opposition and response to treaty rights, off-reservation spearing, and changing elder roles at Lac du Flambeau.

Intertribal and Interracial Marriage

The Ojibwe tribe has long intermarried with other tribes and peoples. The *doodem* (clan) of an individual seeking marriage is very important. Those who belong to a specific clan are forbidden to marry others of the same clan.

Long ago some marriages were arranged. The arranged marriages involved other clans of the Ojibwe nation, other tribes, or non-tribal people. If the marriage was not arranged, specific courting rituals were normally practiced by the Ojibwe.

The first interracial marriages involved the French fur traders who married Ojibwe women. Later Ojibwe men and women married first English, and then Americans. Children of these unions were considered to be *aabitoose* or *wiisaakode* (half-breed).

In the distant past some marriages resulted from raiding Ojibwe war parties who captured women from other tribes. The women would be absorbed into their captor tribes. Over time both the women and children would be considered Ojibwe.

Following the Reservation Period marriages were seldom arranged and partnerships were the result of interaction with others at boarding schools. The period of Indian Civil Conservation Corps at Lac du Flambeau also resulted in intertribal marriages. The travel associated with the World Wars also resulted in new marriages. Today, as long ago, school travel, ceremonial travel, and social gatherings continue to create new marriage relationships between the Ojibwe and others.

Transportation

Transportation has also undergone change over time at Lac du Flambeau. Prior to the Reservation Period, there were few roads in northern Wisconsin. The Ojibwe used an extensive trail system that crossed both waterways and land. The trail system linked Ojibwe to their seasonal harvesting camps, other villages, and other tribes. Travel was easiest when paddling birchbark canoes. The extremely buoyant *wiigwaasi-jiimaan* (birchbark canoe) was lightweight and easily paddled and portaged. The *zhooshkodaabaan* (sled or toboggan) was used for pulling people and gear over the snow. *Agimag* (snow shoes) were typically worn when walking in deep snow. Two types of snowshoes were worn. The longer snowshoe was used on established trails, while the shorter, round bearpaw snowshoe was used in brushy areas off the trail.

Later, the Ojibwe obtained *bezhigoogaanzhiig* (horses) in trade from other tribes and via annuity payments. They did not utilize horses to the extent tribes to the west did. During the Reservation Period some Ojibwe occasionally rode horses. Those who could afford horse-drawn wagons used them for transportation. Few Lac du Flambeau people could initially afford wagons.

Logging operations created the need for the *ishkode-daabaan* (train) and *ishkode daabaan miikana* (railroads) in northern Wisconsin. Trains were needed to transport logs to southern mills. The railroad arrived at the Lac du Flambeau Reservation boundary only to be stopped. The leaders at Lac du Flambeau were very cautious of allowing the railway through their lands. The tribal leadership eventually agreed to allow the train passage. Midwe'asang, then head speaker of the Lac du Flambeau Tribe, announced the decision in 1889. Once established, Lac du Flambeau people traveled by trains for the purpose of shopping, visiting, and adventure.

Mitigo-jiimaanan (wooden boats) with *azheboyaanaakoon* (oars) gradually replaced the birchbark canoe for lake travel within the reservation. Much later, *biiwaabiko jiimaanan* (metal boats) and *akikoons* (outboard motors) became available to some.

The people of Lac du Flambeau eventually obtained *daabaanag* (automobiles). Just as with horsedrawn wagons, it took some time before automobiles became commonly owned. Today, all forms of modern transportation are used by the Lac du Flambeau people.

Religion

Religious ceremonies given to the Ojibwe people are sacred. The Ojibwe believe spiritual power is necessary to attain long and healthy lives. Many Ojibwe people consider it dangerous to discuss specific aspects of religion outside of sacred circles.

Members at Lac du Flambeau continue to perform the Midewiwin (Medicine Dance Ceremony), Ogichidaa Niimii'idiwin (Warriors Dance), and Gichi-Dewe'iigan Niimii'idiwin (Big Drum Dance). The Medicine Dance Ceremony is the original and ancient ceremony bestowed to the people for healing. The Warriors Dance is based on individual dream songs used to transfer healing power. The Big Drum was transferred to the Ojibwe by the Sioux people during the early Reservation Period. The Big Drum religion promotes peace and friendship.

These ceremonies have continued despite attempts to eradicate traditional religious practice. Events that negatively affected traditional religions include bans on ceremonies, wars, boarding school, and gradual acculturation accompanied with loss of the Ojibwe language.

Other religions are also evident at Lac du Flambeau. These include the Native American Peyote, Catholic, Presbyterian, and Baptist Churches. Native American Bible Study groups also assemble here.

Medicine People and Medicines

The Ojibwe are recognized for their knowledge of the natural world and naturally occurring medicines. This knowledge was crucial during times of illness. In the late 1950s western medicine became more available to the peoples of Lac du Flambeau. Most residents were dependent upon traditional medicines until then.

Traditional Ojibwe healing gradually became more difficult to access. Many older tribal members with knowledge have passed on, leaving fewer practitioners of herbal medicines. Many medicine people continue to provide services to those who seek them today, however. Ojibwe healers are not all alike. They have different levels of skill, may specialize in specific areas of the body, or may practice a specific healing approach.

Sports and Leisure

The old forms of sports and leisure practiced by the Ojibwe included *baaga'adowe* (lacrosse), *babasikawewin* (double-ball), *gamaagiwebiinigewin* (snow snake), *makizin ataagewin* (moccasin game), *oninji'iwaataadiwin* (the hand game), and *bagesewin* (bowl game).

Lacrosse was played by many tribes. The Ojibwe only allowed their *ininiwag* (men) to play. The game of lacrosse was played by two opposing teams. Each of the men carried a lacrosse racket, typically made of ash wood. A small rawhide or wood ball was either carried or thrown by the rackets. The team that struck a single pole with the ball scored. Lacrosse was once very popular and has a spiritual origin. Thomas Vennum, a well known author, has spearheaded an effort to revitalize lacrosse in Wisconsin and Minnesota Ojibwe communities. (See Thomas Vennum's *American Indian Lacrosse, Little Brother of War*.)

The *Ojibwe-ikwewag* (ladies) played a game known as double-ball. Each player on opposing teams had *babasikawe'aatig-oog* (two sticks for moving the ball). The *babasikawenag* (double-ball) was either two small buckskin bags or two small bundles of sticks fastened together by a thong. The scoring of the game was similar to lacrosse as the teams attempted to reach the *inaawaa'win* (goal stake) with the double-ball.

Snow snake was a winter game. The Ojibwe carved a stick into the shape of a snake. This carved stick known as *ginebig* (a snake) was then thrown. The snake that traveled the farthest distance was the winner.

Moccasin game is a form of gambling played by men only. In this game four bullets are each hidden under a moccasin. One of the four bullets is marked. The object of the game is to win points by successfully hiding the bullet from the opposing team. Typically three man teams opposed each other in the moccasin game. Each team used a *dewe'iigaans* (small drum) to accompany the singing of moccasin-game songs. The game was highly competitive. Legends tell of fortunes won and lost while playing this game. The game was said to have been outlawed at the site of annuity payment sites. Some losing teams were reported to have caused great disturbances following the loss of their annuity payments. The moccasin game is still played quietly at Lac du Flambeau. In other areas of Ojibwe country it has become a popular tournament game at pow-wows.

Ojibwe also played *oninji'iwaataadiwin* (the hand game). This simple sport involved guessing which hand an object was hidden in. Songs and wagers accompanied this old game as well.

The women of Lac du Flambeau also played the bowl game or dice. Opposing teams would place *biidaakichigan* (small bone figures) into *bagesewinaagan* (wooden bowl used only for the game) and toss them. Various points were assigned, depending on how the figures landed.

A number of different games were played by children, including *bipiinjikanan'owin* (dewclaw game). A set of hollow bones that were originally adjacent to the hoof of a deer was attached to a small string and a sharp needle. The needle was held and the child attempted to drop the small hollow bones onto the needle. *Aadizookewin* (storytelling) was also a leisure activity but served the purpose of teaching as well. (See *Chippewa Customs* by Frances Densmore.)

During and after the boarding school era, new games were introduced to the Ojibwe. These include baseball, basketball, boxing, wrestling, and football. Today, most popular sports are played at Lac du Flambeau. Lac du Flambeau has continued to excel in both individual and team sports. Many who attended boarding schools at Lac du Flambeau and other locations also became musicians.

Language Loss and Revitalization

Many Ojibwe today believe loss of Ojibwe language at Lac du Flambeau resulted from federal policies. These policies were designed to detribalize the Ojibwe and mainstream them into the larger society.

Many today view the boarding school as the beginning of the demise of *Ojibwemowin* (Ojibwe language) in Lac du Flambeau. Children attending school there were forbidden to speak Ojibwe. They were also prohibited from participation in any Ojibwe cultural activities. Physical punishment was dealt to any student who disobeyed these rules. Children attending boarding school were separated from their Ojibwe-speaking families for long periods of time.

Children quickly learned that *Ojibwemowin* could not be used at school. They were taught the use of English language would be necessary to survive. As children became bilingual, Ojibwe language would only be used at home while on school breaks. Many elders have stated that they lost their Ojibwe language while at school. Some chose to learn it while others simply let it go.

The boarding school experience had a deep effect on its students. As the students aged and had families of their own, they chose not to teach the language to their children. When asked, "Why not?" one elder stated, "I didn't want my children or grandchildren being physically beaten for speaking Ojibwe." As a result of boarding school, most people born at Lac du Flambeau after 1930 did not speak Ojibwe as their first language.

Yet the language continued as small groups of fluent elders continued to converse and pass the Ojibwe language to children and grandchildren. Eventually, when it was evident to the Lac du Flambeau Tribe that its original language was being lost, new efforts were created to save the language. In the early 1970s following the fight for Civil Rights, there was a resurgence of Native culture and pride. Many tribes, including Lac du Flambeau, sought to reconnect to their native languages.

Two primary barriers to this effort soon become evident. The first was lack of resources to fund an Ojibwe language program, while the second was limited availability of Ojibwe language teachers. Over time the pool of fluent speakers had diminished greatly.

In 1975 a program called the Wisconsin Native American Language Project began. Native languages spoken in Wisconsin were organized and documented with the assistance of linguists and fluent tribal elders. The project resulted in newly developed curriculum for language teaching. At the end of the project no funds were available in tribal communities to implement the curriculums.

Ojibwe language instruction started for Lac du Flambeau students, despite the lack of adequate funding. Hannah Maulson (Giiwekamigookwe), now in the spirit world, was a key elder in Lac du Flambeau who taught Ojibwe language as a result of Title VII funding. She provided instruction to community members, Lac du Flambeau Public School students, and Lakeland High School students. Giiwekamigookwe also provided Ojibwe language consultation to the Wisconsin Native American Language Project.

Other small community-based language approaches were also attempted. Language teaching elders, also now in the spirit world, included Rose Bobidosh Conto (Ozaawaagiizhigookwe) and Laura Barber Meshigaud (Kookwe).

The Lac du Flambeau tribe had another opportunity to perpetuate Ojibwe language in 1988 when the tribe implemented the Family Circles program. This program used an Ojibwe language and culture based curriculum to combat dysfunction within reservation families. An advisory board made up of tribal elders provided guidance in both cultural and language areas to the project participants. Joe Chosa (Ozaawaabik), Celia DeFoe (Waabanongagokwe), and Reva Chapman (Biiwaabikoons) served as language instructors and members of the Elders Resource Council. The elder Wilber Mitchell (*Bines*) also participated, and Don Carufel, Sr., (Niizho Gaaboo) served as language instructor for the program as well. *Waaswaaganing Ojibwemowin: Ojibwe Language Manual* was completed as a result of the project. Today it is considered a major accomplishment as the dialect used in the manual is nearly one hundred percent Lac du Flambeau.

Following the end of Family Circles, the Lac du Flambeau Tribe continued its pursuit of Ojibwe language and cultural knowledge by funding the Elders Language Program. Language preservation and instruction were the program's primary activities. Language tapes and manuals were also developed with elders guidance. The status of the Lac du Flambeau Ojibwe language was heavily impacted recently with the passing of key elders Reva Chapman, Celia DeFoe, and Wilber Mitchell.

A new approach is underway at Lac du Flambeau to increase the fluency of community members. Other elders are now assisting language staff in meeting Ojibwe language objectives. They include Bill Ackley (Niojibines), Dennis Ackley (Midwe'aange), Don Grey (Midegiizhig), and Marcella Beson. Joe Chosa (Ozaawaabik) also continues to provide key Ojibwe language translations and cultural knowledge. Language preservation activities, instruction, and curricular development continue within the community. Language classes are held two nights a week in the community and Ojibwemowin is taught from Early Head Start through grade 8 at the Lac du Flambeau Public School. A newly designed Ojibwe language curriculum has been implemented here. Initial evaluation of student performance has revealed increased comprehension of basic Ojibwe terms and phrases.

Ozaawaabik (Joe Chosa), a fluent elder, stated, "There was a time when I was very concerned our language was going to be lost, but I no longer feel that way. I believe our language is coming back, as more and more people are using Ojibwemowin today."

Harvesting and Sustenance

The Ojibwe people continue to depend upon the natural resources that were placed here by the Great Spirit. It is important to realize Ojibwe people would suffer starvation and death if unable to secure these resources. The nature and degree of harvesting has changed over the ages; but harvesting has continued and is considered a traditional Ojibwe activity.

The harvest typically follows the cycle of the season and coincides with the availability of specific plants, animals, and fish. Many months within the Ojibwe calendar year describe harvesting activities. Each year is different, thus fish runs, ripening of plants, and availability of animals changes. Seasonal activities are reflected in the names of the months, or "moons," in Ojibwe language:

Ziigwan (Spring):

Iskigamizige Giizis	= April	= Boiling Down Sap Moon
Waabigoni Giizis	= May	= Flowering Moon

Niibin (Summer):

Ode' imini Giizis	= June	= Strawberry Moon
Aabita Niibini Giizis	= July	= Halfway through Summer Moon
Manoominike Giizis	= August	= Wild Rice Making Moon

Dagwaagin (Fall):

Waatebagaa Giizis	= September	= Leaves Changing Color Moon
Binaakwe Giizis	= October	= Raking Moon
Gashkadino Giizis	= November	= Freezing Moon

Biboon (Winter):

Gichi-Manidoo Giizis	= December	= Great Spirit Moon
Manidoo Giizisoons	= January	= Little Moon Spirit
Namebini Giizis	= February	= Sucker Moon
Onaabani Giizis	= March	= Crust on Snow Moon

Some natural resources can be considered primary and others secondary, yet all are important. Primary resources are those that promoted life and met the basic living needs of people. These resources provide food, water, shelter, and clothing. Other resources may not have been harvested as frequently yet are equally important. An example of a secondary resource may be medicinal plants, which served the purpose of restoring health to the ill.

The following section describes Ojibwe people do during the various seasons. The methods have changed through the times as technology has improved.

Ziigwan (Spring)

The harvest cycle started in the spring of the year and coincided with the warming of the earth in April. The Ojibwe referred to this month as *Iskigamizige Giizis* the "Boiling Sap Moon." Warmer days and cold nights encouraged the sap to flow from the maple trees.

Long ago, family groups arrived at the various maple groves to prepare for the sap runs while snow was still on the ground. Valuable maple sugar products came from the boiled-down sap. Ojibwe once depended on these products to last throughout the year.

Much hard work was necessary to obtain maple products. First the Ojibwe would slash through the bark of the maple tree and place a *negwaakwaan* (small wooden sap trough) to guide the *ziinzibaakwadaboo* (maple sap) into a *biskitenaagan* (folded birchbark basket for catching sap). When the baskets filled, the sap would be poured into a large container called an *atoobaan*. The sap was then transferred from the *atoobaan* into large kettles that hung over fire. Next the sap was boiled inside the large kettles. The boiling process was lengthy and required large quantities of firewood and constant supervision as stirring was required.

Various stages of boiling down produced *iskigamizigan* (maple syrup), then *ziigai'iganan* (maple sugar cakes), and eventually *anishinaabe ziinzibaakwad* (maple sugar). *Bigiw* (maple taffy) was also occasionally produced with the use of snow. These maple products were once primary in the diet of Ojibwe. Ojibwe people at Lac du Flambeau continue this tradition each spring.(See *Iskigamizigeyaang geyaabi omaa Waaswaaganing* [We Still Boil Maple Sap Here at Lac du Flambeau] videotape produced by Lac du Flambeau Ojibwe Language Program)

After they made sugar the people would move adjacent to lakes and rivers to harvest fish. In late April to early May walleyed pike and muskellunge or musky would begin to spawn in the shallow waters. The Ojibwe harvested these species and other fish for food.

Fish were obtained by various methods. Some Ojibwe made fish traps by tying small saplings together. They also speared fish at night in shallow water aided by torches and canoes. It is this practice of using a *waaswaagan* (torch) that gave Waaswaaganing (Place of Fishing by Torch Light) its name. Later, when the French witnessed the Ojibwe spearing fish, they named the place Lac du Flambeau (Lake of the Torch).

Bagida'waawin (netting) was another common method for obtaining fish. Harvesting of fish was not limited to spring, but occurred throughout the year. The most effective method at the time was utilized. There was no refrigeration, so harvested fish were either eaten immediately, smoked in smoke houses, or dried over smoldering fires for future use.

The Ojibwe also planted small gardens after the fish harvest and prior to the first berry harvest. Few crops could be grown due to the short growing season. Gardening has been a continuing tradition among the people of Waaswaaganing. In addition to gardens nature provided an abundance of natural foods including wild rice, milkweed, wild potato, berries, fiddlehead ferns, hazelnuts, and apples.

The United States unsuccessfully attempted to create Ojibwe farmers. The government hired resident farmers, who were placed within the reservations to teach the people how to farm. The short growing season, impractical soil types, and associated costs doomed these projects from the start. The other reason for failure was that few Ojibwe people had the desire to become full-time farmers. Small gardens versus large scale farming continue to be more desirable to the Ojibwe at Lac du Flambeau.

The Ojibwe people also harvested *wiigwaas* (birchbark) in the springtime. Birch bark was a highly sought after natural material and was used for many things including, roof covering on lodges, canoes, various storage vessels or baskets, cooking vessels, drying wild rice, ceremonial purposes, and fanning baskets.

Birchbark can be harvested in any season, but early June is the time when it is easiest to do so. The harvest was easier at this time because no rind is present between the outer bark and the inner cambium layers. When cut in the spring, the bark "pops" off the tree. As the year goes on, the rind thickens, until it reaches its peak thickness in the cold months. This type of bark is known as *bibooni-wiigwaas* (winter bark) and is valued for its etching capacity.

Niibin (Summer)

During the summer months, life was relatively easy compared to other seasons of the year. The weather was warm, and there was an abundance of fish, game, and plants to harvest. Ojibwe spent the summer fishing, picking berries, and harvesting other fruits. The people also tended to their gardens at this time. The Ojibwe also hunted whitetail deer during the summer months.

Dagwaagin (Fall)

In late August to early September many Ojibwe concentrated on harvesting wild rice. The Ojibwe realized food would be necessary to survive through the long winter months ahead. A successful wild rice harvest would assure starvation could be avoided. For this reason, the Ojibwe people placed a high priority on the wild rice harvest.

Manoominike ogimaawag (rice chiefs) were selected by the band and given authority to assure that the rice would be harvested properly. After the rice camp was set up, the chief determined who would pick rice in areas of specific rice beds. Two methods were used to harvest wild rice. Harvesters either bundled the rice, or they knocked it off the stocks with slender sticks. Some areas of the rice bed were marked for "tying" and other sections were specified as "knocking areas." The boundaries within the rice bed were either known by the harvesters or marked with stakes. Individuals or teams were given portions of the wild rice bed for harvest preparation.

Those who intended to tie rice would enter their section of the bed to *dakobidoon* (bundle the stalks with basswood inner bark). The bundling process involved tying bunches of individual rice plants together from the middle section to the top of the plant, where the rice seed grows. The now-bundled rice stalks were allowed to ripen with less chance of loss of the valuable seed to birds, wind, or rain storms.

The rice chief determined when the harvest would begin. No one was allowed to enter the rice beds until the chief gave them permission. Violators of this rule were punished by having their canoes taken, or being told to leave the area. When the chief believed the plants to be ripened, the beds were opened. With their hands harvesters bent the bundled rice over their canoes and shook them. Ripe wild rice fell into the boat, while unripe rice clung to the stalks. Later after additional ripening time the bundled rice was untied and the remainder of the rice was knocked into the canoe by striking it with small paddles.

Later in history the State of Wisconsin prohibited the Ojibwe rice bundle method of harvesting. Tying rice was still practiced by some elders and widows at the time it was deemed illegal by the State of Wisconsin.

Not all people bundled rice at this time. Some Ojibwe simply waited for the chiefs to open portions of the ricebed and then knocked the rice. Two people formed a rice harvesting team. The harvesting of rice is most effective with only two people in a canoe. The team consists of a rice harvester who uses sticks to knock rice and a person who propels the *jiimaan* (canoe) forward. *Bawa'iginaatigoog* (rice knocking sticks) are slender round cedar sticks in the range of thirty-four to thirty-eight inches long. The *gaandakii'iganaatig* (long pole used to push the canoe forward) was made of black spruce or tamarack. The pole also has a "Y" stick, made of maple or oak, attached to one end. The push pole allows the team passage through the rice beds, when paddling becomes too difficult.

The push pole is handled while standing, which allows the *gayaandakii'iged* (push-poler) to follow straight lines within the rice field and/or guide the person knocking rice to the ripe rice within the bed. "Bawa'am" means "he or she knocks wild rice." The sticks are skillfully used to gather groups of rice stalk together, then gently knocking the ripened rice off the top of the stalk. Knocking is synonymous with harvesting. Rice harvesters often switched tasks while harvesting rice.

When harvested, the rice is wet and needs to be dried to prevent spoilage. The rice was spread onto birchbark sheets to allow the sun the dry it. The Ojibwe command is "basaan yo'o manoomin," which means "dry this rice."

After drying the next process was *gidasigewin* (parching of the rice). Small fires heated either kettles or tubs, and the rice would be stirred to prevent scorching. Before the Ojibwe obtained kettles certain plants were woven together for this purpose. The woven plants could withstand the heat of the fire without igniting.

Next the Ojibwe removed the rice hulls covering the seeds. They dug a hole in the ground, then lined the hole with buckskin. Some Ojibwe lined the hole with cedar staves. This jigging pit was known as a *bootaagan* by some Ojibwe people. After the roasted rice was poured in an individual would jig, or dance, the rice. To prevent the itchy chaff from touching their skin, the Ojibwe fashioned *mimigoshkam makizinan (*special moccasins with high cuffs). To allow the person jigging the rice better balance, the Ojibwe used two parallel poles above the jigging pit. These poles also assisted in holding much of the body weight off the rice, thus minimizing breakage. This process is known as *mimigoshkamowin* (jigging rice).

Next the Ojibwe used a special birchbark basket called a *nooshkaachinaagan* (winnowing basket), to remove the loosened rice hulls. The rice that had been jigged was poured into the *nooshkaachinaagan*. The rice was thrown upward and caught in the basket, allowing the wind to blow away the loosened rice hulls.

The rice was then hand cleaned in order to remove any remaining hulls. After cleaning the rice was carefully stored away in *makakoon* (birch bark baskets), *giizhik-wanagek-mashkimodensan* (cedar bark bags), or *awesiiwayaanan* (animal skins). Wild rice would stay unspoiled indefinitely when kept in cool, dry places. Rice that was not carried with the families was stored secretly in *asanjigoowin* (caches underground lined with grass), and secured when needed. (See *Manoominikewin omaa Waaswaaganing* [Wild Rice Making Here at Lac du Flambeau 2002] videotape produced by Lac du Flambeau Ojibwe Language Program)

The Ojibwe hunted various waterfowl, primarily in the fall and spring. This harvesting activity coincided with the migration. *Zhiishiibag* (ducks), *nikaawag* (geese), *manoominikeshiig* (ricebirds), and *maajigadeg* (coots) were typically sought for food. Other birds were also harvested including the *baaka'aakwe* (prairie chicken) and *bine* (grouse).

In the fall the Ojibwe gardeners harvested their *gitigaan* (garden) products. After harvesting the garden products were either dried and stored or canned for future use. Favorite garden crops included *opiniig* (potatoes), *zhigaagawaanzhiig* (onions), *okaadaak* (carrots), *oginiig* (tomatoes), *maskodiisimanag* (beans) and *mandaaminag* (corn).

Waawaashkeshiig giiwasewin (hunting of whitetail deer) was another important activity in the fall. The fall hunt for whitetail deer secured meat for the winter months. In the northern winters, extreme cold causes many animals to become scarce. The Ojibwe dried and stored the venison to prevent starvation during the winter months.

The old traditional methods of hunting deer were to use clubs, spears, or bows and arrows. Later in history following the arrival of fur traders the Ojibwe obtained *baashkiziganan* (rifles). The rifle made deer hunting much more effective.

In addition to eating the deer the Ojibwe also used many other parts of the animal for other uses. The brain was used to soften the hide during the tanning process. The *bashkwegin* (buckskin) produced was used to make clothing and footwear. The hooves were used for ornamentation or bells. Various bones were used to make tools, toys, and weapons.

Wanii'igewin (trapping of animals) was also done by the Ojibwe people. Muskrat and beaver were trapped for both food and their fur. Trapping occurred both before and after the lakes froze. Demand for these animals and others increased during the Fur-Trade Era.

Biboon (Winter)

When the winter snows piled high in the northwoods, the Ojibwe sought the *waaboozoog* (rabbit). During this season, most other game animals were difficult to find. First the Ojibwe located rabbit trails and then they hung snares made of braided basswood twine to catch the rabbits. In addition to providing meat the rabbit fur was sewn together to form *waabooyaanan* (blankets). The white-colored winter fur was both soft and warm. The fur was used also on mittens, jackets, and footwear for additional warmth during the cold winter months.

Many Ojibwe tribes have long speared fish through the ice. *Akwawaawin* (spearing fish through the ice), is an ancient tradition still practiced at Lac du Flambeau. The ice spearers have long used the *mitigo-giigoohnzens* (wooden-fish decoy) to lure fish within close range. The Ojibwe speared the fish and following preparation ate them.

The primary fish targeted was the *maashkinoozhii* (muskellunge or musky). To successfully harvest a musky by this method both skill and patience were required. Special equipment was needed to set up and fish by this method. First a chisel (*eshkan*) was used to chop a hole in the ice. Sticks were stood up in the ice around the hole then tied together on top. The sticks looked like a small tipi frame after tying. Boughs from a balsam tree were placed on the ice surrounding the hole, then the framework was covered with hides or blankets. This lodge is called *akwawaa wigawaamens* (small spearing tipi).

The blankets covering the lodge prevented sunlight from entering. Once in the darkened lodge the ice spearer saw clearly into the water. While lying on top of the ice, he dropped a wooden fish decoy attached to a string into the water. When he pulled the string, it caused the decoy to swim about in a circle.

As the musky approached the decoy the decoy was raised, bringing the fish up toward the surface. When the musky was within range, the *anit* (spear) was either dropped or thrown into the fish. The spear was attached to a *biminikawaan* (rope), and the rope was pulled in. The musky was taken out of the water and shaken off onto the ice. The musky was used as an important winter food source by the Ojibwe people. Other fish, if attracted, were also speared. (See *Akwawaawin omaa Waaswaaganing* [Ice Spearing Here at Lac du Flambeau] videotape by Lac du Flambeau Ojibwe Language Program.)

Wisconsin's Restriction of Tribal Gathering Rights

The Ojibwe survived as a hunting, fishing, and gathering society. They knew which natural resources were within their territory and where the resources were located. They also clearly understood the best time to harvest these resources and harvested them conservatively.

Over the generations the Ojibwe had established specific seasonal harvesting sites, located throughout the territories that they eventually ceded to the United States in treaties.

In treaty agreements the Ojibwe retained the right to hunt, fish, and gather within the ceded territories. Following statehood in 1848, Ojibwe access to resources was limited. Various state laws were enacted to protect Wisconsin's resources. These laws did not take into consideration the rights reserved by the Ojibwe.

I identify below some of the state's conservation laws that adversely affected the Ojibwe people who were highly dependent upon natural resources. A short description of the reaffirmation of off-reservation treaty rights follows.

1853: Wisconsin outlawed the practice of gill netting. Gill netting of fish had long been a traditional method employed by the Ojibwe. Ojibwe that attempted to fish using gill nets were arrested, jailed, and fined. Gill netting was done throughout the year by Ojibwe people. Gill nets could be set under the ice or in open water. During the fall prior to the freeze, whitefish were gill netted by the Ojibwe. Walleye, musky, trout, northern pike, and suckerfish were also commonly netted, prepared, and eaten.

1881: Wisconsin established closed seasons on game fish. The Ojibwe were dependent upon the various fish to feed themselves. Again, the state enforced its regulations against Ojibwe harvesting needed fish during the state's closed seasons. Ojibwe were expected to purchase state fishing licenses, and follow state fishing regulations.

1883: Wisconsin shortened its hunting season and also banned night hunting. Ojibwe access to game animals was restricted as a result of this state conservation effort. The Ojibwe had a long history of hunting game as it was needed and their methods of harvesting game included night hunting. Originally, the Ojibwe used torches to light the night, which enabled them to see game animals. These animals were harvested, prepared, and then eaten. The state strictly enforced the new laws, despite treaty right claims by the Ojibwe people.

1887: The State of Wisconsin started employing conservation wardens. This new human resource made it extremely difficult for the Ojibwe to harvest off-reservation. Conservation wardens stopped most Ojibwe people they encountered off-reservation. Once stopped conservation wardens checked the Ojibwe people for state licenses and searched their vehicles. During arrests the wardens confiscated any and all fish or game considered to be illegal. It was not uncommon for Ojibwe deer hunters to be arrested and fined. Firearms used in what the state considered illegal harvesting were often confiscated. These firearms were never returned to their owners and were typically auctioned. Some Ojibwe claim the wardens also seized traps, snowshoes, spears and boats. Regular law enforcement typically cooperated with conservation wardens to assure that all state laws were enforced. Traffic and vehicle safety citations were also frequently issued to Ojibwe attempting to harvest off-reservation.

Despite arrest, jail, and fines, the Ojibwe people continued to hunt, fish, and gather within the ceded territories. The majority of tribal people were still dependent on natural resources to live, as few employment opportunities existed on the reservation.

1901: The State of Wisconsin also attempted to regulate fishing on the reservation. John Blackbird, an Ojibwe from Bad River, was arrested for netting fish within Bad River Reservation waters. Later, a federal court ruled that Wisconsin did not have the right to regulate harvesting within the Ojibwe reservations and Blackbird was released. The court did not address the Ojibwe off-reservation harvesting rights during this trial.

For over eighty years following the release of John Blackbird, Wisconsin continued to arrest, jail, and fine Ojibwe people for breaking state conservation laws off-reservation. Over this same period many precious food resources were confiscated by conservation officers.

Ojibwe Challenge State's Authority to Regulate Off-Reservation Harvesting

The Ojibwe became weary of the state's efforts to impede reserved treaty harvesting rights and realized that the time was right to reaffirm their harvesting rights in the court systems. In the early 1970s the Ojibwe people won two cases involving their fishing rights on Lake Superior. Victory in these two cases led the Ojibwe to argue for all previously held harvesting rights in the ceded territory. This trial (LCO v. Lester Voigt) would begin a long and controversial period in Wisconsin.

The first monumental case involving Ojibwe treaty rights was in Michigan and the second was in Wisconsin. In 1971 People of the State of Michigan v. William Jondreau (Jondreau Decision) reversed a previous court decision made in 1930 (People v. Chosa). The Jondreau Decision reaffirmed the fishing rights of the Keeweenaw Bay Ojibwe. As a result of this ruling, Michigan could no longer enforce its fishing regulations within the waters of Lake Superior against the Keeweenaw Bay people.

In 1972 a similar ruling was handed down in Wisconsin. The case, known as Gurnoe vs. Wisconsin (Gurnoe Decision), favored the Bad River and Red Cliff tribes. Based upon the 1854 Treaty the court ruled that the tribes did indeed have a protected treaty right. The only regulations the State of Wisconsin could enforce would be those necessary to prevent a substantial depletion of the fish supply.

Following the 1974 arrest of Fred and Mike Tribble of Lac Courte Oreilles, the tribe filed suit in Western District Federal Court. The 1975 legal suit requested that the State of Wisconsin cease enforcing state law against tribal members exercising legal treaty rights.

In 1979 Federal Judge James Doyle ruled that the treaty rights of the Ojibwe had been relinquished at the time of the 1854 treaty signing. He also stated that the Presidential Removal Order of 1850 had withdrawn the rights in question. The Ojibwe appealed this decision, and in 1983, the U.S. Court of Appeals, Seventh Circuit, in Chicago reversed Doyle's findings. A three-judge panel decided that Judge Doyle had misinterpreted standard canons of construction while interpreting Indian Law. The Seventh Circuit remanded the case back to Judge Doyle in the Western District Federal Court to determine both the scope of the rights and the degree of state regulation. This case is also commonly referred to as the Voigt Decision as Lester Voigt was the head of Wisconsin's Department of Natural Resources when the suit was filed. It is also known as LCO I.

In 1985 the Seventh Circuit Court ruled that the Ojibwe tribes had the rights to hunt and fish anywhere within the ceded territories. This included privately owned lands. Doyle established a three-phase plan to determine the following:

- the nature and extent of Ojibwe treaty rights,
- the permissible extent to which Wisconsin could regulate Ojibwe treaty rights,
- the damages the tribe was entitled to for Wisconsin's infringement on their rights.

This ruling was known as LCO II, which affirmed Ojibwe rights despite state efforts to stop them from hunting and fishing on private lands within their ceded territory. Judge Doyle completed the first phase with his 1987 ruling known as LCO III. It stated that the Ojibwe could hunt, fish, and gather using any method they wished in the ceded territory at a level that would provide a modest living off the land. The state was given the right to impose restrictions to preserve certain resources and species. The state was also granted the right to exercise laws that would ensure safety.

Judge Doyle passed away in 1987. Judge Barbara Crabb was assigned the task of addressing the second phase. This decision was known as LCO IV. Judge Crabb's decision in 1987 ruled that the state could regulate Ojibwe harvest activities in the interest of conservation and safety but could not deter the Ojibwe from taking what was legally theirs.

In 1988 (LCO V) Judge Crabb ruled that the Ojibwe could not earn a modest living even if they harvested all the resources on the ceded lands. She suggested a plan to limit the fish harvested from the lakes annually.

The fish limiting plan Judge Crabb had suggested was presented in 1989 (LCO VI). Judge Crabb established the safe harvest level, which would identify the number of fish that could be taken without depleting the population. The Ojibwe were entitled to harvest the entire safe harvest level of fish by means of the decision made in LCO III.

In 1990 (LCO VII) Judge Crabb ruled that the Ojibwe were entitled to harvest half of the permissible deer harvest on the ceded territory. She also ruled that the state could ban hunting in the summer and after sundown to ensure public safety. This ruling ended the second phase of the negotiations.

The final phase of Judge Crabb's task was to assess damages Wisconsin owed the Ojibwe for infringing on their treaty rights. In 1990 Judge Crabb's ruling (LCO VIII) shocked the Ojibwe and treaty rights supporters. Judge Crabb ruled that the Eleventh Amendment to the Constitution protected states against lawsuits pursued by tribes. The Ojibwe claim for $300 million in damages was rejected.

In 1991 (LCO IX) Judge Crabb again surprised the Ojibwe and their supporters with her ruling on timber harvesting. She decided that the harvest of timber resources was not a "usual and customary" activity for the Wisconsin Ojibwe. As a result Wisconsin Ojibwe were not allowed to harvest trees for timber. Judge Crabb ruled that the Ojibwe were allowed to gather various forest products without regulation. Examples include firewood, birchbark, and maple sap.

On May 20, 1991, Attorney General James E. Doyle announced that Wisconsin had accepted Judge Crabb's final judgment. In his statement Doyle noted the State of Wisconsin would not attempt to appeal any portion of the case to the United States, Court of Appeals for the Seventh Circuit. Attorney General Doyle stated that many risks were associated with appealing the decisions. He also noted that the state had secured seven key victories while in litigation. They included:

- The tribal claim for $300 million for past monetary damages was denied.
- The tribal claim for timber harvesting rights was rejected. This ruling saved millions for counties.
- The state has ultimate authority to protect and manage the resources in ceded territory.

- Tribal members cannot enter onto privately owned land to exercise their rights.
- Treaty rights do not extend to privately owned stream beds, river bottoms and overflowed lands.
- The Tribe is not entitled to all the available resources necessary to sustain a modest standard of living. The resources must be shared on a 50–50 basis.
- The State can impose on tribal members its boating and safety regulations, even when the Ojibwe are engaged in treaty protected activities. The tribe cannot shine deer or engage in summer hunting.

On May 20, 1991, the six bands of Wisconsin Ojibwe issued a joint statement, which was signed by each of the respective tribal government leaders. The statement outlined the reasons for agreeing not to further appeal the Crabb decision. Tribal leaders announced the objective of securing treaty rights to hunt, fish, and gather had been met and that the decision not to appeal was a gesture of peace and friendship toward the people of Wisconsin. The leaders also added that it was their hope that some day peace and friendship would be reciprocated by the general population and officials of Wisconsin.

Opposition to Treaty Rights and the Response

Both the State of Wisconsin and many of its citizens opposed the Ojibwe exercise of treaty rights. The State of Wisconsin battled through sixteen years of litigation, while many citizens residing in northern Wisconsin attempted to disrupt treaty harvesting. Many frustrated treaty-rights opponents often opposed the state's handling of the case.

Initially there were many reasons why the people of Wisconsin opposed treaty rights. Many mistakenly believed that treaty rights were given to the Ojibwe people by federal courts, when the rights were actually reserved in treaties. The multiple reasons eventually began to focus on two areas, conservation and economics. Treaty opponents speculated that the Ojibwe would over-harvest the resources. The result would be financially devastating to resort owners, restaurant owners, and all other businesspeople in the north.

Data provided by the Great Lakes Indian Fish and Wildlife Commission (GLIFWC) in 1991 clearly showed that state-licensed anglers harvested far more walleye than all the Ojibwe in Wisconsin. The combined walleye harvest by all six bands of Ojibwe spearfishers during the noted years is very small when compared to the total state angling harvest.

Ojibwe Off-reservation Spearfishing Walleye Harvest:

1985	2,761 walleye	1986	6,940 walleye	1987	21,321 walleye
1988	25,969 walleye	1989	16,054 walleye	1990	25,348 walleye
1991	23,018 walleye				

State WDNR estimated that state anglers harvested 600,000 walleyes annually from 834 lakes. The estimate considered that state-licensed angling fishery is not directly controlled. The WDNR arrived at the estimate as a result of partial survey estimates were made based on catches from 34 lakes during the period 1980–1987.

Various studies were made to determine the effect of treaty rights exercise to the fishing tourism. It was determined that significant changes to Wisconsin's tourism economy were occurring prior to the exercise of treaty rights. Declining occupancy at resorts was associated with the age and quality of the facilities and not exercise of treaty right. Many people were also buying summer homes instead of staying at resorts.

In the summer and fall of 1987 Jack Gray, survey conductor for the UW Extension interviewed 1,704 people from area hotels, resorts, and private campgrounds. Gray concluded that "too much marketing is geared toward fishing," as his study indicated that while 100% of the visitors could have fished, merely 8.3% of those surveyed actually stated it was their main reason for the trip. (See also *Chippewa Spearing Season, Separating Myth from Fact*, Great Lakes Indian Fish & Wildlife Commission 1989 and *Masinaigan*, January/February 1990, GLIFWC)

Off-reservation Spearfishing

Springtime spearfishing was the most controversial treaty right exercised. During this period, walleye and musky, both prized game fish, were harvested by Ojibwe spearfishers. Treaty opponents, without any ecological data, assumed that the spearing of spawning walleyes was extremely detrimental to the lakes. A common misconception forwarded by treaty opponents was that the Ojibwe did large-scale spearing of egg-laden females and trophy class fish. Opponents of spearfishing often overlooked the fact that annually, prior to the ice forming, large numbers of female walleye with eggs were hooked, by non-Ojibwe ice fishing anglers, using tip-ups. Data obtained by GLIFWC clearly proved that the majority of walleye harvested by the Ojibwe were male and less than twenty inches in length. (See GLIFWC, *Annual Treaty Fishing Statistics*)

The Lac du Flambeau Ojibwe were renowned spearfishing people prior to the exercise of off-reservation treaty rights. The Ojibwe name for Lac du Flambeau is *Waaswaaganing*, which refers to the use of torches while spearfishing. The Lac du Flambeau people were the most visible and most active spearfishing tribe in Wisconsin during the treaty rights struggle.

Three primary groups organized following the Voigt Decision. These groups include anti-treaty groups, the Waswagon Treaty Association, and treaty rights support groups.

The primary anti-treaty groups started up in areas adjacent to Lac du Flambeau. These groups include: Wisconsin Alliance for Rights and Resources (WARR) 1984–1987 led by Larry Peterson of Park Falls, Wisconsin, was one group. Peterson also formed Protect American's Rights and Resources (PARR) in 1985. Stop Treaty Abuse–Wisconsin (STA–W) was formed in 1987 by Dean Crist and Al Soik of Minocqua.

During the mid 1980s and early 1990s PARR and STA–W organized protests at boat landings and lakes speared by the Lac du Flambeau people. These lakes were primarily in Vilas, Oneida, and Iron counties. The protests were aimed at stopping the Lac du Flambeau and other Ojibwe tribes from exercising their treaty rights.

In response to growing violence in 1989, an organization called the Waswagon Treaty Association (WTA) was formed at Lac du Flambeau. The organization immediately took a leadership role. Original members included Tom and Laura Maulson, Nick and Charlotte Hockings, Gibby Chapman, Bobby Chapman, Dorothy Thoms, Anita and Art Koser, Maggie Johnson, Scott Smith, Freddie Maulson, and Goldie Larson. The group promoted the off-reservation use of treaty rights. Many but not all spearfishers from Lac du Flambeau were members of this association. WTA was often in conflict with the Lac du Flambeau tribal government, the State of Wisconsin, and anti-treaty groups.

Boat landings were often jammed with protester boats and people. Loud whistleblowing, racial insults, death threats, and rock throwing commonly occurred. Protesters often carried signs, with various messages, including:

"Spear an Indian, Save a Walleye,"	"Abrogate, Don't Negotiate"
"Send Rambo to Flambeau,"	"Spearing Sucks"
"Timber Niggers Go Home,"	"Spear This" (picture of pointed handgun)

Protesters also commonly hung dummies dressed to represent Ojibwe with ropes around their necks. Heads of other dummies were painted with headbands and feathers attached to them and spears pierced through them.

The Ojibwe spearfishers were subjected to terrible abuse just to get onto the water. Once on the water additional danger was waiting. It was common for protesters in boats to create dangerous wakes, ram spearfishing boats, throw rocks, and shoot objects from wrist rocket slingshots. Ojibwe also were fired at with rifles and shotguns. Attempts to place pipe bombs in lakes to be speared were also documented. Ojibwe reported having vehicles tampered with or vandalized while parked at landings. They also reported problems while en route or returning from spearfishing. Ojibwe vehicles were either rammed or forced off the roadways. The protesters also placed concrete walleyes into the lakes to damage spears.

Local WDNR and law enforcement made few arrests for these acts and parallels can easily be drawn to race relations in the Deep South. The crowds of protesters became increasingly larger and more difficult to control. The Ojibwe continued to complain about inadequate protection from law enforcement. The Ojibwe believed that the sheriffs of Vilas, Oneida, and Iron counties all held anti-treaty attitudes. Crowd control and increasing violence led the state to increase law enforcement presence at boat landings with county law enforcement officers from across the state. National Guard armories were also put on alert and asked to be ready to respond to calls for aid by law enforcement.

Non-Ojibwe founded treaty-rights support groups as the violence escalated at spearing sites. Witness for Non-Violence was formed in Milwaukee. This group provided support from 1988–1992. They attempted to promote peace while documenting abuses the Ojibwe endured at the hands of protesters. Midwest Treaty Network (MTN) included a number of support groups from Wisconsin. MTN also included larger urban groups from Madison, the Twin Cities, and Chicago. This organization coordinated spring boat landing witness efforts. It also played a large role in attempting to educate Midwest residents about treaty rights. Honor Our Neighbor's Origins and Rights (HONOR) also supported treaty rights. This national human rights coalition focused on Native American issues during the struggle. The groups mentioned above and others had a consistent presence at boat landings and lakes during the protests. Once their role was known, treaty rights supporters also became targets. They, too, endured racial taunting, threats, and physical violence.

Assisted by the American Civil Liberties Union, on March 7, 1991, the Lac du Flambeau Tribe claimed that civil and safety rights were not being upheld and requested that STA–W and three county sheriffs be reprimanded. The tribe and its witnesses stated that county sheriffs were not providing adequate protection to spearfishers or their vehicles while at the landings. The tribe also identified the tactics being used by STA–W against the spearfishers, their families, and treaty supporters as dangerous and violent. Crucial evidence in the injunction request was the documentation in the form of photos, videotape, audio tape, and notes, made by witnesses and spearfishers.

Judge Crabb threw out the request against law enforcement, and determined that the state and counties' law enforcement plan was adequate. She did, however, rule that STA–W disruptions would need to cease. She agreed that STA–W had the right to voice opposition to exercise of treaty rights, but also ruled that the First Amendment does not provide anyone the right to threaten, assault, or commit battery. Judge Crabb granted the injunction and prohibited STA–W and its followers from doing the following seven actions:

- assaulting or battering any member of Lac du Flambeau Tribe or his/her family members on any landing or lake within the ceded territory;
- intentionally creating wakes on waters to interfere with spearfishing;
- planting decoys in any waterway;
- intentionally blocking spearing boats from moving;
- shining lights into the eyes of spearfishers;
- playing leapfrog or other actions impeding the progress of spearing boats;
- taking any other action that is intended to or may reasonably be expected to interfere with spearing rights.

Dean Crist continued to make threats following the injunction hearing, but not directly aimed at the tribes. He instead suggested that the WDNR obtain helmets and made comments to the press warning the WDNR that when spearing began in 1991 the lakes would become "extremely dangerous."

Following the STA rally in Minocqua in April 1991 treaty opponents agreed that it was necessary to continue to protest spearfishing. On April 20, 1991, another racial incident took place involving treaty rights protesters and a witness. James Mincey, a witness from Madison, went to Sand Lake to observe the treaty fishing. Mincey is an African-American. For nearly one hour Mincey was surrounded by treaty opponents and was pushed, had racial slurs shouted at him, and had his life threatened by them. Kathleen Hart, another witness present, believed that Mincey would be killed that night. Treaty supporters from a distant lake eventually arrived. Law enforcement stated that it was a near-riot by both sides.

Following this incident, the anti-treaty movement eventually unraveled. Many people now realized that treaty rights were here to stay. The concept of a friendly northern Wisconsin had been badly tarnished as a result of the treaty protests as many Wisconsin newspapers and television stations had a presence during the protests.

Accurate public information also helped to reduce tensions. GLIFWC frequently published information about treaty rights and harvests. Data collected at boat landings by creel clerks clearly showed the harvest levels of Ojibwe spearfishers to be minimal and well within the safe harvest levels established in courts. GLIFWC also provided conservation enforcement through its wardens that were cross-deputized by the State of Wisconsin.

Many believe that the primary reason spearfishing protests ended was the injunction filed by Lac du Flambeau. Those who would interfere with Ojibwe exercising off-reservation treaty rights would now be subject to both state and federal laws. Disorderly conduct charges were filed by district attorneys' in state circuit courts. The fines for disorderly conduct were minimal. Those who would interfere with Ojibwe spearfishers as described by Judge Crabb in March of 1991 would be subject to stiffer sentencing under civil rights statutes. The overt opposition to treaty right exercise was effectively ended as a result. Following the 1991 spearfishing season boat landing protests grew smaller and smaller. Today boat landing protests no longer occur.

The Ojibwe pursued a nonviolent approach throughout the treaty rights struggle, despite extreme antagonism. Those who speared and those who supported the cause did so at the risk of life and limb. Many spearfishers believed if the rights were not exercised, they would be lost. The spearfishers, their families, and supporters are very courageous people.

Today Ojibwe people continue to quietly hunt, fish, and gather off-reservation as our ancestors did. Most Ojibwe view the exercise of harvesting rights as central to our heritage. They also believe maintaining a traditional diet is important to good health. (See Larry Nesper's *The Walleye War: The Struggle for Ojibwe Spearfishing and Treaty Rights* and Walt Bresette and Rick Whaley's *Walleye Warriors: The Chippewa Treaty Rights Story*.)

Changing Elder Roles at Lac du Flambeau

The elders of Waaswaaganing have assisted in preserving the history of Lac du Flambeau. The community history is both intriguing and complex. Previously, Ojibwe people passed on history orally. No single elder knew or was expected to know the complete history. They simply recounted what they had been told by previous generations.

Elders of the tribe were considered knowledgeable and wise. In Ojibwe elders are called *gitchi-aya'aa* or "s/he that is greater." Elders held leadership roles in councils and traditional ceremonies. They clearly understood both the methods and variables within the highly important harvest cycle and also generally made reasonable decisions based upon life experiences. For these reasons and others elders were held in high esteem by the Native community.

Previously, Ojibwe family groups typically included elders. Elders were able to pass information to their descendants on a daily basis. In this fashion cultural knowledge flowed freely among the generations.

Elders who once lived with their families had specific roles. In addition to being knowledge keepers and teachers they were also child care providers, cooks, food providers, and participants in harvest activities.

The roles of elders began to change in Lac du Flambeau over time for different reasons. One change that affected Ojibwe elders was the loss of harvesting rights and methods. Following placement on reservations the Ojibwe were no longer able to move about freely. The previous hunting and gathering society was lost. The State of Wisconsin typically arrested and/or fined Native Americans for exercising traditional gathering activities off-reservation. This barrier, coupled with changes in technology, led to the loss of tasks for elders within the sugarbush, fishing, hunting, and wild rice harvests.

Families structure also changed as a result of boarding school. Children who were previously being instructed by parents and grandparents were now absent from the home. Only the very young remained at home. The role of elders as instructors for school-age children was nearly eliminated at that time.

Another factor that affected the role of elders was dependence on non-Ojibwe goods. Cloth, steel tools, and foods once unknown to the Ojibwe eventually became necessary. The Ojibwe needed jobs to earn the money that would enable them to acquire such goods. The time spent working these jobs in turn changed the old life-style. The old ways that led people to be totally dependent on natural resources were diminishing. Young and middle-aged adults no longer participated with elders in typical Ojibwe harvesting activities. Many harvesting activities were too difficult for elders to engage in alone and thus were not done at all.

After the closing of the boarding school working parents did become dependent upon elders for child care. When employment was available, elders would provide child care during and after school hours. Parents with jobs indirectly boosted the role of elders during periods of increased employment opportunity.

Another factor that greatly changed the roles of elders at Lac du Flambeau was housing. Previously, fewer homes were available, and it was not uncommon for grandparents or even great-grandparents to live with their families. As more housing became available, families were separated. Young Ojibwe families moved to various housing locations within the reservation separate from their elders. As these individuals moved into elderhood, they retained these homes and lived independently away from their children and grandchildren. This increase in housing decreased daily interactions between elders and their families. Many elders with large extended families, however, enjoy frequent visits by their children, grandchildren, and great-grandchildren. Elders also enjoy the company of elder friends within the community.

The advent of nursing homes also affected elders' lives. In the early 1970s some aged elders were removed from the community to be cared for in nursing home facilities located off reservation. Most elders placed in the nursing home were not very happy. Typically few other Ojibwe elders resided in the same facility. The foreign environment coupled with inability of relatives to visit contributed to the elders' sadness. Many people at Lac du Flambeau desire a tribally owned and operated nursing home for our Ojibwe elders. This continues to be a difficult goal as the resources required to build and staff such a facility here have yet to be realized.

Today, those elders who can live independently continue to do so as long as possible. Eventually the time comes when either family members are required to move into the elder's home to provide care or the elder moves in with a son or daughter. Most Ojibwe elders choose to remain at home.

In the early 1980s Elks Point Senior Residential Complex was built at Lac du Flambeau. Elders now had a group complex to reside in at Moss (Mud) Lake. This concept was not traditional but one borrowed from American society as the Ojibwe had previously cared for their elders within their own homes.

Despite these changing times, Ojibwe elders are still the primary sources of knowledge within the community. Within Ojibwe culture roles are clearly defined. Elders continue to be keepers of wisdom as they have accumulated experience and knowledge over their long lives. Younger generations continue to expect elders to share their experience.

Stories shared here by the Lac du Flambeau Elders provide a powerful message to today's generation. The stories display the age-old traditions of storytelling and oration within the Ojibwe Nation.

As the historical overview has shown, overt attempts were made to destroy the Ojibwe culture. As the generations passed, fewer people related our history in great detail. Some elders have stated, "Fewer people are interested in what happened long ago." Different factors may have contributed to the suppression of our history, but the stories of the past have continued.

By understanding the larger history of the Ojibwe we begin to understand why elders of this era carried the attitudes and beliefs they display today. As we examine these stories both deeper meanings and greater respect for our elders are attained. These stories are a wonderful gift, for we continue to draw upon previous events to guide our way into the future just as our ancestors have done for generations.

Leon C. Valliere is currently administrator of the Lac du Flambeau Ojibwe Language Program. He is a received an A.A. from Haskell Indian Junior College in Lawrence, Kansas, and a B.S. from the University of Wisconsin–Stout in Menomonie. His interests include Ojibwe language, ceremonial music, and birchbark canoe construction.

Ojibwe Sounds

Ojibwe has fewer vowels and consonants than English. Seven vowel sounds are used in Ojibwe language. They include *a, aa, e, i, ii, o,* and *oo.*

Here are examples of how these vowels are produced:

	English	**Ojibwe**
a	<u>a</u>bout	agim=snowshoe
aa	f<u>a</u>ther	aabajitoon=use it
e	s<u>ay</u>	ayaabe=buck deer
i	<u>i</u>f	indaw=I am
ii	s<u>ee</u>n	aaniindi=where
o	<u>o</u>bey	ozhibii'ige=he writes
	b<u>oo</u>k	agow=these animate objects
oo	dr<u>ew</u>	boozhoo=hello

The following consonants are used in Ojibwe and are parallel to English sounds:

b, ch, d, g, h, j, k, m, n, p, s, sh, t, w, y, z, zh and **'** *(glottal stop)*

The glottal stop is written with an apostrophe, and is used to mark a position where the sound cuts off in flow. An English example would be the sound between the two syllables of the expression "uh-oh." In written Ojibwe the apostrophe also separates sets of vowels.

ode'=her or his heart   ma'iingan=wolf

Ojibwe also has nasal vowels. To show that this vowel must be nasalized, we often use "hn" at the end of the vowel sound to represent "hold nose."

giigoohn=fish (singular)   giigoohnyag=fish (plural)

Other sounds occurring in Ojibwe include the diphthong in English words pie, lye, cry, and my. In Ojibwe writing, the sound is marked as "*ay.*"

omood<u>ay</u>=bottle

Another sound present in Ojibwe is parallel to the English word "church p<u>ew</u>." In Ojibwe the sound is written "iw."

        i'iw=that inanimate object   iniw=those inanimate objects
        agiw=those animate objects

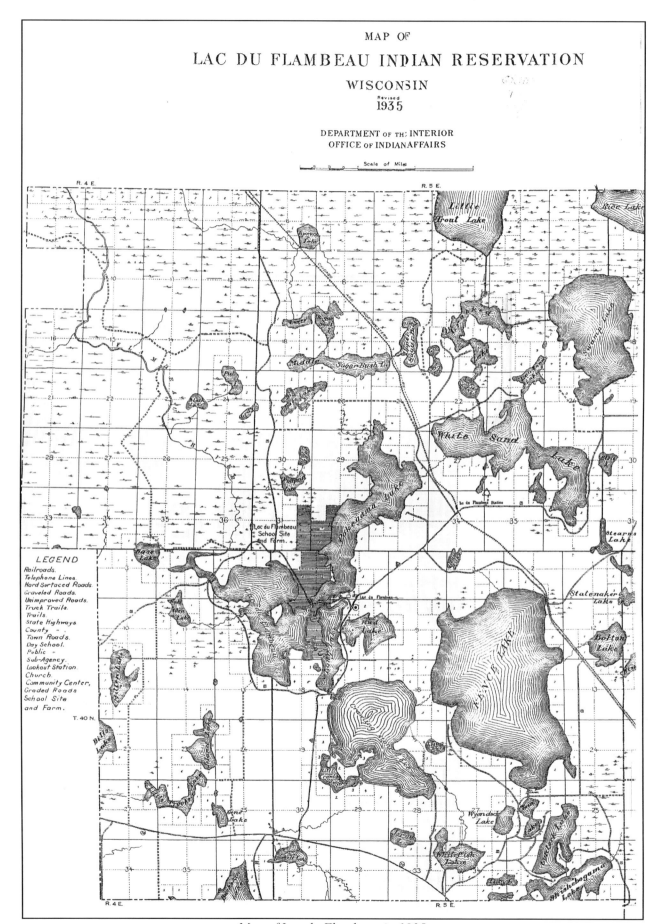

Map of Lac du Flambeau in 1935

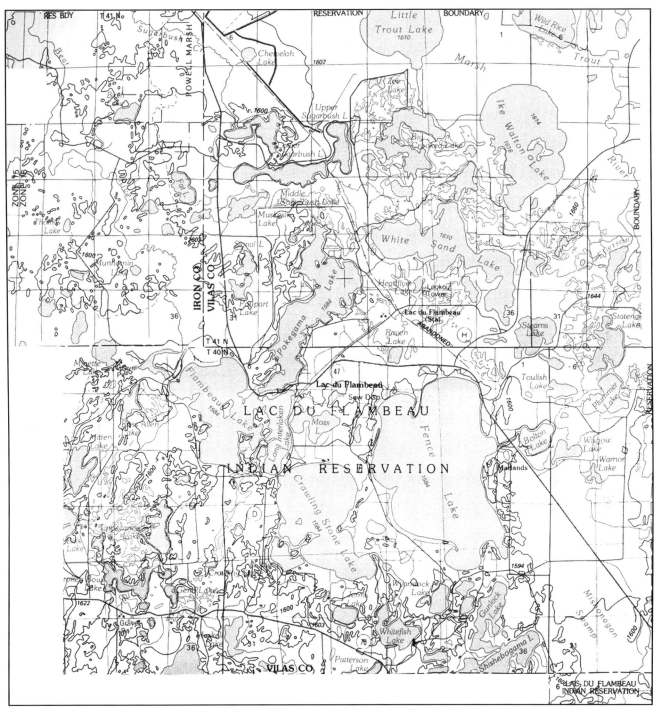

Map of Lac du Flambeau today

Chief Buffalo

Family and wigwam in winter

Maurice Big John playing in front of summer wigwam

Old Indian Village

Bear River Dance Grounds

Dancers at Bear River

Dancers at Bear River
(Big George Skye in foreground)

Women making beadwork

Medicine Rock

Strawberry Island

Whitefeather with ceremonial pipe

George W. Brown, Sr., with lacrosse stick

Main Street Lac du Flambeau, circa 1904

BIA Agency complex seen from Pokegama lake. From far left to right: Superintendent's office (with chimney), warehouse, boys' dormitory (white exposed building), sewing room to its left, laundry, and girls' dormitory on end

Children and staff at the BIA boarding school

Children in boarding school classroom

Boys in uniform at boarding school

*Father Oderic Derenthal with children
dressed for Confirmation*

Team and loggers

Lumber mill in Lac du Flambeau

Planing mill

Yeschek's Crawling Stone Lodge resort

Community Presbyterian Church

Downtown Lac du Flambeau, circa 1940

Post office in downtown Lac du Flambeau, near end of train line

Baseball players

Indian Bowl next to Museum

Round House as it looks today

William Wildcat, Sr. Community Center

George W. Brown, Jr. Museum and Cultural Center

Lake of the Torches Casino Resort and Convention Center

Lac du Flambeau Tribal Fish Hatchery

Hatching Jars, where 30-45 million walleye eggs are raised annually for restocking area lakes

Agnes Archdale and Liza Brown

Agnes and Liza (Elizabeth) were born to Mary Cadotte Cobb and George Cobb, Sr., in Couderay, Wisconsin, on the Lac Courte Oreilles reservation west of Lac du Flambeau. Agnes was born on November 11, 1912, and Liza was born March 6, 1915. They both went to public school in Couderay. After their father passed away their mother moved to Lac du Flambeau, where she worked as a cook in the government boarding school and raised her children in the Old Village. Agnes and Liza both attended Haskell Institute in Lawrence, Kansas, where they got their high school diplomas. Agnes went on to take business courses there after graduation.

Agnes met her husband, Mervin Archdale, while a student at Haskell. He was an Assiniboine from the Fort Peck Reservation in Montana. Agnes moved to Montana with Mervin, and they had two children, Mervin Jr., now living in Colorado Springs, and Magel, who lives in

Crandon, Wisconsin. Agnes and Mervin returned to Lac du Flambeau in 1936 and lived here the rest of their lives. Agnes worked as a clerk for many years, first in the Lac du Flambeau Post Office and later at the Lac du Flambeau Town Hall. After Mervin passed away, Agnes traveled to Florida in the winters to stay with their sister, Gertrude Goodwin.

After graduating from Haskell Liza returned to Lac du Flambeau and in 1940 married Jimmy Brown from Lac du Flambeau. Liza went with Jimmy to Manitowoc, Wisconsin, where he was employed in the shipyards, and she worked in the hotel where they stayed. They returned to Lac du Flambeau and seventeen years after getting married had their daughter Susie (Poupart). Both Liza and Agnes lived in Lac du Flambeau the last years of their lives, spending much time with their children and grandchildren, nieces, and nephews. In her later years Liza also worked as a foster grandparent at the grade school, one of her greatest joys, where all the children knew her as "Grandma Liza."

Liza and Agnes recall their childhood in Lac du Flambeau and Couderay in their interview, and tell stories about their relatives, especially their mother and grandparents who helped raise them. They have many recollections of the once-thriving downtown Lac du Flambeau with its many resorts, stores, restaurants, and small businesses as well. They also describe in detail the dances held at "the park" or Bear River Pow-Wow Grounds, and what life was like in the Old Village. Their advice to young people is to "get all the education they can get" and "stay busy."

Interview with Agnes Archdale and Liza Brown

This interview was conducted by Verdaine Farmilant.

Agnes: Waabanaasinookwe [is my Ojibwe name]. "Early Morning Clouds," I was told. In fact, I have three Indian names, so does Liza. But these are kind of nicknames. Kowiinzii,[1] that's "Jelly"—my grandma used to make chokecherry jelly, and chokecherries are the hardest thing to make into jelly. They don't gel. It was more like a heavy syrup, and I was always eating that or getting into it when I was just a little girl. My Uncle Frank [Cadotte], he's the one who gave me that name. I was always into the jelly. Kowiinzii.

He used to give me the names. In fact that name was given to me after I was born, Shtigwaan.[2] That means "Head." I was bald-headed . . . absolutely bald. And my mother used to make bonnets, and I wore bonnets all the time. You don't see those any more. I always had one on. [laughs] I'm not going to say she was ashamed of me, but I just didn't have any hair. And then my uncle used to come along and he'd say, "Take that cap off." He'd take my bonnet off. Shtigwaan. That's what he called me. And to the day he died, he called me that.

Liza: I've got Gimaakwe.[3] I've got lots of them. Hoyot. Shinot.[4] Otootamindimooyenh.[5] Those are mine, my grandma and grandpa gave me those names, and Uncle Frank. Gimaakwe I know, that's "Bossy Woman" [laughs] or "Head Lady." But I don't know what the others mean. Mindimooyenh, that's an old woman, but I don't know.

Agnes: Shinot was the name of some lady in Reserve, I remember that name.

Liza: I don't know what "Hoyot" means. But when we went to see Grandma, we'd go up to her, we'd say "Niin Gimaakwe Hoyot.[6] Otootamindimoyenh." And that's the way I kissed her, you know. And she [Agnes] would go up to her and say "Niin" and give her all her Indian names. All the time.

Agnes: Our grandma lived in Reserve, and we lived in Couderay.[7] And we used to go to Reserve every now and then to see, to stay a week or two with our grandparents, Liza and I.

----

[1] According to Agnes, Kowiinzii means "Jelly." Because she came from Lac Courte Oreilles, her dialect might be slightly different from Lac du Flambeau Ojibwe. According to Joe Chosa, in the Lac du Flambeau dialect Kowiinzii could be a short form of the word *akiwenzii* meaning 'old man.'

[2] Shtigwaan is short for *oshtigwaan*, which as she says means 'head.'

[3] Gimaakwe is a short form of *ogimaakwe* meaning 'chief woman.'

[4] We have been unable to find a translation for Hoyot, but Shinot was the commonly used Ojibwe rendering of the proper name Charlotte. Since the "l" sound does not exist in Ojibwe, "n" would be substituted.

[5] According to Joe Chosa, in the Lac du Flambeau dialect *otootamindimoyenh* means 'all old lady.'

[6] *Niin* means 'I' or, as in this case, 'I am.'

[7] Reserve and Couderay are two towns on the Lac Courte Oreilles reservation about a hundred miles west of Lac du Flambeau.

Frank Cadotte, Jr., scraping a buckskin hide

Sometimes we'd stay all summer. And the way we'd go there, we didn't have a car. You had to either take a team of horses or something or walk. The mailman used to go there three times a week, and he had what they called a "sulky." It was a two-wheeler cart and had a seat. And then he used to put the mailbags down on the floor. Our mother would probably ask him if we could ride with him to Reserve, because that's where he was going. And that's the way we'd go. We'd stay there two, three weeks, sometimes a month, with our grandparents. There used to be a grocery store in Reserve, and our grandpa would go to the grocery store and he'd tell them, whenever they saw her and I come into the store, they were to give us anything we wanted, like candy, gum, or nuts. We used to think our grandpa was rich. At that time we knew the value of money, because we didn't have much of anything.

Mary Cadotte Cobb Martin [was our mother's name]. Frank Cadotte, Sr., was our grandfather, he was a senior and then my Uncle Frank was Frank Cadotte, Jr. . . . . That was another thing we did not question my mother about. How did she get from Flambeau to Couderay? Where did she meet our father? He was from Barron, Wisconsin,[8] and that's where some of his family still live. I keep in touch sometimes, at least once or twice a year, with the family. Then there's another family from Illinois. I think she's making a family tree of the Cobb family. She would be our cousin. . . .

---

[8] Barron is about forty miles south of Lac Courte Oreilles.

Our parents were caretakers at a lodge, when Frank, our brother, was born. He got killed in an auto accident in '52 in Fifield. He was working for the BIA, the Indian police. In our family there was Frank, my brother, myself, then Liza, then Billy, and then there was Dotsy that died. She died of tuberculosis. Then there was two little ones that died in infancy. Then Georgie, Joseph.[9] I call him Georgie, his baptismal name is Joseph. He's the last of the Cobbs. Then Gertrude Schroeder.

My father's name was George Cobb. [My mother] became Mary Cadotte Cobb. My grandfather [on my father's side], I didn't know them, they were from Barron, around Rice Lake, Cameron. They were white. They came to visit us once, do you remember that, Liza? . . . Seems to me they came from the old country, Scotland, Ireland, wherever. I always said we were Scotch but my cousin from Barron says, "We're not Scotch, we're Irish." I said, "Well, I was always told I was Scotch, so I'm still Scotch." Our dad always said he was a Scotchman. He had no Indian at all in him. It's our mother that was a full blood.

Liza: I always wondered how my mother and father met. We never asked them.

Agnes: And they never offered to tell us either. They were just there.

Liza: And they were together until our father died.

*   *   *

Agnes: Our grandpa died here, in Flambeau. He used to come to Flambeau and take care of business. He used to be a policeman, when they lived on the reservation here. My grandma was a Catfish. She was a very pretty lady, her name was Margaret. My grandpa and grandma were both from here, but how they migrated over to Reserve is still a mystery and we'll never know. That's where they lived over in Reserve, at that time they called it Reserve but now it's not even mentioned I don't think.

Koobide[10] [our mother's grandmother], we don't know if she had an English name.

Liza: She lived with us in Couderay.

Agnes: My mother took care of her. And you know, we didn't know what illnesses there were until now, you think back of it, and you think, well that must be what she had—Alzheimer's or whatever.

Liza: Because she was forgetful. You had to watch her all the time. You had to see that she didn't play with matches, because we started the wood fire with paper and matches and kindling. And it was right by the stove. And my dad was always afraid she'd take that and light that basket of kindling you know. I vaguely remember her, but I remember that. I remember when she got away from us too.

---

[9] Joseph Cobb, Sr., whom she calls Georgie, passed away in January 1998.

[10] *Koobide* (also pronounced as *koobie*) means 'great-grandmother' in Ojibwe and is still a commonly used term of endearment for a great-grandmother or grandmother.

Agnes: Yes I remember. It was a bitter, bitter cold winter day. Wintertime.

Liza: In the morning, my dad went through the kitchen there. Her bed was right behind the stove, or close to the stove. And she was gone, and he went outside and looked for her. He went and looked in the toilet and she wasn't there. And he saw her tracks going out of the yard. I don't know if she had her moccasins on or if she was in her stocking feet. We were in the house, and my dad come and told my ma that Koobide was gone. Well, then he went looking for her.

Agnes: He hitched up the team and the sled, and they put hot bricks in the sled where the hay was, in case they found her those bricks would keep her warm. . . . She walked quite a ways, it was between Couderay and Signor.[11] Closer to Signor.

Liza: That's a long way for an old lady to walk with just a shawl over her. . . . And it used to get like fifty below, sometimes more.

*   *   *

Liza: I came to Flambeau right after Pa died. Ma got a job in the government school, she was a cook.

Agnes: Maybe some of them going to boarding school at that time—I never went there and never knew too much about it—they might remember her.

Liza: Billy went there to the government school, but I didn't. I was too busy taking care of kids!

Agnes: When we lived in Couderay, Pa worked for Beckerdal Lumber Company until he died. At that time, the mothers didn't work, they took care of their home and their children. Only our mother, she took care of sick people.

She was always going to the neighbors and taking care of them, so consequently it left Liza and I taking care of the little ones. And we learned how to make bread and everything else, we could keep house just like our mother did. That's what she taught us.

Liza: We used to bake bread. Agnes would mix the bread, and she had to stand on the chair sometimes, you know, mix it and knead it down.

Agnes: I remember one time I didn't know how to make loaves. There was somebody sick all the time, and Ma would be the one taking care of them. Well anyhow she left, and I don't know if she set that bread or what before she left, but anyhow we were left to take care of the bread. And the kids too. I didn't know how to make loaves, I just didn't know . . . so there was another lady, she had kids that we played with. We had time for fun, you know, it wasn't all work. Well this lady came, I could see her coming down the road, and I told Liza, ah, here comes Aunt Mary. We used to call her Aunt Mary, we were not related. I said, "Here comes Aunt Mary, she'll know how to make bread." Sure enough she came to the house. . . . So we told her to come in, and I told her that

---

[11] Signor, the village she mentions, no longer appears on the map. This is often the case with smaller towns, villages, or Indian settlements.

we had bread to bake but I didn't know how to make the loaves. So she showed us how to make loaves of bread.

Liza: You didn't only make two or three loaves, you made like ten or twelve loaves of bread. Plus biscuits.

Agnes: Our oldest brother was Frank Cobb. . . . He married George Brown's sister, Tillie or Matilda Brown. . . . I come next, my husband's from Montana, he was from the Fort Peck Reservation. He was an Assiniboine. I met him at Haskell,[12] and we had two children, a boy and a girl. Our son lives in Colorado Springs, he was in the Navy, he retired after twenty years of service. Mervin Archdale.[13] He took up dentistry, prosthetics, making porcelain teeth. . . . That's what he took up when he was in the Navy. When he came out of the Navy, he carried on his profession. He went into business for himself, he put a lab in his home. He used to take orders from dentists in Colorado Springs, making plates and what not. He married a girl from Arbor Vitae, and they've got three daughters.

The oldest lives in Colorado Springs and she has two children.[14] The youngest daughter lives in Denver and she has one daughter.[15] The second daughter lives in Phoenix. She works for Motorola. . . . I have three great-grandchildren out there.

Magel, she lives in Crandon, and she has two children, a boy and a girl. She's married to an Ison, well known down there in that area.

Liza: I have one child. I married Jimmy in 1940, Jimmy Brown. His mom and dad were George and Sadie Brown. And we were married I think almost seventeen years before we had Susie, or Mary, her real name. We call her Susie. She's the only one we had. Her dad used to ask me, "Liz, do you realize how old we're going to be when Sweetie is going to high school?" I said, "Sure but I'm not telling you, you should know." Well he never lived to see her graduate, when she went to Minocqua High School. He died before she graduated. And then she went to Wausau and went to that technical school down there. . . .

Then she got a job in the plant, and then she met her husband, Buster Poupart, and they got married. They were married quite three or four years, before they had a little boy. That's Blue. His name is Charles Bluejacket Poupart, we call him Blue. Then ten years later they had little Jimmy,[16] his name is James Willis. He was named after Willis Allen. Jimmy and Willis were just like brothers, they were brought up together, on the [boarding school] campus. And he's four years old now. And I worked at the—it seems like I've worked all my life. Even when we came to

---

[12] Haskell Indian School, also known as the Haskell Institute, in Lawrence, Kansas, was another early BIA boarding school, founded in 1884. Chippewas were often listed as the second largest tribe at the school, which was the most intertribal of all boarding schools. Haskell offered education and training beyond the typical eight-year program and in 1964 became Haskell Indian Junior College, now termed Haskell Indian Nations University.

[13] Agnes's husband's name was Mervin Archdale, Sr.

[14] The oldest granddaughter's name is Penny.

[15] The youngest granddaughter's name is Bernice.

[16] Jimmy is Liza's husband, James Brown, whose friend from the boarding school was Willis Allen, also from Lac du Flambeau.

Flambeau, I used to go out to the resort and take care of kids. [To Agnes] I don't know, you cooked or something out at the resort?

Billy Cobb lives in Arizona, I don't know what his wife's name is. He was married to Reva Chapman. But her name was Sagasunk then, and they had one son [Tony]. I think Billy went to the west coast when Frankie was there, and Billy went over there.

Agnes: No, they went during the war. Mervin and Billy went to Vancouver, Washington to work at the aluminum plant out there. Frank went out there too, he was stationed in Fort Lewis at the time.

Liza: . . . About two Christmases ago, Billy came home and he brought Tony with him, and that's the first time we saw Tony since he was four years old. I took him over to Reva's, and he's been here a couple times since then. He knows where to go now, that's where he goes. This last time he brought his brother Frank—Billy had some other children by Dory. I know there was Frank and Mary. . . . This past month Tony came home again, and he brought his brother Frank with him. They come over to the school to see me. Mrs. Jubert said, "You can bring him in here, Lize, or you can go out in the hall, whatever you want to do." Good thing I went in the hall because as soon as I saw Frank, I knew who he was because he looks just like my brother Frank. And I knew Billy had a son named Frank. And I started to cry, and I couldn't talk to him. And I had him bawling [laughs] and he was hugging and squeezing me. . . .

Agnes: [The next youngest sibling is] Dotsy—Anna Marie Cobb. But she went by the name of Dotsy. Some of these girls from here know her, they went to school together. Dotsy would've been in her sixties.

She was about eighteen when she died.

Liza: She died of tuberculosis. She stayed with Jimmy and I, when she came from Agwajing? She stayed in our house. And we lived in an old shack. That's where Jimmy and I lived. And when Dotsy came home, she wanted to stay with us. She came from Agwajing, that was a sanatorium in Minnesota, near Bemidji. I was there, too, before she—I stayed there almost a year.

Agnes: She was very young when she died.

Liza: I don't think she was eighteen yet. Anyways she came home and Jimmy said she can stay with us if she wants to. Because that shop, it sure wasn't warm, and it was airy. And that's what she needed was fresh air. So we went and got blankets—the window was up above her. We took the window out, and you could put it back in again. Her bed was beneath that window.

And then right across from her was another window just like it. She really had fresh air, and we would, even in the wintertime, we'd open the windows and wrap her up in blankets. And we'd leave those windows open for about fifteen, twenty minutes. [After Dotsy came] two little babies who died. George was the last of the Cobbs.

Agnes: Then there was George. He married Margaret Doud. . . . Then my mother married George Schroeder, and she had Gertrude. She's the baby of the family.

Liza: And Gertrude has one daughter, Jolene.

*   *   *

Liza: [I was born] March 6, 1915, in Couderay. Maybe it was in Devil's Lake, because I remember I was real small when we lived in Devil's Lake.

Agnes: I was born 11–11–12, November 11, 1912. I'm eighty-three, and she's eighty-one.

Liza: I moved here [to Flambeau] on New Year's Day in 1930. I brought Georgie with me. . . . Georgie was just a little baby, he was just walking. My mother sent George Schroeder after us.

Agnes: [I've lived here] since 1936. I got married in 1934, then I got married, went back to work in Lansing, Michigan, then came back here and stopped to see my mother and family. Then I went on to Montana, where Mervin was. I lived out there for a year and a half. What a difference the climate and everything was, compared to our woods and lakes and whatnot. Over there at the time it was just barren country. Mervin's mother said, I think you better take her back home because she's going to get sick here. I've lived here since '36, and I'm still here!

*   *   *

Liza: We never thought of being poor, because we always had something to eat, and the love and care of our folks.

Agnes: We lived on a farm. But like I say, we never considered ourselves poor. We were rich in love and caring for one another. That was our life. And everybody was just a person. People. We never thought of segregation or different nationalities. We were just people. We all lived together and got along with everybody. Went to Couderay school and graduated from there. . . .

Liza: There was Polish, Norwegians, Swedes, Indians, and we all went to school together. In a big room, from first grade to however high it went—eighth. All in that one room.

Agnes: That school is still standing there. It was a public school.

*   *   *

Agnes: I know what Liza and I used to do when we were kids. They used to have pow-wows in Reserve. Right across from where my grandma and grandpa lived, they had a pow-wow ground there. My grandpa always dressed up in his costume, a beautiful costume that my grandmother made. Like I said, she was an invalid, she could not walk. But he strung the frame and had it hanging from the ceiling, had a rope or a string, whatever, and hung the frame there, and she worked on it while sitting on her bed, beading. She did all that beadwork that you saw in those pictures [of their grandfather Frank Cadotte Sr.].

Liza: I don't remember how he had the chairs, but there was two chairs back there, and then there was an ironing board and that was padded with real heavy old blankets or whatever he padded it with, and her back was up against that board. And she sat like that, all day long until dusk, beading. And when it got dark where she couldn't see any more, because we had lamps then, grandpa would take that frame away. Grandpa would get her pipe then and she'd tamp the tobacco down in it. But she'd let me light her pipe, and I'd blow that smoke out, and I thought that was just great. [laughs] That was the only time she'd smoke, after she'd had her meal and then she'd smoke.

She must've had rheumatism, she couldn't move at all from her waist down. She couldn't stand up. I don't know how, he'd get her under the shoulders and lift her when she needed to move. She couldn't talk English, they talked Indian. We talked Indian. I used to be able to talk real good when I was young. But then when I moved up here I lost all that. I went to classes too, but it doesn't sound like the way they used to talk to us.

Agnes: We used to say our prayers in Indian. . . . We spent a lot of time with our grandma. Even when we were children. Because we lived on a farm, an area that must have been owned by the family, the Cadotte family, because our Uncle Frank lived up on a hill. Then we came down the road a bit, Grandma and Grandpa, then Koobide and her husband. And Aunt Katie . . . and our family was the end. When you come into that area, Devil's Lake, it's a big open space. And ours was the first house. . . .

Liza: Why don't you tell her the truth? [laughs] We used to sleep with Grandpa you know. We used to wake up, and we'd just lay there and wait for him, he'd dress us. You know, put our shoes and stockings on. Well, we often talked about that, her and I. Can you believe that we just lay in that darn bed until Grandpa come with our clothes and dress us? [laughs] He would.

Agnes: And he did the cooking.

Liza: If we couldn't dress ourselves, we sure couldn't cook! [everyone laughs]

*   *   *

Agnes: I went to public school in Couderay. . . . After my father died, I began begging my mother to let me go away to school. At that time she was trying to raise the family on no income whatsoever. But she used to get from the county, at that time they called it a mother's pension. But they did not include—if you were sixteen or older, you did not come under that. So Frank and I did not come under that, we had to go out and get jobs, if we could find a job. So that's why I wanted to go away to school. She let me go to Haskell. Because that's where she went to school—my mother and my Uncle Frank and my Aunt Katie, all three of them went to school at Haskell. It's one of the oldest Indian schools, Carlisle's the oldest.

I wanted to take nursing but they would not let me, I was too young when I went to Haskell. So I just went through the high school academics.

*   *   *

Liza: [In Couderay] I didn't finish the eighth grade when Ma went to Flambeau. Because I stayed home and took care of the kids. You [Agnes] went to Haskell.

Agnes: The fall of 1929 I went to Haskell. . . . When Pa was gone, I figured that was my chance to go to school. Really I don't know what would've happened if we would've continued our education, if it weren't for the government school.

Liza: You had already graduated from high school when I went there [to Haskell]. You were in your first year of commercial [school] when I went there. . . .

Agnes: Those were good days. . . . I went on to business school after high school. They had everything there, they had nurse's training. . . . At the time I graduated, that was the Depression, they had no jobs available. But I was on the Civil Service Register.[17] But my education's helped throughout the years.

Liza: I work at the school, I work during summer school too.

*   *   *

Liza: I worked in the kitchen. I worked out at the Island Club all the time. Then after I got married, Jimmy got a job in the shipyards in Manitowoc. And I went to Manitowac. . . . There was a restaurant in the hotel we stayed at. I washed dishes: washed them by hand, dried them by hand, scrubbed floors, wooden floors. They had to be white when I got done with them. I was no stranger to washing dishes and scrubbing.

Agnes: Well that's the way it was when we were children. We had a big house, we had to scrub those floors from one end to the other, and they were all hardwood floors. No rugs, you know. We done our own washing, pump water, carry water, do farm chores.

*   *   *

Liza: I mean there were big stores [in the town of Lac du Flambeau].

Agnes: Filling stations, Western Union, the Fireside.[18] Where the Fireside is, is where I started when I started at the post office. I worked there. . . . You know where the post office is now, and the library? I remember [Verdaine's father's restaurant there]. And Schillman's had their filling station on the other side of the road. I remember that, when the post office was where the Fireside is now, that's where I started working. No indoor plumbing, you had to go outside. I retired from the post office after twenty-five years, I retired in '72. Where the print shop is now? That used to be the post office [after it was at the Fireside location], that's where I retired from. Jim Stuart was the postmaster when I was in there, and then Jack Oldenberg was the postmaster when I retired.

---

[17] Civil Service Register was a method of appointing government employees based on competitive examinations.

[18] The Fireside restaurant is in downtown Lac du Flambeau, on the site of the former post office.

Downtown Lac du Flambeau, circa 1950s

Liza: Do you remember the ice cream parlor? There was an ice cream parlor there, Peterson's.

Agnes: Yeah, don't you know George Wilson? George Wilson, he had an ice cream parlor. He had a grocery store there too. See that building we were talking about? What was that blind person's . . . ?

Not Woodman's Hall, that was further back, on the edge of that, in that Y there. We used to go there for dances.

I remember when the Flame was going full blast as a resort and rooms. Then across the street from that was Gauthier's, Grandma Gauthier's store. We took over the kitchen in the Flame. We ran the dining room one summer. Then there was the Dew Drop Inn, right across from Jeanne Murray's. They used to have the Dew Drop Inn, that was Keene's, Dukie Keene's folks. They used to sell beer. . . . Then there was a filling station there. That took care of that block.

Then the next block, Barb Severeid's. There used to be a post office in there. And then Wilson had that next building, he had a grocery store there. Then the next was Mabel Gauthier's gift shop. It was on the same side as the library. I don't know when she moved it across the street to where it is today. Then Aschenbrenner's store, a big grocery store there. Then Eliot's garage. Then the next street was where the Chamber of Commerce building was.

Liza: There used to be a Ladies Aid house there too. . . . They moved into that white house. And then there was a tall building there, where Jimmy was born in town. Remember there was a tall building there?

Agnes: That was Oldenberg's, where he had his store there. . . .

Liza: There was a tall building there that had an upstairs to it. That's where Jimmy was born, I forgot what they called it. That's where Sadie had Jimmy. And then they moved over to the campus,[19] they lived over on the campus by John Allen and his wife and his family. . . .You know Ellen and Bill MacArthur? There was one [school] there by where they live [on the street behind the new casino], they called it the Little Red Schoolhouse. . . . They used to call that Silk Stocking Avenue. [laughs] I don't know [why], they had crazy names for places. It was a red schoolhouse, had a big bell on it. Jimmy and that Oldenberg girl were the first ones who went to school there, I think they were the only ones who graduated too.

Agnes: Where Dillman's is, Ben C. Gauthier had a resort there. That's where I worked. In the kitchen, and then I used to wait tables. [Resorts] and guiding, that's the only jobs there were [in the 1930s when they came to Flambeau.]

We lived in the old Indian village, in that area when we first came to Flambeau, Mervin and I. Our mother had already gone, she went back to New Post.

Liza: I think Gus Martin come to Flambeau and visited one time, and he met our mother. They knew each other before . . . Katie, our Aunt Katie, married his brother. But I don't really know how he. . . . I just think he come to Flambeau and took her! [laughs] Took her away from us. . . .

Agnes: When they used to have dances, they used to have them at the Bear River . . . at that time they didn't call it the Bear River. Do you remember what they called that?

Liza: I don't know—the dancing grounds. They didn't call it "the park"[20] then either.

Agnes: I guess that Round House is still out there.[21] There used to be a road that come down, right down at the end of that road there, on the lake side, and we used to do beadwork. She did beadwork, I used to do beadwork. . . . And we used to sell it from our house. We'd string a string across the window, and hang our bracelets, whatever we were making. And the tourists would stop and buy, you know. That's the way we sold. I never took my beadwork to a shop to sell.

* * *

Liza: I remember I was there when they adopted Mr. Cornelius into the tribe. And they called him Aandeg, "Crow." And my father-in-law carved a big totem pole, and they put a big crow on top. I don't know if it was a stuffed crow or what, but it looked real to me. And they put it on the end, and it was out by Cornelius' all those years.

Agnes: They used to dance where the new casino is now, in that pine. . . . Just like ordinary pow-wows or dances. I don't know if it was for the public.

---

[19] The campus refers to the boarding school grounds.

[20] The current Bear River Pow-Wow Grounds was called by different names in different eras. Formerly the Bear River was called the Flambeau River, and the pow-wow grounds was formerly called "the pageant grounds," the "dance grounds," or simply "the park."

[21] The Round House is the round building where Big Drum services are held in the Old Village.

Original Round House

Liza: Then they'd dance out at the park. They didn't cut any of those trees down when they were camping there. They never cut trees. They just put their wigwams in amongst the trees. Then they had a dancing ring. But they brushed it, you know.

*   *   *

Agnes: I'd tell them [a young person], get all the education they can possibly get. That's something that they cannot take away from you, what you learn. I always think of that myself: They might take everything away from me, but they cannot take the education I learned. They can't take that away from you. And it's helped me many times.

Liza: Stay busy. I've worked all my life.

Gilbert J. Chapman

Gilbert Joseph Chapman was born October 10, 1910, to Robert Chapman and Mary McArthur in Lac du Flambeau. He attended the government boarding school here and later the Mt. Pleasant, Michigan, boarding school, where he was a star football player. He married Marion Norma Valliere, also from Lac du Flambeau, on January 31, 1931, at the age of twenty-one. They had five girls and two boys and also three infant sons who died at birth.

He was one of the first tribal policemen in Lac du Flambeau and worked as a police officer for both the Tribe and the BIA for thirteen years. A man of many skills, he also worked in the logging camps, the Indian Conservation Corps (ICC), and on the railroad as a repairman or "section worker." He was a veteran of World War II, serving three years in the Army; he was stationed in the Philippines with a regiment that was preparing to invade Japan when Hiroshima was bombed. Gib was also an excellent hunter and a wonderful storyteller with a sharp memory, as his narrative illustrates.

In his interview Gib talks about his experiences as a logger, ICC worker, railroad repairman, and policeman, including transporting patients the long hundred miles from Lac du Flambeau to the "Indian Hospital" in Hayward. He also describes life in the boarding schools, playing on the football team, the Depression, life in the old village, visiting with the elders, medicine men, and Strawberry Island. He tells many funny stories, including one about "Big George" Skye and another about a cat that lost its head. He talks about the many veterans in his family and about how they lived in the old days, hunting, snaring rabbits, using fish traps, drying fish, and making maple sugar. He ends the interview by encouraging young people to live a clean life and respect both others and the earth rather than littering or polluting it: "This is a beautiful country and we should keep it that way." Gib passed away on August 24, 1997.

Interview with Gilbert Chapman, Sr.

This interview was conducted by Phyllis White, Gib's daughter, and Beth Tornes.

My name is Gilbert Joseph Chapman. I had an Indian name, but I don't remember it. I think my aunt gave it to me, but I'm not sure. I was pretty small. My father was Robert Chapman; my mother was Mary MacArthur. [My grandparents on my father's side were] Joseph and Louise Chapman, on my mother's side, William and Sophie MacArthur. [They were Irish] on my grandfather's side. They were from Antigo, I think, as far as I know. Around Sheldon, Unity. My uncle, my granddad's brother, owned a farm there at Unity. . . . They never talked much about where they come from, but they homesteaded down through there.

The Indians [would spend the winter south], they would come up here in the springtime. That was on my mother's side. Her mother was born and raised in Flambeau. Her parents went down as far as Eau Claire, they'd winter there, then they'd come back in the spring. Then they'd move south, it's a little warmer down there, I guess, and there was a little more game. I had five brothers and five sisters. I was born October 9, 1910, I think at Lac du Flambeau, I'm not sure. I've lived here all my life. I got seven [children]. There's Phyllis, Gerald, Yvonne, Norma, Bub, Lorraine, and Julia.

*   *   *

It wasn't much to do around here. There was no cars here, so you didn't travel much . . . just swim, play ball, that's about all. There was nothing to do. When we was kids with slingshots, we'd hunt red squirrels. We'd fish. Not too often. My mother'd want some fish, want us to go fishing. She would give us five pennies, and we'd buy two cents worth of hooks and three cents worth of candy. We'd go fishing then.

In the wintertime, it was pretty hard here. No work, there was no work here. My parents and my Grandmother Chapman [had the most influence on me]. I used to stay with her quite a bit. She owned there [by Hutton's Creek] but she had a house right up here by the Catholic church. I helped her, I'd milk cows when she got older—I was older too.

I attended the public school here and the boarding school here. It was up here by where Simpson's Molding Plant is there. You went to school half a day, and you worked half a day. You'd go one morning, the next day you'd go in the afternoon. And you'd work the rest of the time. It was more like the military. You had a uniform, and every place you went you had to march. I think they found it easier to control a group of boys like that.

Boys at boarding school

I worked on the farm, farm work, they called it.[1] Milk cows, harness the horses, unharness them at 4:00. We started milking about six o'clock in the morning. They had quite a big herd of cattle. And they raised their own gardens, they raised potatoes, 'bagies,[2] and fall we'd have to help harvest potatoes. Not much else. You couldn't go home anytime you wanted to, you know, after school you had to stay right there. . . . The lights went off at a certain time. Around 9:00 the lights went out. They had their own generator there for electricity. They had their own heat, steam heat.

They had just the general [classes], arithmetic and so on. They didn't have many subjects like you have today. History, geography, reading and writing. That's about all. I missed a lot of school, when I went to public school I had trouble with my eyes and couldn't go to school. I went to Mt. Pleasant[3] in 1927 or '28, I think it was. The coach come up here and try to get some guys [to play on the football team]. And then about ten of us went, and I stayed there until after the football season was over. And I ran away from school, hopped the train. Just I and my cousin, we come back together. Took us about a week. Freight trains, one passenger train. It was cold, in November. Snowed a little bit. We'd get it in upper Michigan, then the people that run the train, the conductor, they didn't bother us. Let us ride. Then when they had to unload freight, we'd help them. There wasn't too much, sometimes just a few articles we'd unload. And a few articles to load, we'd help them. Otherwise the conductor and brakeman would have to do it.

---

[1] The boarding school complex included a working farm with pigs, horses, cows, a vegetable garden, and, across Pokegama Lake, a large cornfield. The children had to work half the day, as Gib describes, and attended classes the rest of the day.

[2] "Bagies" is the short form of the Lac du Flambeau name "rutabagies," for rutabagas.

[3] Mount Pleasant, Michigan, was the location of another Bureau of Indian Affairs boarding school.

There was no high school then. The nearest one was Rhinelander,[4] in horse and buggy days you couldn't go down there. People here didn't have money to pay board, so they didn't have much chance. The older ones, older than I, they went to Carlisle.[5] But they discontinued that, I think. And later Haskell come up, Haskell Indian School. But I never went there neither.

[Mt. Pleasant was] just the same thing [as Flambeau boarding school]. You marched every place you went. They'd have shows, silent pictures once a week. You had to even march to them. And then just go in groups, you'd march. There's a section for boys and a section for girls. I liked football though. I was left guard. I was the heaviest guy on the team, I weighed 175 pounds. I was a star on the team, I was a pretty good player. All the government employees would all cheer. The high school, they'd watch our games, they'd cheer for us too. They called them "normals," the schools, like a college. It was a lot of fun anyways.

I could [speak Ojibwe]. My mother could talk it fluently. But after awhile, I'd ask her a word, she couldn't remember it because she had no one to talk to. It just gradually disappears. Now some of the words I never thought of come back to me once in a while. My cousin lives in Chicago, I was down visiting him one night. He asked me how to say tobacco, and of all the things in the world I couldn't remember it until I got back here. I remembered "asemaa." But I had to get back here before I even thought of it!

I remember [my classmates here] Elmer Graveen and Clarence Graveen, there was some older boys but they're all dead now, just about all of them.

*   *   *

My ma was a housewife. My dad guided—he did odd work, you know, whenever he could find work. Wasn't much work up here. Work in the logging camps in the wintertime.[6] He didn't come home every night, they stayed right at the camps because they got up pretty early in the morning, worked pretty late at night. And after he got older, he worked in the CC camp; I worked in a CC camp too.[7] We built roads, cleared the roads. Right-of-ways, burn all the brush. Summer

---

[4] Rhinelander is located forty-five miles southeast of Lac du Flambeau.

[5] The Carlisle Indian Industrial School was founded in 1879 in the remains of an old cavalry barracks in Carlisle, Pennsylvania. It was the first government boarding school, and its first residents were Chiricahua Apache children, thus beginning a long history of forced assimilation, whereby boarding schools took Indian children from their families and suppressed their Native culture, language, and religion.

[6] The logging camps began in 1886, and the sawmill was built in 1894 soon after the advent of the Chicago and Northwestern railroad. The sawmill's operations ended in 1913. Men from Lac du Flambeau were hired to cut trees, drive teams of horses hauling lumber, and work in the mill.

[7] CC camp refers to the ICC or Indian Conservation Corps camp, which employed men in the 1930s and 1940s to carry out public works projects: In Flambeau these included such projects as the dam between Bear River and Flambeau Lake, the River Road Bridge, and the Tribal Fish Hatchery. Men from different tribes came to live at the ICC camp, located on Flambeau Lake, where they were housed, fed, and paid a minimal wage. WPA, or Works

CC camp at Lac du Flambeau

and winter. And the road building crew would come behind. Then I drove a truck up there most of the time.

My grandfather was a Civil War veteran.[8] My uncle on my mother's side, he was a veteran of World War I.[9] And my aunt was married to an Indian guy, he was from Minnesota, he was in the Marines. He was in the Spanish-American War.[10] And my relatives in World War II, and my nephew in Vietnam, Robert Chapman the Third. And one nephew by marriage was killed in Korea.[11] And my wife's brother's boy.

My grandfather's buried up here in the Presbyterian cemetery, the one who fought in the Civil War. He just said it was terrible, he wished that I would never have to go.

I was in there a year. I got as far as the Philippines, that's where they were staging for the invasion of Japan. I never seen no action, I was just built up on the invasion of Japan proper. But the atomic bomb ended that, so I was quite happy too. I was assigned to the decoy invasion. We were going to hit it in the middle. The real invasion was going to be in the north and south side of Japan.

*   *   *

Progress Administration, was a federal agency (1935–1943) begun by Franklin D. Roosevelt to insititute and administer public works projects in order to relieve national unemployment following the Great Depression.

[8] Gib's grandfather, John Chapman, was the Civil War Veteran. He is buried in the Presbyterian church cemetery in Lac du Flambeau.

[9] His uncle on his mother's side was Robert MacArthur, a World War I vet.

[10] When asked about this, Gib's family was uncertain of the name of Gib's aunt's husband from Minnesota, the Marine who fought in the Spanish-American War.

[11] His nephew by marriage killed in Korea was Carlton ("Corky") Valliere. (See also Georgian Kinstedt's interview: Corky was her brother.)

My cousin told me that my grandfather and his brother, his brother was taller than him—my grandfather on my mother's side.[12] They lived on Trout Lake, on an island, there was eleven acres there.[13] They went up through the winter—they snowshoed across country to Fifield, robbed a bank. My cousin said they got $1,500 dollars, that's what my cousin told me. Said they got away with it. I guess they lived pretty high when they got back.

My uncles, out on the island, they made moonshine there too. They wouldn't let none of us kids go there where they were. My grandmother and grandfather told us not to go up there, so we didn't. We didn't know what they were doing, we was just kids.

*   *   *

They used to play moccasin games.[14] It's just like you see on TV, they have those shells? Instead of shells they had moccasins. They had a little, I don't know what they had under there. But the guy would put his hand under each one, you know. There were three moccasins, and the guys, they'd bet. And the guy had a stick and he'd tap the moccasin. He'd tap it, if he didn't flip it he could flip the next one, any one of them. That's the way they played that. They'd bet on which moccasin that thing was under. They played that hour upon hour. Just the men would play it. Each one would have to wait his turn. And if a guy won, he got a chance to put the thing under. The winner, if he hit it, the object that was under the moccasin, if he hit the right one, he'd get a chance to work that. I imagine that game went on years and years and years and years.

I don't know what they played for, after awhile they played for money. Before that, they never had money then. They'd play for arrows or bows or feathers. I imagine before they bet different things—tobacco, probably headdresses.

I remember my grandma, Grandma Chapman, used to take me to the squaw dance.[15] You changed presents, you know. And whatever you give them, they try to give you back the same thing. Just the women [danced].

[13] Trout Lake is located near the northern edge of the reservation from which several Lac du Flambeau families originated. According to Phyllis White, Gib's daughter, his grandmother taught the children the Ojibwe language while growing up there, and his grandfather taught them English.

[14] The moccasin game is a game of chance that consists of hiding small objects such as a bullet or stone under a moccasin. Typically four men play, in two teams, although Gib says only three played when he watched. After the object is hidden the opposing man or team tries to guess which moccasin it is under, striking the moccasin with a stick and flipping it over. For further description of the moccasin game see Frances Densmore, *Chippewa Customs* (Washington, DC: United States Government Printing Office, 1929), 114–115.

[15] Squaw Dance or Woman's Dance (Ikwe niimi'idiiwin) is a ceremonial dance performed by women. It typically includes a feast and a giveaway.

There was a lot of government policeman before me. I started in 1930—in the thirties. I was Indian police for five years.[16] The price of food was going up, they didn't pay much, maybe $50 a month. And I had kids, so I quit. I cut pulp a little while, then I went into the Army. Then I was town police for seven years. Thirteen years altogether. I worked on the town crew for twelve years. I worked for Patterson's[17] for about five years too. And I worked for the railroad. Took care of the tracks. Sections [they called them]. Section hand, had a section boss. And two guys, sometimes three guys, depending on how much work they got, they'd bring in sections from there. Working on the railroad, used to go pretty near up to Mercer and all the way down to about Miskonagon Swamp there, that's where we'd turn around. The rest of it's Woodruff.[18]

*   *   *

[The biggest change was] when they put streets in. Otherwise, all mud. Just dirt. There weren't too many buildings like there is now. And they got Aschenbrenner to come in, he built a store.[19] There were only two stores here. Oldenberg's and Ben Gauthier's. And Oldenberg's was the first one. The only way to get to Woodruff then was to go out on [County Highway] D, and hit [Highway] 70 and go in. It was crooked. Then go into Woodruff. And between Woodruff and Minocqua, after you cross that little pond on the right coming this way? From there on there was no buildings. You got right into Woodruff and that big store, that Super 3, that was on the Main Street. Carl Oldenberg had it, the first time anyone owned a Model T Ford. He parked it right in front of his store.

Those roads were wagon roads though. The wagon road went from right close by Angler's there. That's where I pretty near got stuck. Then it went down along Miskonagon, just above the railroad bridge. That's where them Indians would go. Take that road.

*   *   *

---

[16] The current tribal police station and judicial center is named in honor of Gib, the Gilbert J. Chapman Senior Judicial Center. Phyllis says she encouraged the tribe to name it after her father while he was still living and similarly to name the George W. Brown, Jr. Lac du Flambeau Chippewa Museum after George. In a resolution the tribe adopted both names for these buildings.

[17] Patterson Lumber in Minocqua, the town south of Lac du Flambeau.

[18] The Chicago and Northwestern Railroad, which ran between Chicago and the Twin Cities, was first built in 1889 and served to bring many tourists to the area. It was later used to transport lumber to the large cities. Mercer, at the northern edge of the part Gib worked on, is about fifteen miles north of Lac du Flambeau. Woodruff is the town thirteen miles south of the reservation. "Miskonagan Swamp" (though spelled Mishonagan, most of the elders Gib's age pronounce it with a "k") is on the southern edge of the reservation, northwest of Woodruff.

[19] Aschenbrenner's was a grocery store as were Oldenberg's and Gauthier's, which also sold native crafts to tourists and formed part of the Gauthier resort.

Railroad crossing near Woodruff

Main Street, Lac du Flambeau, 1904

My uncle raised popcorn here. A guy found out they could sell it, like in Chicago. So a bunch of them got together, they all had their own land, it was allotted, and planted popcorn. The government give them two horses. My uncle heard that mules were better workers. They worked good all right, but they had to go from here to the depot, two miles, you know. By the time you got about halfway, the train was about due. He would've made it but the mule started balking. It was in the fall, kind of cool. And the mule wouldn't move. He got out, everything! So a guy come back, he said you better hurry up. He said, "I can't get this mule to go, I don't know what's the matter with it." "Build a fire under it. He'll move." He moved all right, but just pulled the wagon over! He never got his popcorn to the train. Moved over and the fire started to burn the wagon, and the corn started popping, and the two mules froze to death, they thought it was snowing!

Another one, there's a guy down there in Merrill, he moved up here as he got old. He said there was a little shack, his father was working there. They hadn't logged this far yet, at Merrill. Mother had an old cat that she told him, take that cat out and kill it. He had an old single-shot .22. Went out to check his snares, took the cat and put it in a bag and took it out. . . . Got out there, and he took the cat out and shot it in the head. Cat would kick awhile, he watched it, and then he checked his snares. Come back and his mother said, "I thought I told you to kill that cat!" Said, "I did! Shot it in the head, I seen it kick!" "Look under the stove," he looked under there and sure enough, the cat was there. "God," he said, "I'll take it out tomorrow. I'm a set some more snares. So I'll take my hatchet with me." He did. Took that cat out, shot it in the head again. This time he didn't want it to go home. Cut the head off'n it. Then he come back and Mother said, "I thought I told you to kill the cat! It's under the stove!" He looked under there and sure enough, the cat was under there. He said "I don't know how it got there, oh my, I know it's dead, I cut the head off!" She said, "Well, the cat come home carrying its head in its mouth."

*   *   *

Make beadwork mostly, moccasins [to make money]. That's all they had! And the prices wasn't very much, well the price of food wasn't much. God you'd get fifty cents worth of sugar, my mother used to—in the summer they'd pick berries. They'd can them, sometimes they didn't have enough money to buy sugar, they'd can them just like that you know, and when they got money they used them, they'd put sugar in them. Pick strawberries, raspberries. Blueberries mostly, though. Out here, past the second bridge on [County Highway] D there. When I was a kid, that was all open, all the way to Buckskin Lake. Oh there was little clumps of trees. Had wild horses run wild out there, must have been two or three hundred horses out there.

If you had a house like this, and you wanted a garden in back, you had to put a fence around because horses and cows . . . everyone had one or two cows. You'd buy milk, ten cents a gallon. No refrigerators then.

*   *   *

Dancers near site of former sawmill

Not many [celebrations back then]. They'd have pow-wows, certain times of the year they celebrated something, you know. Then they'd dance, you know. In later years when the tourists started coming, then they'd dance, you know, they'd make a little money there. By dancing.

They'd have medicine dances[20] every once in awhile. Every fall they'd have a harvest dance, and dance in the spring, you know. Just like the Indians always did, you know, to the Great Spirit. To make the garden good, you know.

They had certain spots they'd dance at. Up there by the casino was one of them. And that's about the only one they had, where they had the pow-wows. There were a bunch of pine there, you know. I'd drive by there, that's where the old planing mill used to be, right where the (old) casino is today. Right by the museum, that's where the sawmill was. They had a fence like across that [hot pond].

*   *   *

No work, nothing [during the Depression]. The government give us sheep and flour and stuff. Those sheep, I must have been six, seven years old when they sent them up here. Molasses, tea, sugar, salt pork, then they come up with them sheep. God, them sheep must have been killed or froze to death out West. Whole sheep. Dead, they were froze about five years I think. I got one of them, I stuck it out there and a dog come along, a couple dogs. Looked at it, started barking, turn around and run back! [laughs] Yeah, there [was] just nahthing, there was hardly no meat on them!

---

[20] "Medicine dances" refers to the Midewin dances. (See Introduction.)

That's what I did when I was Indian police, all the old Indians, they called them rations.[21] I'd go out once a month. As Indian police that was part of my job to give old people as they come. I used to give them a lot, too. [chuckles] Beans, tea, molasses, sugar, baking powder . . . that's about all. You couldn't keep any of it, because it'd freeze, you know.

Wasn't that many deer then. My uncle told me, before I was born, you'd hunt deer, if you found a deer track, you stayed with it. Because of all that pine, there was no food under there. All that needle killed everything. Till after they logged it, then the deer started coming. Used to migrate, that's why they called it Fence Lake.[22] Indians cut down trees, you know. And they'd leave openings, that's where the deers would migrate south. And they would get salt, they had to go pretty near up to Ironwood there, to get salt. Then they'd stay here, after they started logging here. . . . I guess there were green little hardwood patches. Then they'd start going back in the fall. That's where they'd kill them, shoot them, in those little openings.

*   *   *

The old ladies would go and visit one another. You see, I used to go and check out the village, a lot of old people out there. About every morning, if I didn't have something else, I'd go and check on them.

Walked in the house and sit down, pretty soon a knock on the door. I was talking to Jim Bell. The other old guy said, "Jim Bell live there?" Started talking, pretty soon another, the wife would answer the door, old guy come in and sit down. Never said a word. I talked to Jim some more, finally the old guy got up and walked out the door. He'd come over and visit with that guy. But they never said a word! They didn't have much news, there was no newspapers or anything.

That's when Big George,[23] he spent a year in prison. Waupan. Killed a guy worked for the railroad. Section worker, they were building a railroad then, north of us. I guess they were drinking. That guy, didn't want to give him any more whiskey, phht! Picked up a shovel, hit him in the head, killed him. They said, "You killed a white man. That's why you're here."

"Oh no, no, no. I didn't kill no white man." He killed a Swede! No, that's what he . . . then he got up, they told him to raise his right hand and swear. To tell the truth, the whole truth, and nothing but the truth. He got up, and he would try to swear, but he didn't know too many words!

---

[21] The BIA provided "rations" or food items to families and elders at various times, consisting of such staples as flour, sugar, and canned goods, as Gib describes. Today's "commodities" replace these as the common method of food distribution by the BIA.

[22] Fence Lake is the largest of the reservation lakes, named, as Gib tells us, for the fences that Indian hunters built out of brush to "corral" deer as they migrated south for the winter. They would put out salt to attract the deer as people do today.

[23] Big George Skye was an extremely large man, over seven feet tall, and as a result a popular subject for tourist photographs.

George Skye

[laughs] They were cussing! He was a great big guy, Jesus. His one hand was as big as my two. Big George Skye. There's two George Skyes, the younger one was as big as I was.

*   *   *

Just that [Strawberry Island] and the big rock[24] out there [were considered sacred places]. I always put tobacco out there. Like they had a big—back of Ben Poupart's house, up at the village? Had a medicine wigwam. Christ, that thing was big! From here to that house over there long [gestures across the street, about fifty yards]. Just like a wigwam, only long. They'd have medicine dances. I watched them shake a wigwam too. Jiisikii.[25] My uncle, my mother's uncle, he had one arm. He'd shake that, and poles that big, I know damn well he couldn't shake that, that thing would flop like that, [flops his hand in all directions] every direction. He'd pound the medicine drum in there. See a medicine drum is little, only about like this [holds his hands out about eight inches

[24] Strawberry Island and Medicine Rock, "the big rock." (See Introduction.)

[25] Jiisikii means "He Shakes a Teepee" and refers to a healing ceremony or *jiisikiiwin* during which a wigwam or teepee shakes. For more on *jiisikiiwin* see Densmore, *Chippewa Customs*, 44–46.

around]. It's round. They ain't like the big drum, you know. Medicine drum, that one guy would pound it like that and sing, you know. [When the wigwam shook] it sounded like wind to me. We'd get right close to it, and watch it. Clarence Graveen, he went over [laughs] and, "That must be the devil." He got some holy water and [shakes his hand as if sprinkling water], "Chase that away from there!" They caught him.

Them men . . . my dad used to live on Chicog Street, it was all opening in there, pines there. Them guys would gamble in there, take a blanket and gamble, play poker. I and my friend Clarence . . . had a lot of little rocks like this in my pocket. I seen them guys going out there, and there weren't enough there yet to play, so I and my friend we'd climb up in a pine tree. Got out there, we could see the tent. We could hide up there, you know. Geez . . . then they started to play. My dad was in that too, pick them little stones up you know. We'd set still, not make a noise, you know. Them rocks was on that blanket. Then one of those guys would get up and walk around. . . . They got too much for [laughs], there must have been a bad spirit or something, they all quit and went! He pretty near give us a way.

Bert Sky, he'd make fireballs, they talked about it.[26] My grandma, she believed in it, Grandma Chapman. Had Jim Grey, old Bearskin [medicine men]. Some of them, they didn't do much, you know. They never talked about it, though, like we talk about it now.

[Bert Sky] made fireballs all the time. My grandma tried to explain it to me. He was either like a dog or something, you know.[27] He was like in a trance, when he's . . . when they go.

My uncle [laughs] he went hunting, there was snow on the ground. They had rifles then, they had old muzzle-loaders. His moccasins got thin on the bottom so his wife sewed on a sole, another sole, you know. He was hunting and it got warm. And that thread must've broke, and just the heels were holding it.

And he'd walk, he was walking, my mother told me this. Walking, and he could hear it—them things would fly up in the air and they'd, like somebody stepping behind, you know. Jeez, he'd turn around, quick, you know, and nahthing! He'd start again, sing a couple Indian songs you know, walk again. All at once he got scared, I guess, and he took off. He ran about half a mile to get home. He got in there, he was telling his wife. She picked up his moccasins, and hang them up to dry you know? And she seen them, and she started laughing. [laughs] They found out what they were, you know.

Another old Indian, right up where the school is, he had an old horse. He had a field back there, he planted potatoes back there. All fall he had his hoe on his horse, no saddle. Hoe, couple pails there. He had a shotgun [laughs]. Riding out there, partridges, ruffled grouse were there. He

---

[26] Bert Sky, Jim Grey, and Bearskin were a few of the medicine men of Gib's day. Bert Sky (named after his Indian name Binewigiizhig meaning "Bird in the Sky") was known for making "fireballs," which suddenly appeared moving through the woods, over buildings, or across lakes, and were considered a sign of potential harm.

[27] Some medicine men, including Sky, were believed to have the power to "shapeshift" or transform themselves into dogs, bears, or other animals and back into humans.

Bert Sky on right with his brother John Martin on left

stopped the horse and he shot. And that horse turned up in the air, he went, and down he come! The horse come back home to the barn, and he had to walk all the way back there! [laughs] He never realized, you know, that horse was never, a gun never fired on it before, you know.

Another one, old John Beson, hunting with his son-in-law, Charlie Poupart, Old Charlie. Trying to catch a porcupine, he had an old muzzle loader. Porcupine ran in a hollow long, at least that long [holds his hands out three feet], a big cat. Old man crawled in there, he seen he couldn't catch a porcupine, so he picked up his gun, and that concussion knocked him out! Charlie, he come out, he couldn't find him. But he happened to look at that log, and just his moccasins were sticking out! [laughter all around]

*   *   *

[When I was a policeman] I used to stay up all night and walk the streets. I didn't come home until four o'clock in the morning when the bakery would open up, and I'd come home. There was me alone. Then they hired another one. Then there was two, and the town had quite a few of them too. . . . I had a house and the coal. Electricity was paid for. Government furnished me a car, furnished the gas, everything.

But I was more of an ambulance driver. I used to make, the only hospital they'd go to was Hayward,[28] I'd make two, three trips sometimes a day. Sick people. I'd make it in three hours, over and back. But jeez in the middle of the night they'd get me up. I'd balk though, one time a woman was going to have a baby. Take her down, I said, I'm not going to take her down alone. What the hell am I going to do with her? Well take your wife. My wife isn't working for the government, I said, no. They should have sent her before, last week they should have sent her. I'm not going to take her. She was in labor. She had her baby, it was stillborn. I guess the doctor was scared.

And I had a niece, about two o'clock in the morning, came and got me. Clyde's little girl, Pansy. Jeez, it was about ten miles from Hayward where she died.

[There was no hospital in Woodruff then] the nearest hospital was in Rhinelander, in Lake Tomahawk.

*   *   *

Stayed about two weeks out there camping, beyond Wipagaki. Them people had a resort there on Sand Lake. They'd come up there and fish. Catch any fish, my dad said, asked them guys if they had any luck, no. He said are you coming back this way tomorrow? Yes, he said, we're going to fish, we're going home day after tomorrow. He told my daughter, bring us some bread. Bring your boat over here, bring your stringer here. They had ten nice bass on there. Them guys come back the next day alright. Jesus Christ, we had enough stuff there to camp for another two weeks Then we had a cousin, my brother, too big rocks like that, water was about this deep [spreads his hands apart three feet], they moved all those big rocks in a circle so that the fish couldn't get out, kept them in there. Them guys didn't get any fish. My dad said, "Here, bring your boat over here." They had an old dip net, my brother and my cousin. They got all them fish out of there, there was about fifteen of them, great big bass like that [holds his hands about twenty inches apart]. Jeez, them guys were happy. So they at least had fish to go back with, anyways.

*   *   *

[People got around with] horse and buggy. . . . There were trails in some places. Like where the bowl[29] is, there's a trail going up through there and one up through the cemetery, and come out

---

[28] The nearest "Indian Hospital" was in Hayward, Wisconsin, about a hundred miles west of Lac du Flambeau on the Lac Courte Oreilles reservation. Local hospitals at the time such as those Gib mentions refused to treat Indian patients. It was not until the 1960s that Indians received treatment at the nearby hospital in Minocqua.

[29] The Indian Bowl in downtown Flambeau, where dances are held for tourists (See Introduction.)

Bob Pine with birch bark canoe

up on the road. Otherwise you went by around by Simpson's[30] and walked up. All dirt roads, wagon roads. My grandma had an old horse, called her Daisy. That's how we got our boat from Pokegama to Sand Lake. I went with my dad, we took it over the day before, put it on Sand Lake, so we could . . . about a mile there. Then take the horse back, my brothers and my cousin did. Then we'd come back, and Dad had the boat loaded to go.

That was a long time ago, fishing. I like to fish. I used to like to fish. Used to go fishing brook trout a couple times a week. There's some little streams here. Phyllis used to eat them.[31]

Those little bitty streams out here, Johnson Springs, one by the tower, by the mineral station there. There's two springs there, then right across it. Up past Mercer, go out on the sheep ranch, those little springs. We used to fish all of them.

Oh God, I liked to hunt ducks. One time I had a vacation coming from Indian police. Went hunting ducks, I had ducks piled up on the porch, in a cord about that high [holds his hand four feet high].

*   *   *

He was good to me [his neighbor, Bob Pine]. Let me drive his horses. Then he got a Model T. . . . I used to go down and watch him make canoes.[32] He wanted me to come down there every day, he'd have taught me how but that's when I had to go to the hospital all the time. Last time I

---

[30] Simpson's Electric Plant.

[31] Phyllis White, Gib's daughter, who interviewed him.

[32] Bob Pine was a well known canoe maker in Lac du Flambeau.

was down there I had to hurry back and take somebody to the hospital. Then when they'd bring them, sometime they'd bring them all the way from Hayward, sometimes I'd have to meet them halfway. Some of them died, I just took them right into the hospital. Let them take care of it. I had to go up in Michigan, Lac Vieux Desert,[33] Indian settlement there. I had to go and pick a woman up there.

Where the gravel pit is down there [on Highway D], they had a pest house out there.[34] My grandma told me about it. We used to go by there, that old road going to her place. The road didn't go through by the gravel pit then. It went around this other way, around the gravel. They'd take them if they had smallpox, typhoid fever, they'd take them out there. If they died, they buried them right there. I was just wondering if they ever dug up any bones there. [That gravel pit] is getting pretty close to where that road was.[35] Towards Pokegama. You take Oberland's Point Road, it's an old road that used to go in there.

I don't know what they did there. She just said there was people buried out there. When they got so sick they couldn't do anything, to confine them. That one road, you had to walk through there, went right by it, went out by Gerry's fish ponds out there.[36] There was three houses out there, her house, my aunt Rose's house, my Dad's house. Used to be springs there—they had a pump where the springs come out of the ground. My grandmother—ox and dirt, banked it up. Way up on the hill, close to the top, put a wooden trough in there. She'd build it up with rocks. That's where that water'd run out, run out and run all the way down to the creek. There was a couple more springs there. We never used a pump, you'd go down there and put your pail down on the rock, when it filled up you'd pick it up, put the other one down—two pails. My grandma, she lived there, that's where she'd put that, it was just *cold* water too. She'd set her milk in there.

I'm about the only one who knows how to make an old Indian fish trap. Now you can make a quick one, chicken wire and stuff like that. But this is all wood. Used to go with my grandmother early in the morning, sun would be just coming up. In the spring. We'd go down there, crows would be getting in there [the trap] so we got two more sticks like that, put alders in there. Put alders over the top, and crows wouldn't go in there because they'd think it was a trap—you know, it was dark

---

[33] Lac Vieux Desert is an Ojibwe reservation just over the northern Wisconsin border in Upper Michigan about thirty-five miles northeast of Lac du Flambeau.

[34] The "pest house" refers to a building where those afflicted with smallpox or typhoid, both highly contagious and deadly diseases, were forced to live. Some Lac du Flambeau elders have said that these diseases were introduced in the community when the government gave infected blankets to the Indian people.

[35] The area where this pest house was located is now the site of a large gravel pit owned by the tribe. According to Gib, as the pit expanded it approached the road leading to the pest house and the burial grounds where those afflicted were laid to rest.

[36] Gib is referring to the tribe's fish-rearing ponds on Pokegama Lake, near Hutton's Creek. His father Jim, grandmother Eloise Chapman, and aunt Rose lived out there, and Gib spent a great deal of time with them there as well. Phyllis says they were caretakers for the Huttons. "Gerry" is Gib's grandson Gerry White, a Fish and Game employee who works at the fish ponds.

in there. And the fish'd go down, the back end was slanted a little bit like that. Fish would get in there and they'd flop and die.

So every morning we'd get fish. Muskies, suckers, walleyes. The creek wasn't very deep, about like that [holds his hand about two feet high].[37] In the dry season doesn't run too much. In the spring it always, that ice you know would melt and that snow water would run into the lake. She'd run high then. The suckers—muskies and walleyes we ate, suckers she'd sun dry them. They'd build a rack like that [moves his hands to show sticks on a rack] up there, cut the heads and split them down the middle like that so they could open up. Put them on there.

I and my cousin, we got a whole bunch of suckers. Never did again after that. She bawled us out for taking more than we could use, you know. She said, "But I'll use them, I'll dry them." He and I had to go get wood, dry popple, put it under there. I said, "You have to have smoke to dry them?" She said, "No, that heat keeps the flies away." So the blowflies wouldn't get on them or anything. It's that heat from that wood you know, it doesn't take much. It's that heat going up.

And all that next winter, I stayed with her most the time.

*   *   *

[She'd make baskets] about that long [holds his hands about two feet apart] I guess, for maple sugar and sugar cakes, wild rice.[38] And she'd lace them with a cover on and seal them. No bugs would get in there. Birch bark, basswood. Basswood is just as good as birch bark. No bugs will get in there. You don't see them any more—you used to see a lot of little canoes for flowers, you know. You'd make them, I guess you'd get a dollar for them. . . . Because if you make a plant holder out of that, that dirt won't hurt that birch bark. It won't rot. . . .

I'd carry sap. Cut wood, carry wood.[39] I and my brother, he'd come after me on Friday, didn't go to school on Friday afternoon. Went up by Stearns Lake Road there. Then there was no road there, just that old wagon road. It was washboard, logs and stuff. Jeez, there was a lot of bluegills, I and my brother would start catching them.

Nice bluegills. Took them out, my grandma's sister and her boy, they'd start cleaning fish. Had them right that night too.

---

[37] Hutton's Creek at the time had walleyes, muskies and suckers running in it: Today it is still a spawning bed for suckers, which people harvest in early spring. The fish trap Gib describes was probably a football-shaped trap made of willow with bait at one end and an opening at the other, which fish could not swim out of once they swam in because of sticks facing inwards at the opening.

[38] These birch bark baskets or "makaks" were traditional cone-shaped baskets, larger at the bottom, with a tight-fitting lid to keep dirt and bugs out. Rice and sugar stored in these "makaks" could last for many years.

[39] He is describing maple sugaring at the familys' Stearns Lake sugarbush, as well as at his grandmother's sugarbush by Pokegama Lake.

It was awful when you first got to sugar camp. Go in that wigwam, that hole up there on top, that smoke in there. . . . Jeez, your eyes would be all bloodshot. About a week after that, you. . . . And she had one out here across Pokegama there. Used to go there with her.

*   *   *

My grandmother, in the spring, she'd make a tonic. It was out of popple.[40] You take the bark off the tree and then scrape fine bark under it, you know. Scrape that and dry it. Then she'd boil it. And that was spring tonic we had to take every spring for a couple days. A tablespoon full. And bitter! That was really bitter.

And then when we'd get sore throats, she had, she called it "golden thread."[41] It's a root, it grows around here. You'd boil that and you'd gargle with that.

My Grandma MacArthur, she's the one that made the—we called it sweet medicine. I don't know what it was, they had an Indian name for it too. If you was constipated, they'd give you that. It was bark and different roots. And then she had another one that looked pretty near the same. If you had diarrhea, they'd give it to you, and it'd stop the diarrhea too.

They had all their own home remedies. And then skunk grease. That was for cold, or something. They'd rub it on you, you know. It didn't smell like skunk, it was just oily, you know. And then bear grease, they used that for the hair. And nobody killed bear up here just then.

But my stepdad,[42] he loved bear meat. My mother told me he could eat that for breakfast, dinner, and supper. One time I killed five bear, I gave them all to him. He really liked it. He liked all kinds of game. He used to hunt, but after he got older his eyesight wasn't too good. He bought an old pair of glasses so he could read, but he couldn't see with them.

I hunted with him one time. I shot a doe and a buck come out where he was. So I saw him watching him. He jumped in the creek, and he shot, and he killed it. And I always kidded him about—he didn't hit the deer, the deer drownded! [laughs]

He give the gun to me, he said, "I borrowed it." "Keep it," he said. "I ain't gonna hunt no more." And his father told me, he knew I hunted, because I used to give my mother venison. And my stepfather's dad, he stayed with them. He told me about hunting. He said, "You want to go in September. August and September, go and look on the south side of a hill. That's where them buck lay there so their horns will dry, you know." I told my brother-in-law that, he said, "Jeez, I've

---

[40] "Popple" or aspen trees (*Populus tremuoides*) are very common in the northwoods and have many uses including medicinal, as he describes.

[41] Golden thread is a medicinal plant with bright golden flowers that blossom in springtime. As Gib's stories demonstrate, the Lac du Flambeau Ojibwe people were very knowledgeable about medicinal plants and continue to use them in their everyday lives to cure all kinds of ailments.

[42] Gib's stepfather was George Sharlow.

hunted a lot, that's the first time I ever know that! It stands to reason, too," he said. "The sun hitting the horns, it would dry them out."

*   *   *

And you know that Chippewas never fought against the whites? Did you know that? No, they never fought against the whites, the Chippewas. Not here. They fought other tribes. I think that's why they moved out of the east.[43] That Senecas was a great nation. Large, they had a lot of allies. I think they just chased the Chippewas here, because this was Sioux country and they moved in from the east. Some come south of Lake Superior, the ones in Canada went north of Lake Superior. Because there's a lot, I don't know how many thousands of Chippewa. We're the fourth biggest tribe, that's Chippewas in the United States. But they don't count the ones outside! There's probably more in Canada than there are here.

My grandmother would try to tell me [about the battle with the Sioux on Strawberry Island].[44] She said—she was pretty small I guess. She said she seen a hatchet up on a oak tree [on the island]. She didn't know if they took it or not.

*   *   *

We played lacrosse with a string tied between two sticks.[45] We didn't have no lacrosse rackets, you know. The old people that owned them, they wouldn't let them go. They always kept them. Kept them where they was dry and wouldn't let no kids play with them. We'd get a stick and cut a stick off, put short sticks on either side of that string, throw it up. Hit a post, a tree. You had to hit that, then you got a score. . . .

Yeah, we'd hunt. Go hunting partridge. I lived right across from the school, I could race home, ask my ma for a quarter, and go up and get five shotgun shells. Go bird hunting. Go right back to the house, towards the old people's housing there? Go back in there and get enough for a meal. Ruffled grouse. I was lucky one time, went back there, two of them was walking, they'd walk till their heads got right in line. I shot and I come home with six.

---

[43] There are different versions of the Ojibwe migration story, though they all say that at one time the Anishinaabe (comprising the Ojibwe, Potawatomi, and Odawa people) migrated from the eastern Atlantic region to their current territory in the Upper Midwest and Canada.

[44] The battle between the Dakota and the Ojibwe. (See Introduction.)

[45] Lacrosse is a traditional Ojibwe game in which a wooden ball is tossed with a racket typically made with a loop of bent sapling and with a pocket of woven rawhide in the loop where the ball is carried and thrown. Gib and his companions improvise a lacrosse racket with sticks. The goal is to carry the ball to the goalposts, two sticks with a crossbar, or in this case a tree.

We'd snare in the winter. You didn't have much time, you know, you'd get through a Friday, Saturday morning you'd go and set snares, Sunday you'd have to go and pick them up. A lot of rabbits here. My brother helped a guy who didn't know how to snare too good, they got ten, I got nine. I had ten snares, only got nine rabbits. That's what we'd do. . . . Christmas vacation we got two weeks. So we'd snare, and ice fish.[46] I made a living here, no work. I set lines on Flambeau Lake. Got ten cents a pound for walleyes. Now they're four dollars, five a pound. . . . I made my living that way.

*   *   *

[I'd tell a young person] not to use dope. Not to drink too much. Or to destroy another person's property. When they break the benches and pull the flowers up on the street, it makes no sense. That belongs to them as much as it belongs to me or any member of the tribe! The parents should realize that and teach the kids not to destroy stuff. Someday after all the older people are gone, they're going to own. Do they want it to look like a garbage dump, or don't they care? We only live once, and we should have a beautiful country. This is a beautiful country, and we should keep it that way. They shouldn't destroy their own country, their own reservation.

Just like I was taught, be home at a certain time at night and don't touch something that don't belong to you. When I was a kid, the people would pull up the boats—leave the fishing poles. The kids would stand there and look at them and just wish we could have something like that. Nowadays you can't leave a boat with anything in it, they steal or destroy it.

[My kids] they stayed home. None of them ever left the yard unless I said so. There was a big line of pine trees back there. I don't know why the rest of the people can't do that.

---

[46] Snaring rabbits with a wire loop hung over a rabbit trail and ice fishing with either lines or spears, are two wintertime subsistence activities.

Reva Chapman

Reva Chapman was born on May 15, 1915. She had two Indian names, Biiwaabokoons ("Steel Wires") and Zhaawashkobinesikwe ("Bluebird Woman"). Her parents were Jim Sagasunk ("When the Sun First Comes Above the Horizon") and Mary Ackley (Niizho-Asinokwe, or "Two Winds Blowing Woman"). She had six brothers and one sister. She was married to William Cobb and later to Orville Chapman. She had six children.

Reva lived all her life in the Old Indian Village, until her elder years when she moved to town. In her interview she talks about life in the village and in the sugar camp by Sugarbush Lake, where the family moved to every spring. She talks about gardening, drying and eating deer meat, making clothes, playing outside, and generally having a happy childhood. She also describes the harsh life at the government boarding school. She talks about the importance of praying and using tobacco life every day of her life, and her narrative ends "Some of the memories are good. And some kind of bad. But I enjoyed life. I still enjoy life." In these lines, we see her positive outlook and gentle spirit. She was devoted to her children and grandchildren, some of whom she raised, and was always teaching about Indian ways, whether it was an Ojibwe word or phrase or how to make hominy soup and fry bread. She was also an avid reader, and in her elder years she read a book or magazine every night before going to sleep.

Though Reva does not talk about it in the interview, she also played an important role in the revitalization of the Ojibwe language in Lac du Flambeau. She and Cecilia Defoe began teaching in the Family Circles Program in 1987, later joined by Joe Chosa. This language revitalization effort continues in today's Ojibwe Language Program. She worked in the Ojibwe Language Program until the last year of her life, generously sharing her vast knowledge of the Ojibwe language and culture with her fellow teachers, students, children, and grandchildren. She was the last surviving speaker of the Old Village dialect of Lac du Flambeau Ojibwe language when she walked on, on May 23, 2001.

Interview with Reva Chapman

This interview was conducted by Marilyn Conto.

I have two Ojibwe names.[1] I have two namesakes. My name is Biiwaabikoons and my other name is Zhaawashkobinesikwe, that's my other name. My namesakes are the ones that are heirs to Strawberry Island, the Whitefeathers. John Whitefeather, he had a dream about electricity, electrical wires, you know, before all this here came about, and he said the wires went all over, you know, in the sky, in the earth, and down below. And that's what he was dreaming about. That's what he dreamt about, and he said that they were powerful, they were real powerful and strong. And he said I would get strength from this dream, because, you know, he dreamt about something like that. And so I believe him today because I'm still going, and I'm still very strong and still very much alive. I've got a lot of responsibility but I'm doing the best I can.

That was the first name, Biiwaabikoons. That means, you know, wires. I guess that's what it means. Then my other name is bluebird, bluebird woman. It's like a thunderbird, you know, thunderbird lady. That's the way I describe it, that's the way I translate it. And I think I got a good translation for it. But it does mean bluebird lady. But then we always think of a thunderbird, and everything was sacred in that naming ceremony. So I don't know how old I was when I was named, but those were my two names.

And I got real close to those people. They lived at the point, they were out there by that big rock,[2] right around that area. When we were in the Old Village,[3] we all knew one another, you know. So I got to know them pretty well, and I used to visit them quite a bit. I don't think they had any children, there was never any children there. But I saw the picture in that paper, and it just brought back all these memories.

Those Indians put out a feast for a naming ceremony.[4] They give the people that they choose to name their child a certain amount of time. Whenever a man or woman has a dream or, you know, has a name ready for the baby, that's when they tell them that it's time, you know, they'll be able to name the baby. I don't know if I was a baby then or just a kid, I don't really know. They usually

---

[1] Reva was born May 15, 1915. (She does not give her birth date in the interview.)

[2] The "big rock" is Medicine Rock, at the end of a point on the western shore of Flambeau Lake. Believed to have been brought here by Wenaboozhoo, it has a sacred significance to the Lac du Flambeau Ojibwe.

[3] The "Old Village" is the older settlement of Ojibwe people, as opposed to the "town," which grew up around the sawmill after the logging industry came to the area. The Old Village was considered to be the more traditional community, where Indian religions were practiced and ceremonies were held. Also, fluent speakers in the Old Village had a distinct dialect of Ojibwe language.

[4] The Naming Ceremony is the ceremony wherein a child (or in later times an adult) is given a name in Ojibwe by a namesake or "awenh= en," who receives the name in a dream or vision or after seeing something unique that inspired the name.

John Whitefeather and his wife

name them when they're babies though, that was long ago. They didn't wait till they grew up, like they do now.

*　　　*　　　*

My dad's name was Sagasunk. In the white man's style, it was Jim Sagasunk. And that's my surname, Sagasunk. That means when the sunbeams are just coming through, and the sun is going to be appearing on the horizon . . . just when it comes up above the horizon, and the sunbeams come first. And I guess I'm the last Sagasunk in this world now. [My mother's] Indian name was Niizhoo'aasinookwe. I guess that means, I could never translate that very much, but I did think of, I don't know if there's such a thing as two winds together blowing. That's the way I translate it, the way I understand it. Niizhoo'aasin, that's two. Niizhoo'aasinookwe.

[Her maiden name was] Mary Ackley. That's another name she went by. Because long ago they never had white people's names you know; they never had English names. I guess my grandpa is the one that—I can't tell you because I really don't know myself, I can never get that explained to me. But old man Bearskin is the one that was her dad. So really, she didn't go by Bearskin, though—she never went by that name. But he raised her and you know, because my grandma gave her up to my grandparents, and so my grandparents raised my ma. And that was Bearskin. . . . My dad lost his first wife and he asked my grandpa for my ma. And then my ma consented to—be my ma [laughs]—and I guess that's the way they met.

Frank Link and Mary Sagasunk

Bearskin (Makwayaan), Reva's grandfather

I had a lot of brothers. I guess there was a few that she lost. I have five brothers that I knew. Then I have one sister, she died almost two years ago. It will be two years in February. Margaret. Do you remember her? We used to travel with your ma a lot. She lived by where Dorothy Poupart lives, in a little house. My oldest brother was John, his name was John. My next brother's name was Philip. My next brother's name was Lawrence. And the other brother's name was Victor. And then my youngest brother's name was Clarence. And then Margaret was the baby. And then we had another baby. . . . His name was Freddy. But she lost that baby when he was small. [Sighs] So, my goodness, I had six brothers. That's a large family, huh?

*   *   *

We lived out [by] the Sugarbush Lake. In fact, I'm an heir to part of that land there. We had a home out there, and we lived out there during sugarbush time. We lived out there, and it was a home to me. We lived out there, and my father farmed out there. He grew potatoes and beans and corn, and the transportation we had was horse and buggy. . . . We lived out the Sugarbush, we made our own sugar.

We picked berries, and ma would can 'em. She dried her meat, we didn't have refrigerators, she dried her meat. Smoked it and dried it. And then when that meat, when she'd cook it, it was just delicious, that meat, you know, deer meat. Then we had our own potatoes, carrots, and dad would have all that. And he'd give us a little piece of a garden for my sister and I. And we'd plant. "There's the seeds," he says, "you plant what you want." So I'd plant beans, and cucumbers, and a little section—my garden was about this size [points to the width of the room, about twelve feet] and then her garden was about this wide. But she profited on hers 'cause she had lettuce, she grew lettuce, and the neighbors next door loved those salads. And she would sell her lettuce. I couldn't sell nothing 'cause I just had peas and carrots or something. And we learned to take care of our gardens. Our gardens were just perfect, in rows, like that. Showed us how to make an even, you know, an even line to grow the carrots. But he planted corn, and he planted the potatoes, and he planted the rutabagies. But we just grew vegetables, onions, things like that. Kind of hard to remember a lot of that because I have to dig it out of my head. You know, all this happened so long ago.

But I had a good time. I had a good life. I still enjoy my life.

I'm glad to wake up in the morning. "Reva, get up. Time to go to work." [laughs] I talk to myself somewhat. "Come on. Don't be mad today." That's when I do my praying. I do a lot of praying, like Joe says, we all do. Have my tobacco, throw it outside, stand out there, pray. I feel good after, you know, after I get through, and I come in the house, and I do my cooking, wake the kids up. The kids are starting to be a little bit responsible, they get up on their own now.

*   *   *

Old Village

My dad was the head of the family, and we had to go by his rules. It was just a plain family, you know, mother, father, and children. And we were pretty well organized. I had to help cook, that cooking was stirring potatoes, and you know, we used to have big meals in the morning, shoot. Have biscuits and potatoes, boiled potatoes, boiled meat, deer meat, and then we used to have this—she'd fry the pork, you know, and we'd have like a grease dish at the table. Then we'd have the pork, you know, and we'd use that for our potatoes, like people use butter. Well, that was a old-fashioned meal. And then we drank tea, sometimes coffee, but it was mostly tea. And we'd all sit around the table, and I'd have to be the one to fill up the vegetable dish or go get some more bread, you know, I was the waitress. Yeah, that brings back a lot of memories.

My mother trained me to make beadwork and sew. I used to try to sew after I got to be about twelve years old, I was in school. I used to try to make my own clothes. And when I went to high school, I was real good then. I made my own prom dress and my own suits. There used to be a style, they call 'em farmerettes, and I used to just love that. I'd put those on on hot days and when my dad would be, you know, when I'd expect him home I'd take 'em off because he didn't like that revealing, you know. It was like regular bib overalls, but they were made of colorful material, and then a bare back, you know, it had those little ties in the back.

*   *   *

We were mostly all one clan in the Village,[5] and that was the Fish Clan. And there was quite a few in the Bear Clan and Marten Clan, but not as big as the Fish Clan. We were all doodems,

---

[5] Fish ("Awaasii") Clan is one of the seven clans of the Ojibwe and was the largest clan in the village. *Doodem* is the Ojibwe word for clan. The clan system was a form of social and political governance whereby each clan had its

that's what you call doodem. My father was Fish Clan, and my mother, I would say, was like a Bear Clan because her father was a Bear Clan, and that was the old . . . his name was Bearskin. . . . [There have been] quite a bit of changes. The whole town has changed, the Village. There's no more village, just a few houses down there now. Before there used to be homes, all from by the frog ponds all around the lake, and my namesakes lived way up out that way. You know, all around the lake. Except by the big curve there, there was no homes there, except your ma, your grandma [Rose and Roy]. And across the road, there was an old man that lived there. And I'll always remember that spring, we used to go over there and drink water out of that spring by your house. Your ma was my friend. They were very attractive girls, they were real nice-looking girls. I used to like them. Now and then we'd see them, but most of the time . . . 'cause they lived across the lake. I remember your grandpa, he was a little man. Your ma's uncle, Jack, I used to know him. He was my friend. Jack Roy. I remember he was my friend. We used to trade books. . . . I still read a lot. You know, I got a big wide bed, and half of that bed is full of magazines and papers and books; I just reach over and grab a book. You know, anytime at night when I can't sleep, and I go to sleep again. I just love to read. I just go into a different world, you know.

I'm glad I have eyes yet. I don't know what I'd do without eyes. I still make beadwork, too, now and then. I crochet. But I haven't been doing that lately because I got too many kids! The only time when I have time is when they're in school. And then I have to use that time to clean the house and, you know, put my food on.

*   *   *

I remember I used to have a good time, play house, I used to make my own dolls. And we never had no store dolls or anything like that, you know. I had playmates across the road, there was Mrs., her name was Margaret White Scott, Pearl Potts, that Pearl Davidson, she just died. And my sister and Elsie Skye, Violet Skye, all the Negani girls. There was quite a few that were living there at the time. . . . We were all chummy, we used to have good timesWe'd pick berries, and we'd play cards, that was when we got a little bit older and knew how to play cards, and go fishing, play house in the woods, you know. I don't know, we just created our own fun. And it was all clean fun. Nothing like the way it is today. We never said we were bored because we created our own fun. Course we

function in the community and its special place in ceremonies.
> The Crane and Loon clans were chieftains, those people with natural leadership abilities;
> The Fish or Water clan people were the intellectuals, philosophers, mediators;
> Bear clan provided the protectors, policing the borders of the village to keep out intruders. They also became expert at knowing which herbs and medicines could be harvested and used;
> Marten clan was the warrior clan;
> Deer clan were the gentlest people, the poets;
> From the Bird clan came the spiritual leaders of the people.
—From Edward Benton-Benai, *The Mishomis Book: The Voice of the Ojibwe* (St. Paul, MN: Red House School, 1988), 74–76.

used to have to wash dishes and help clean the house, you know. Yeah, I had a happy childhood, and today I feel like thanking my people, that they gave me that kind of a childhood. We never got spankings, we just never did anything to deserve a spanking, there was no such thing as a spanking. Until we got involved with the government school.[6] My ma would threaten us, I'm gonna tell your dad, and we'd have to behave ourselves. My dad would, he mostly said, "taa, taa," like that, in such a way that we knew he was mad at us. I was afraid of that "taa." That's all I know, that they were good people, and I'm glad today that they raised me, the way I am today. And that is the way I am today.

I'm gonna live a good life, the rest of my days, I plan to do that, you know. I don't plan to change my life, I'm just gonna live it the way the Great Spirit wants me to live. I pray every day, I try to pray. Offer my tobacco. I pray for the kids, I pray for people that are sick, and then I pray for myself. You know, please don't let me say anything unkind. But it's hard to raise kids without saying. . . . [laughs] You've got to discipline 'em. So sometimes I just say, oh forgive me.

*   *   *

I went to the government school in Flambeau. My dad took me there and entered me in school. Then I went to Tomah, Wisconsin, for a year, then I went back to Flambeau, they added some more grades and so I stayed there, finished the ninth grade. And then I went to Flandreau, South Dakota.[7] I stayed there till I finished school. And then I got a job in Minneapolis, taking care of a crippled lady. Then I came home. Then when they started that, what do you call it, Flambeau, that Indian Park, where they dance now by the river, Bear River. We didn't call it Bear River that time. We called it the Indian Park. That was Flambeau River at one time. And when I came back from Milwaukee, everything was changed, they call it the Bear River now.

The Niijii is where the government school used to be. We had reading, writing, and arithmetic. We went to kindergarten, right up to the sixth grade. We had math, English, and reading. We used to have penmanship. I liked it, but it was more like a military school. You had to march to classes, you'd get punished. Just like Celia says, you'd really get punished. But I was never involved in being punished though. Like I say, my father raised me, and I wasn't perfect, but I just never got involved in anything very wrong. They would really beat those girls. Like Celia

---

[6] The government school was a BIA school, opened in 1895 in operation until 1931, where Native children were forced to attend after being removed from their homes. They were forbidden to wear traditional clothing, practice their religion, speak the Ojibwe language or follow any Indian customs. Any usage of the native language or customs, even accidental, resulted in severe punishment by school staff. In later years the building was called the Niijii Center (*niijii* means 'friend') and converted into offices for the Family Circle's AODA prevention program, including Ojibwe language classes. Reva and her "chum" Celia Defoe would joke that once they were beaten for speaking their language there, and now they are teaching it in the same building!

[7] Flandreau, South Dakota is the location of a BIA boarding school where many graduates of the Lac du Flambeau boarding school attended high school.

says, we were punished. We were getting ready to bathe, for baths, and we were all lined up. And there was a girl ahead of me, about two people ahead, and she was talking to me. So I got out of line. I made that mistake, I got out of line. Then that matron saw me getting out of line. I quick got back in line, but I was too late. So when I got up to her, she says, "What did you get out of line for?" I said, "Well I was talking to this girl," I said, "she was asking about. . . ." It was so long time ago that I don't remember what it was about. Boy, did she smack me in the face. She slapped me just hard. Wow. And of course I cried. And I went in, took a bath and everything, and I came out. And when I got out there in the hall, who should be standing there. My dad. And he knew that I had been crying, and he says, "What's the matter," he says. "What happened?" So I told him that lady hit me on the face. Oh, and he was real angry. And he says, "Come on with me," he says, and we went right upstairs to that head matron. Oh, she talked to my dad, my dad wanted to know why I got hit like that for. And I was kind of crying yet, and oh geez, my dad got really sick with those ladies. See, he just came just about that time that happened. If he'd got there a little bit sooner, he would've saw that lady hit me. So that's all I remember about getting hit.

I would get punished for the other kids. Like if somebody got into something, we'd all get punished for that girl, you know, if somebody did something. And we wouldn't even know sometimes why we'd be marching around and marching around and marching around. That's the way they punished us.

Then we'd have to kneel. Then we'd kneel, and oh, that was tiresome. Or stand in a corner and just stand there for hours at a time. We'd march to the tables, we'd march and the bell would ring and then we'd sit down. Then the bell would ring again, then we could start eating. It's one of these little things [waves her hand down, as if hitting a bell on a desk], I think they still make them. Then we could eat. They'd give us a certain length of time to eat. Then when that bell rings again, we couldn't put anything else in our mouths anymore. That's the way they served us at the dining hall. And then the bell would ring, and we'd all have to go stand in line again. The bell would ring again, and we'd march out.

We used to have to make up our beds, of course. We'd have to do that in the morning right away when we got out of bed. We'd have to make our beds, and we'd have to be trained as how to make 'em. We did that. . . . We had good dormitories after the kids made up their beds, you know. The dormitory was good, nice. Of course they used to mop it up and all that. Just like when we had that mopping day,[8] it was Saturday. Well, that's what it is, that's how come we named that Saturday mopping day, scrubbing day. We all had to do all that—they'd appoint different ones to wash dishes, and appoint different ones to work in the kitchen, and appoint ones that used to clean the steps. Oh, we all had our chores to do, different things we had to do. People would say though they're the good old days, they bring back memories. But some of the memories are good. And some kind of bad. But I enjoyed life. I still enjoy life.

---

[8] The word for Saturday in Ojibwe is *giziibiigisaginige-giizhigad* which means 'floor washing day.' As Reva explains, this word came from the practice of making the children clean floors and the rest of the boarding school on Saturdays.

Ben Chosa

Ben Chosa was born on Mud Lake, now called Moss Lake, Lac du Flambeau, on March 19, 1929. He began fishing around age five and learned to fish as well as hunt and trap from his father and others. As a young man he guided fishermen as well, which he continues to do today, a skill which he learned from his elders and his father, who made his living from guiding and trapping. He has guided many visitors to the reservation, including President Dwight D. Eisenhower. In his interview Ben describes in great detail his apprenticeship as one who lives off the land, practicing all the traditional ways of food gathering, and also remembers vividly how the "old timers" used to live on the reservation. He notes with sadness how the quality of the environment has declined over the years, especially the water quality, and remembers how his family used to drink clean water from the lakes of Lac du Flambeau.

Ben still guides on the reservation today, one of several active Native guides. He can be found on nearly any given day in his fishing boat, plying the waters of Flambeau and other area lakes for fish, and spearing and fishing through the ice in the winter. Over the years he has passed on his extensive knowledge of fishing and guiding to younger tribal members and would very much like to see the long tradition of guiding fishermen carried on in Lac du Flambeau. He is a lively and humorous storyteller, as the interview shows. He lives in Lac du Flambeau today with his daughter Barbara, who conducted this interview.

From left to right: Rose (Chosa), John Chicog, and Bertha (Big John)

Interview with Ben Chosa

This interview was conducted by Barbara Olson, Ben's daughter.

My name is Ben Chosa, but I do not have an Ojibwe name. My father's name is Ben Chosa, my mother's name was Rose. Her maiden name was Rose Chicog. My grandfather's name [on my father's side] was Henry Chosa. [My grandmother's name was] Angeline Chosa, but her maiden name was Artishon [Ben pronounces it "Artishaw," as in the French pronunciation]. My mother's father was John Chicog, my grandfather. I never knew her name, she (my grandmother) had an Indian name but I can't remember it right now. She was a medicine woman, she was blind. I remember her. I may have seen my grandfather, but I don't remember him, because I was very young. He moved from here, and I was interested in him, so I went and asked Archie Mosay because he'd moved over into the St. Croix area. I went and asked the head medicine man over there, I gave him tobacco, and he told me to come back in three or four days, and I did.

So then he gave me the history of John Chicog. They used to call him Jack over there, his name was John though. He moved from there, he went to Danbury,[1] but he had a woman in St. Croix, and they had children there. I never did determine how many children he had, two or three, then he moved to Danbury. From Danbury he went across into Minnesota, across the border from Danbury there somewheres. And he had a woman over there, too, you know all great chiefs have many wives, they say. He was chief.

---

[1] Danbury is a town on the St. Croix (Chippewa) reservation in western Wisconsin, which is comprised of five parcels of land spread across three counties near the St. Croix River, which forms the border between Wisconsin and Minnesota.

So he eventually came back to Danbury and he owned a hotel there. . . . The man who was giving me information, Archie, he said he didn't know what happened to that, because he used to stay in a house behind the hotel. Then some woman took care of the hotel for him. So when John Chicog died, Archie didn't know what happened to the property. So that's what I could determine about my grandfather, John Chicog.

So I have relatives there. His children's children are there yet. Chicogs on the St. Croix reservation. As to my grandmother, I don't know much about her, who she was. Never could find out what her maiden name was, but I do believe that she was related to the LaCass's, because all those old people over there in the Indian village . . . the LaCass's, they'd have me over, I'd stay over, and they took care of me. I belong to the Bear Clan.

I was born on Moss Lake, what used to be Mud Lake, on the northeast end over there. I was born on the reservation. A lot of the Indians here were not born on the reservation; they were born in Woodruff or Hayward. So I was born on the reservation.

Henry Chosa was the son of old Joe Chosa, who would've been my great-grandfather. And they're from L'Anse-Baraga area.[2] There's a lot of Chosas up there yet, relatives of mine. And he was one of eighteen brothers. And there was one girl there. I never did find out her name.

An interesting thing, Grandfather Henry told me, he said when he became thirteen years old his father kicked him out. But he did that with all the boys, when they became thirteen years old, he'd kick 'em out. He'd put a sack of flour on their shoulder, tell 'em "Get out, you're on your own now." So Grandfather Henry was laughing when he told me that. "I was the dumb one," he says. "I asked him, 'What do I do with this flour?'" And he says his dad told him, "I don't care what you do with it. Throw it on the ground!" he says. "It's yours." [laughs] So that was his stake, he could take off with that, do what he want with it. He became very self-sufficient, all of the Chosas were very self-sufficient because of that I guess. They either made it, or they didn't.

Henry was the only one [who came to Flambeau]. When he got kicked out I suppose he came here. Wandered through here working through the woods and stuff. When he was very young he worked in the woods for three years, and he told me this himself, he worked for three years, and he saved all his money. He didn't know how much he had, over a hundred dollars for three years work. And he came to town in L'Anse-Baraga there, and the local bootlegger got hold of him as he was going by, invited him in. And gave him alcohol. Whiskey. So he says he woke up back at his place where he was staying. And his money was in a tobacco pouch. And the tobacco pouch was gone. So he took his rifle and he walked back there, he said there was a picket fence there. He called this guy out. Told me his name, but I can't remember his name. And he says he wanted his money, so they got to arguing there, and the guy says, "I don't know what happened to your money, when you left here you were drunk."

[2] L'Anse-Baraga refers to the two towns in the L'Anse (Chippewa) reservation, located in the upper peninsula of Michigan, on L'Anse Bay. This bay, with the adjoining Keweenaw Bay, is the largest gulf of Lake Superior.

"No, you robbed me," he says. "You give me my money or I'm going to shoot you." The guy says, "Get outta here, you ain't got no money," and my grandfather shot him. On the spot. Went back to where he was staying and the police came and got him. Took him back over and asked why he shot that guy. He said because he robbed him. He asked, "Well can you identify your money?" He said, "I had my money in a buckskin bag," he said, "a buckskin pouch." And he told him how much he had, including the change. So the guy was laying there, and they went over and searched him. And in his pocket was the money. So he got ten years for manslaughter in the Michigan State Prison. And he served that. To the day, he said. When they said ten years it was ten years. There was no time off for good behavior or parole or anything. But he served ten years in the Michigan state prison for manslaughter. . . .

I heard they [my mother and father] met in the boarding school over here, the government boarding school. They met while they were there I think. Anyway, they were childhood sweethearts. So while my father was there, there were seven boys caught talking the Ojibwe language. And they lined them up against the building, which is incidentally still standing there. Lined them up alongside of it. . . . They lined them up there and at that time the boys got horsewhipped for talking Ojibwe. What I'm telling you now is a matter of court record in Chicago—he testified on behalf of the Indians there, at the Appeals Court in Chicago, that's how I found this out.

And they were talking to the judge, and he told the judge that story, about how he was going to get horsewhipped. I guess he was about two or three boys down the line getting horsewhipped. When it came to his turn, the judge asked him, who were these men? He said they were grown Oneida men, that's who they had there for disciplinarians. And they were going to horsewhip them, for talking the Ojibwe language. So when it came to his turn, he says he took the whip away from the man that was going to horsewhip him. He was thirteen years old at the time, incidentally. And the judge asked him, "What did you do?" And he said, "I thoroughly thrashed him and all the rest of them. All three of them," he said. "I thoroughly thrashed them." And so the judge said, "Well, what were you going to do now? What did you do then?" And he said, "I knew that I was going to prison for that." "So," he said. "I ran, I took a left there, and I went along the shore there to my mother's house. Which was by the church there. And I got in my canoe and I went down the Bear River. I left the reservation."

So you asked me how he met my mother—well, then when he was around his late twenties to early thirties, he came back here to the reservation and he married his childhood sweetheart, who was my mother. . . .

May, Betty, Yolanda, and Virginia. There are four girls [in the family], in that order, oldest to the youngest. Then there's me, I'm the oldest boy, Mike, Edward, and Alan, he's the youngest one.

[I was born] March 19, 1929, over on Moss Lake. They said I was born in a wigwam, but I don't know that. I've been in this house here since 1982. I acquired this house from the tribal council, because my house had been destroyed by arson. . . . I own this house.

Ben Chosa, Sr.

[Children] that I know of? Many, but the only ones here that I claim are two, one is Linda, and the other is yourself, Barbara.

*   *   *

One of the first things I remember is going spearing with my father. And I was riding on a sled. I remember walking too, but I must've got tired, and he must've put me up on a sled. Pulling a sled, we went to Lower Sugarbush [Lake]. And I remember he had a big teepee there, a tent with blankets underneath it. He was on one side, and I was on the other. It was in April—ice was bad then, I know that. So he said, "Here." He gave me the decoy. "You pull the decoy for a while." So I pulled the decoy, and then he kind of leaned back, and he went to sleep. [laughs] I knew he was asleep because he was snoring. So I pulled the decoy, and a big musky came. So I started hollering, "There's a fish here!" He kind of woke up a little bit and said, "Spear him!" And I remember I couldn't get the spear up; it was too heavy for me. So he reached over, and he grabbed the spear and boom, he got the musky. And that was one of my earliest memories, I must've been four or five years old.

The other thing I remember about my early childhood; we used to have a big garden. Must have been, oh, three acres. A field there where we lived. We had a great big vegetable garden and the rest was planted in potatoes and corn. I remember we used to get our potatoes and invite all the people who wanted them to take the rest of the potatoes. We had a lot of potatoes, which of course was a big staple, and I remember we used to can. Can vegetables and everything at that time. We had ducks and chickens, a lot of ducks. I remember my job was to go around and collect eggs.

There were a lot of ducks, and we must've ate duck eggs, too, and chicken eggs. And I remember he had a big flatbed truck, like a logging truck. He used to get wood in that. And I don't know where we were to this day, but he was getting wood and his truck was kind of parked on top of the hill. And how kids are—I think I was standing on top of the seat playing driving, you know [holds his hands as if gripping a steering wheel]. . . . And I inadvertently took it out of gear and started down that hill. And I remember him running, and I remember looking up on the bank up here, he was running [laughs], and I was picking up speed, and I guess he jumped in the truck.

There was something the matter with that shifting lever . . . because afterwards he made a slingshot, and he put it around there to hold the shifting lever. So we came back, and I had the slingshot, and they were plowing the field over there. And there were robins flying around, you know how they do on a freshly plowed field. And I remember standing by the house with that slingshot shooting this and that, and I was happy I had a slingshot. A robin sat on the post there and I went plunk! [He shoots an invisible slingshot.] Got the robin. And that was the end of my slingshot [laughs], he broke it up! I killed a robin, you know. He told me, "Never kill anything that you're not going to eat." I remember that, that's what he told me.

So anyway I didn't have no slingshot, but those are some of my childhood memories. And fishing, I started fishing then, too, about that time, I was five or six years old. I started fishing then because I had a flat-bottom boat and all the older ones, even the men would come and get me because I had a boat. And I'd use, oh, cast-off rods of my father's and things like this to fish with. Baits and stuff. And fish. They'd troll around for muskies and fish for walleyes and things like that.

I started learning very early how to fish, I must've been six or seven years old. By the time I was eight I was already learning how to spear through the ice, seven, eight years old, using my father's decoy. Because when I was eight years old I made my first decoy. I copied my father's, tried to make it like his. Looked like his to me. Got the lead, did everything he did, melted the lead, and put it in there, put fins on it and so forth. But then I went and tried it out; it wouldn't work.

I remember I was sitting there, and I was looking at it, and he came and said, "What's the matter? You made a decoy." "Yeah," and I says, "It don't work." "Well, what did it do?" "It went backwards." [laughs] "It went backwards!" "Let me look at it," he said, so he looked at it, and he adjusted where you put the line. We used to have a piece of tin with holes in it, that's where you put your snap and swivel, so it . . . so the balance would be proper.

And he told me why that was like that, and where the fins had to be placed—he showed me exactly what had to be done. He adjusted, and I took it back out there, and it worked! My first decoy, I made it when I was eight years old. Carved it out of—I don't know what, a piece of wood around the house I guess. So those are some of my childhood memories.

There were many people who influenced me, not just my father, because he was always busy trapping or guiding or trying to feed eight to ten kids. So he was always gone. So I spent a lot of time with my grandmother. She taught me a lot too. . . . But many other people had an influence on my life, especially a lot of the older people. Older men. They taught me a lot. I don't know why they did it, but they would come over to the house and get me. Say, "Come on, we're going here" or "We're going there."

I was sitting there one day and here comes Joe Jack. Father of the Jacks here now. He came over one day and said, "Come on, come with me. We're going hunting." So I got ready and went with him, this was early in the morning, and we went. Now for some reason he took me out there, and I don't know where, but he taught me how to do what they call "rattle up a deer," using deer horns. We went to one spot, and he told me why we were there, the wind was a certain way and so forth. It was close to the runway or something, I guess. And he tried it there, and nothing happened.

But he would rattle those horns like that [shakes his hands as if rattling two horns together] and he would stick them in the bushes, and he'd shake them—to me it was comical. And he'd get up there, and he'd jump around and stomp his feet around there, and he'd sit back down and wait. Fifteen minutes, he did that two or three times, nothing came, then said, "Well, let's go somewhere else, nothing around here." So we went to another spot, we were sitting along the edge of a swamp, kind of a hill there, and he did the same thing. [Shakes his hands again.] Rattled those horns, thrashed the bushes with them, stomped his feet around there. Did it two or three times, and about the third time he did that, a buck came over that hill. Come running down here just comical, jumping around here and there, looking, and come down there and stopped, looking around. And he shot the buck! So he taught me how to rattle up a deer using horns.

And a lot of those guys said, "You're going to go fishing with me." So we'd go fishing. They'd teach me different places to fish and how to fish and why. Taught me a lot of things about fishing. Like Earl Cross, Senior—"Fishtrap," Big Louie Saint Germaine, LaBarges, Henry and Sam LaBarge, and Firpo. All those old timers taught me a lot about fishing. Ben Poupart, Paul Poupart, Bill Poupart—they all taught me how to fish. I don't know why they'd teach me. But they did teach me. They would single me out and take me and show me, "Now you follow me today. I'll show you these spots to fish. And use this and use that, use this type of rig," and so forth. They would tell me these things. From about the age of eight, nine on, till I was fifteen, sixteen years old. By then I was row trolling.[3] Eleven, twelve years old I was row trolling, muskies. And I was fishing muskies a lot because I was catching a lot of muskies at that time.

I'd catch maybe half a dozen muskies in one day. Some big ones in there, thirty, forty pounders, and nothing but row trolling. I had no motor or no casting rod even. Wasn't very much later that they started getting level wind wheels,[4] but we couldn't even cast then. Because there was no level wind wheels, and the rods weren't very good. They used to use pool cues, make a musky rod out of a pool cue, put eyes on it. Big Louie used to do that a lot, and everybody else copied him. So you could have a rod, a good stiff rod, make it out of a pool cue.

---

[3] Row trolling refers to trolling (dragging the bait along behind the boat to attract fish) as you row the boat.

[4] Level wind wheel is a reel on a fishing rod that winds the line evenly, back and forth, so that it is level.

"Big Louie" St. Germaine (at right) guiding

Sam LaBarge holding a musky

Earl Cross, Senior ("Fishtrap")

And that's what we did. And that's who taught me, all these people you know, the old timers, had an influence on me. Not only my father and my grandmother, but a lot of the old timers. They all taught me these things. I don't know why. I think part of it was I was willing to learn or exhibited something to them that indicated that I wanted to learn about certain things. About everything. Taught me how to build a wigwam and how to hunt.

I remember I used to go out to old Charlie LaCass's place. Got out there, and he said, "We're going to stay out there about a week" and "We're going to go hunting." So then we'd go, Charlie LaCass and three or four other guys. "Johnny Forty-five"—that's what they called John Wayman—was over there too. We'd go hunting, us boys would go hunting. They'd take us, but we ran. We had no car or anything, so we ran. They'd tell us where to go, "These three are going to go over here and watch; these three are going to make a drive," and so forth. "We'll give you fifteen minutes to get over here, and then we'll start the drive."

And we got the deer. They used to make a bundle, they'd call it, where you'd get the deer and throw it over your back. And you ran as far as you could with the deer on your back. Then switch it over to one of the other boys. And we ran everywhere we went them days. So a lot of people had a lot of influence on my life.

I don't think any child liked school, but you had to go school, so you made the best of it and did the best you could. I remember when I was going to grade school I went to the public school, which is now Simpson Electric Plant. They also had a government school where a lot of them went. . . . I used to get a new pair of high-top boots in the fall, and they were to last me all during the school year. And they never did. About March, my boots would give out, and then I wore moccasins to school. And as soon as it got warm enough, I went barefoot. You'd go barefoot all summer. Till fall, buy a new pair of boots again. I'd get high-top boots, that was the thing in those days. But they'd never last, I remember that. So that's where I went to school, graduated from the grade school
there.

My classmates are all scattered around town now, but a lot of them have died. Alcoholism took a lot of them. [To Barbara:] Your uncle Minok was one of my classmates, Earl Cross Junior. Ed Brisk, Carlton Valliere, he got killed in the Korean War. Hiram Valliere, he's still here. George Wolfe, he's still here. Frankie Doud, but he was a couple grades below me. Delores Carufel, she married someone over in Lake Tomahawk I guess. I remember a lot of them. Phyllis Chapman— Phyllis White.

My father was primarily a fishing guide. In those days they had the CC camp here, and WPA, work programs instituted by President Roosevelt. And they used to get a dollar a day in WPA, I think they worked six days a week or something like that. They were raising families, and on the CC camps they had to stay out there. They got $21 dollars a month and room and board. Some clothes, too, I guess. So these are the things my father did, he was primarily a fishing guide, and then, too, he was a trapper. And that's the way he was able to raise his family. From his guide wages and from trapping.

He was one of the biggest trappers in northern Wisconsin; he got to be partners with Pete Christensen. And they trapped. I remember I went one time, I was in school, and he asked me to go look at his trapline with him. He said Pete was out looking at one trapline, and I and him was to go look at the other trapline. We started after school on Friday, and we looked at traps. We wound up in Oconomowoc, Wisconsin, the end of his trapline. It's almost all the way down the state, and I remember we had twenty or thirty mink, which was a lot of money in those days. That was the end of his trapline, then we came back and looked at traps all the way back again. Picked up a big pile of mink, trapping mink. Pete was similarly looking at another trapline that extended as far.

So they were big trappers, in two weeks they trapped maybe a thousand muskrats. Plus beaver, they'd have beaver . . . holy! And work, they'd be gone before daylight, they'd be back after dark, and they'd skin and they'd stretch until the wee hours. I used to help them skin and stretch muskrats. They would work on the mink and the beaver-- we had our whole house hung with dried pelts, and I guess Pete had his house the same way. So it was a lot of work, but he made a lot of money, big money for those days. That was his primary source of income.

[The lumber mill] was still standing into the twenties, I guess. Where the museum is now, that was the end of the line for the Chicago-Northwestern train. It would come out there, then it would back in, stay overnight, and it would leave in the morning. You can still see the old track lines going out, that was the end of the line for them. They'd overnight there, for many years they did that, I remember the train backing in and staying overnight. And they'd take off in the morning. . . . That's how a lot of the tourists got up here, too; it was the only way up here. It was dependable and fast.

Otherwise they had to drive up from Chicago or wherever they came from, and it'd take them a long time to get here. Take two three days to get here by car, because there was no roads like there are today. I remember my father told me, him and my mother went to Detroit to work. Said he wanted to go over there and work, he was a high steel man there.[5] He had to work two, three years, and he bought a brand new Buick, it was one of those touring cars. I remember he made a truck out of it afterwards. A big old thing with the canvas top on it, you see pictures of them. He said it took him maybe two weeks to drive from Detroit.

He had to come through Chicago, and then it took a week from Chicago to get up here with the car. The roads were so bad, mudholes and everything, go here and go there, get lost—no roads! But he got up here with that big old Buick, yeah, I remember it too. It was a big old car. Made a truck out of it, like I said.

I was in the Korean War. Joe Chosa, he's a cousin of mine, my dad's brother's son, he was in the Second World War. My brother Mike, he was in the Vietnam War. My father, he joined up;

---

[5] A high steel man is a man who works building skyscrapers, which Ben's father did in Detroit.

I think he was one of the first ones ever in the military service from here. Although they don't recognize that, because he was—I think it was 1909 when he joined up, and he had to lie his age to get in. I remember that. But he got in, and he was in the cavalry, and he chased Pancho Villa around the New Mexico border country. And he stayed in until they discharged him after the war ended, he didn't go overseas. But when they discharged him down there in the New Mexico territory, he became a sheriff in a border town. Some old fellow told me that, I didn't learn it from my father. He never talked about it. . . . So our family members have been in the Spanish-American War, First World War, Second World War, Korean War, Vietnam War, all of them honorably discharged. . . .

Chief Geneshteno was my great-great-grandfather on that side of the family. You've got to understand a little bit about the history of that. In the 1850s they had what was known as a Removal Order,[6] part of it was to remove all the Indians in this area to specific reservations. And there was a lot of Indians scattered, family members and bands and groups of Indians all over around here. Like the Waymans, they came from over around Sugar Camp. My family, they had a band of Indians over at big Trout Lake. My great-great-grandfather was Chief Geneshteno, he signed a treaty as Chief of the Trout Lake band.

So when they had the Removal Order they removed all these Indians to Lac du Flambeau and Mole Lake and Hayward and Odanah and forced them into reservations at that time. The landing area at Trout Lake was one of the places they stayed. The other place they stayed was on the island, that big island over there, and at the outlet. They had camps there. He was chief, and he signed the treaty as chief there, and when they removed him from there he became second chief of Lac du Flambeau, and I understand after that he became first chief of Lac du Flambeau. So that was Geneshteno. . . . My grandfather John Chicog—he was the grandson of Chief Geneshteno.

So I'm the great-great-grandson of that Chief. Incidentally, about that part of it, I liked to go over and visit George Sharlow. There were two brothers here, George and Joe Sharlow. Joe Sharlow, he's the grandfather of Buddy LaBarge—Melvin LaBarge. I'd go visit George—I'd go over there because I knew that his wife Mary baked bread every morning, and she'd have a fresh pan of biscuits on the table.

---

[6] In 1852 Chief Buffalo, with other Ojibwe chiefs, journeyed with his delegates from LaPointe, on Madeleine Island to Washington, DC, to meet with President Millard Fillmore in order to request that the Ojibwe not be forcibly removed to west of the Mississippi but be allowed to remain on established reservations in Wisconsin. President Zachary Taylor had issued a removal order in 1850, which shocked and outraged the Ojibwe, especially those who had signed the 1842 treaty guaranteeing them permanent reservation homelands. Chief Buffalo was over ninety years old when he led this delegation by canoe, train, and on foot. Once in DC, they drew up a document detailing their grievances and were successful in persuading the president to rescind the removal order. (See Introduction.) For more on Chief Buffalo and his journey, see Walter Bresette and Rick Whaley, *Walleye Warriors: The Chippewa Treaty Rights Story* (Warner, NH: Tongues of Green Fire Press, 1999); Ronald N. Satz, *The Reserved Rights of Wisconsin's Chippewa Indians in Historical Perspective* (Madison: Wisconsin Academy of Sciences, Arts and Letters, 1991); and William Warren, *History of the Ojibwe* (http://www.ancestry.com/search/db.aspx?dbid=4011).

So when I'd go in and knock on the door, he'd say [in a gruff voice], "Come on in." He'd be sitting at the table, drinking tea. He'd look at me and say [in a harsh tone], "Young Ben Chosie— What do you want here? You don't belong around here! You belong over at Trout Lake." And I'd have to argue with him, "No, no I belong here, I was born here. I'm on the roll." "No, you belong at Trout Lake," he said, "You're from Trout Lake."

He knew my history. Of my grandfather, where he came from. And he would tease me about it like that. "Sit down," he'd say. "Want some tea?" I'd tell him, yeah. And a pan of biscuits would be there covered up with a fresh, clean dishcloth. He knew I wanted a biscuit, so he'd give me a biscuit, and I'd sit there and I'd talk to him. And he'd tell me a lot of stuff and talk and laugh. He was a good old man, that guy George, George Sharlow.

So he knew that. *I* didn't know it. Now I know that he was always teasing me, you know. So that's where Geneshteno came from. Two of the branches of my family, one came from L'Anse-Baraga, and the other came from Trout Lake. My grandfather Henry Chosa, he left here. Divorced my grandmother, and he went and settled in northern Minnesota, had children up there too. Here he had my Aunt Betty, who was Betty Chosa Baylis, Elizabeth her name was, we call her Aunt Betty. And Joe Chosa, Senior, he left here and he went to Minnesota by his father Henry; that's Joe Chosa's father. And he died up there, Joe's father; he was on the lake up there making ice, and he got an appendicitis attack and his partner had to snowshoe out and get help, and when they come back, he was found dead in the sleeping bag. Died of an appendicitis attack. My grandfather Henry, he died in Ely, Minnesota. He had a home up there on Basswood Lake. John, my grandfather John; he died in Danbury. John Chicog. So those are some of my relatives.

Lac du Flambeau has changed dramatically from when I was a child to now. Been a lot of environmental changes and a lot of changes in the reservation, especially housing. That's a sore spot with me, housing. Because when I was young, everybody owned their own home. I think maybe ninety-five percent or maybe higher than that, Indians owned their own home. So the government came along and said, well your house is unfit for habitation. And they said we're going to tear your house down, and we're going to build you a new house. So everybody agreed to that, and they built them a new house, and they started charging them rent. Said well you owe rent now. And come from ninety-some percent homeownership to ninety-some percent rental. They didn't own their homes anymore. And that's the way it stands today. Very few people own their own homes now. And that was a bad thing that they did that to them, it was a money-making thing. And now they're saddled with the rental.

And Flambeau housing, Chippewa Housing or whatever they call it, wasn't very good, and I still don't think it's any good myself. Although I own my home, there are many, many people that don't. And they continue to pay rent. With no possibility in their lifetime of owning their home, although I think some of that is changing.[7] I remember Peterson, Injun Peterson, he came to me, he came to this house and sat down and talked to me. Because he says, "I finished paying for my house. But they won't give it to me," he says. So I went and researched it, and we helped him acquire his home. They said, "Well he can't own his home because that house was built in a block of homes, so many houses, and until all of them are paid for, even though you have paid for your home, you don't own your home." But he acquired his home in tribal council action, I guess. I don't think that was right. But I understand that's changing now, as they pay for these homes I think they're acquiring them now. Some of them.

Power and sewer is another thing. I remember when I was young, my father was tribal chairman, president of the tribe. He came to me and various other young people, he asked us to go around, because we were getting a per capita payment. I forget what it was, we'd filed land claims, I forget what it was, amounted to two, three million dollars. Which was a lot of money in those days, and we all would have got two, three hundred dollars I suppose. And they asked us to take that money and build a water and sewer facility here. They told us that we would never have to ever again experience high prices for water, and there'd be water for everybody, water and sewer. Now I understand that we're just as high as everybody else in the surrounding area, the surrounding township, we pay just as much as they do. Yet we sacrificed our money, gave our money so that we would not have to do that. Now we pay very high water and sewer. A flat fee, even if you don't use the water, you're still charged.

And for me it's a sore spot, because I know the history of that. I was the one who went around with the young people, said let's do it, don't have to pump water no more, carry water, stuff like that. So now we have to pay a high price for water, even though we gave our money for that.

I've seen one thing I'm very concerned about, two things actually. I think if I live long enough, I will see the last full-blooded Lac du Flambeau Indian die. I am not a full-blood, I am thirteen-sixteenths Ojibwe and three-sixteenths French. But I think I will see, if I live long enough, I will see the last of the full-blooded Lac du Flambeau Indians go. Then there will be no more full-blooded Lac du Flambeau Indians here. They'll be gone like the dinosaur. And that's a sad thing when you say that about a people. To see the last of our people gone, our full-blooded. That is very sad, very sad to me.

The other change I've seen is the deterioration of our old people. When I was young, there was a lot of old people—eighty, ninety years old. I remember they used to paddle in with canoes to get their mail, go shopping, come in from the village, and I'd see them all over the reservation. Old people! Eighty, ninety years old, active! I'd see them out cutting wood, and doing everything, making wild rice and trapping and doing all these things. Now I understand one of the oldest,

---

[7] In the years since this interview was conducted, the tribe has increased the number of rent-to-own homes as well as offering programs to help with purchasing houses. More tribal members are buying their own homes as a result, though there is still a housing shortage on the reservation.

eighty-eight, is one of our oldest members now. There used to be a lot of them a hundred and ninety years old here. And we have no old people here no more! It's of great concern to me that our ability to live a long time is gone now.

I think it has a lot to do with the environment, environmental change. In my lifetime there were still people living in wigwams! There used to be a lot of people who moved out of their house in the summertime and moved into their wigwam. Oh a lot of people had a wigwam by their house. They'd move in there, stay in there all summer, then move back in their house in the fall, when we got cold again. They were active outside. They ate different. They ate their own vegetables, a lot of wild game and fish. I think that has a lot to do with it: the environmental change was too quick. Eighty, ninety years ago, they were in the bushes, so to speak. So now they live in houses. The environmental change for us as a people has come too fast.

Alcohol, drugs. All these drugs, all the chemical additives to food is killing us off with cancer. And I don't believe we can ever go back to the way we were, but at least we can do more, eat more of the homegrown foods, and have gardens again. A lot of people had vegetable gardens. They had community projects for vegetable gardens and things like that. They'd go work there, then when it comes harvest time they were included in the harvest, take the vegetables. So these things have all contributed to that change.

Deterioration in the water quality, especially on our lakes, has been astronomical. Some lakes now are so polluted that we can't eat the fish, or we're not supposed to eat the fish. Although a lot of people still do. I've seen where, especially like say on Pokegama Lake, my grandmother and I used to go in a canoe over to Mills Point after an electrical storm. You could see the stunned whitefish down to twenty-five feet! I remember when I used to fish walleyes I could see them down there, twenty-five feet. Then I'd fish them. Now you can't see down there ten feet.

So the water has deteriorated. A lot of that of course has to do with the logging, they've logged all these lakes around here, everything was covered with pine. A great filtering system. So the waters were pure. Took all the pine, now they've got all leaf trees around. And that has added to water quality change in that it became more acidic, hostile to fish and all that grows in the water, and all that swims in the water. Became hostile to them and polluted the water because of the combination of the air quality that dropped a lot of acid rain, combined with the acidity of the leaf trees in the water, has combined to leach the mercury out of the bedrock of the lakes, causing an increase in mercury.

And of course I suppose the fish don't repropogate the lakes properly because of that, they're not able to, because the young die—poisoned. And some lakes—there was very few homes on these lakes, now there's wall-to-wall homes all the way around. Their septic systems are right there, right on the lake, so all that drains off into the water table, into the lake. The scientists say, oh don't worry about the acidity and everything else. It just poisons the water, it'll just kill everything in the lake but it won't hurt you. That's what they say! That acid rain, that poison and pollution don't just fall on the lake! Lakes are collection points—it falls all over. What is it doing to all the rest of the food chain? Poisoning it, and poisoning us in the process.

The water quality in my lifetime has deteriorated to that point where there's not as many fish. There's many reasons for that, I suppose, the tremendous fishing pressure we have here being one. The other, water quality—I believe that if the lakes were surrounded again by a band even three hundred feet deep of pine only, rather than your leaf trees, that they would prevent those leaves from falling into the water and deteriorating and releasing their acid. That would take care of some of the acid. I think that would do much to, in the long term, eliminate some of the acidity in the water and clear up the lakes.

Interesting sideline to that, I was in Odanah, and I talked to a woman who was then a 103 years old. And I talked to her and asked her how it was when she was young on the reservation. She said she remembered—I asked her specifically about how they lost the reservation, they lost most of their reservation, about eighty-five percent of it is gone, the rest is owned by tribal members. She said the timber people bought up the land, some people didn't even know they were selling the land. They'd get them drunk, and they'd sign their papers, they'd say put your X mark here, and they'd lose their land like that to the timber industry. And I heard they did the same things here in Flambeau. She said when she was young the Bad River was like a trout stream, it was just clear. Now she says you can't even see down there one foot.

She believed the reason for that was all the timber was removed; the topsoil washed off and polluted the river. I think the same thing happened here, but not to that extent. The timber was gone, that filtering system was gone. That's why a band three hundred-foot thick of pine would keep the leaves from blowing in there. Tell people they have to plant pine, take out the other trees. Plant pine around the shores again. It might be difficult to do, legal and otherwise, but I think it could be done. Septic systems must be improved to the extent that minimal damage should be done by septic systems. And they have the knowledge to do that today.

When I was young nobody had outboard motors. You rowed wherever you went, fished, and that's the way they did it. They used to haul you eight, ten boats at a time with those big launches. And they were inboard motors, so very little pollution got in the water. But now the discharge of the motor itself is into the water. And that kills the fish—I remember seeing all kinds of little fish when I was young, thousands of little fish around the lakes, shores, and all over the place. Pinheads they used to call them, the hatch.

Now you don't see that anymore. I think that has a great deal to do in my lifetime with the influx of the outboard motor now, the releases of gases right into the water; it kills a lot of those little fish. They lay right up on the surface like that. . . . I don't know what we can do about the outboard motor; there's a lot of laws, but they're not being enforced. Jet skis, the big boats, there should be a limit as to the horsepower on the boats. They could license all the motors—the bigger the motor, the more license fee you have to pay. That would start limiting them. . . there should be a limit on the size of the motor, should be a limit on hourly usage, not to disturb the people that fish. I've had them come roaring right by me, roar right up to me, five, six feet away, say, "Hey how are they biting?" [laughs] "Get out of here, what the heck's the matter with you, don't you know any better!" Almost sink you too.

I was once in Squirrel Lake, there was a sign right up there "Loon Habitat: Do Not Disturb," and some guy with a big outboard motor went right straight up to the nest. And those loons were just crying, they were off the nest, they had eggs in there or young even. I went over there and chased him away. . . . They do disturb them, especially loons, and they'll chase them with their motors, around and around, follow them all over the lake, stop right up next to them. The loons are trying to protect their young. I've seen it; I don't like it. They'll go next to the eagle nest to along the shore, and disturb the eagles. Come right up there to the nest, and hollering and taking pictures and doing everything to disturb them. There should be more protection of our environment, more protection of the wildlife. . . .

Those are some of the changes that I've seen. I'm concerned because of our people, those things are killing off our young people. A lot of people are dying of cancer. Young yet, forty, fifty years old, they're dying of cancer. That's why we don't have any old people. You have to be pretty tough to survive here, to be eighty even. They used to be in their nineties, people a hundred years old walking around here. Active too. Those are some of the changes that I've seen.

*   *   *

Most of them worked in the woods [to make their living], lumber industry. A lot of them guided, I remember there used to be fifty guides here, over fifty guides. Fishing guides, and they were raising families on those guide wages. I remember when I started guiding when I was young, we were getting three dollars a day! Where if you worked with the WPA or CCCs you were making $21 a month, maybe a dollar a day for WPA. Guiding they were getting $3 a day, so they used to guide. Guide two days, and they made more than they made all week in WPA. So a lot of them were guides, and they were raising families. I am probably the last active one of those fifty-some guides. Some of them are still alive. John Christensen, Buckshot, he's still alive. There's still quite a few of them alive that did guide. But I'm the only active left, I guess, out of that bunch. I still guide, not much, but I still do guide. So that's how they made their living. Trapped, fished—they lived off the resources is what they did.

When I was a kid, I remember going to my grandmother's house, and I'd go over there, and then she would dress me up. I used to have a whole buckskin outfit. And from there I'd walk out to the pow-wow grounds, out to the village, and they used to have a pow-wow out there lasted a week. I would go over there, and pretty soon some old lady would come and get me, and she'd say well, you're going to stay with us here, and I'd stay out there. I suppose some of my relative was out there, old people. Naomi, Naomi LaCass and the rest of them. I would stay out there and dance, and I remember those cars would be parked all the way down to what is now Wayman Road, parked on both sides there. And they rode all the way in—there'd be a lot of people there. They'd have a pow-wow for a week. They used to have Fourth of July celebration in town here I remember. Now where the police station is there used to be a garage there; I can't remember the name of that garage now. But Hunt's store was right there, too; old man Oldenberg used to run that store. That used to be the finish line for a race, used to start up by the community center up there, the old dirt road, board sidewalks. They'd have a horse race; you'd see them coming down, a cloud of dust, and the thundering of hooves! And they'd race to the finish line there; that'd be the finish line. That was a big thing, the Fourth of July here in those days. And of course they had the stands here, they'd have baseball, and they'd have a rodeo, used to have a rodeo too. . . .

And pow-wows, they used to have a lot of pow-wows, not just the one they call the Bear River pow-wow. But they used to have more than that, all kinds of them. Used to have them in the spring, in the fall, and in the summer. They used to have a lot of pow-wows here celebrating various things. Veteran's Day pow-wow. . . . They used to have a lot of pow-wows here, but now they don't have those any more.

*   *   *

I do remember the Depressions years; it was a tough time around here. Although I think we fared better than a lot of the surrounding communities because of the fishing. Like I said, there were fifty guides here, and they were being paid top wages. And it seemed it was the best guiding in the thirties and early forties. I don't know why that is, but there was a lot of money people around here. People who had money came up here to fish and vacation, they stayed two or three weeks at a time. So guides were being paid $3 a day. I remember my father, he always had a car, but there were only about five or six cars on the whole reservation. . . .

I remember we were the first ones to have a radio. I remember Sunday afternoon we used to have a whole houseful of people sitting around listening to the radio. They would listen to radio broadcasts like "The Shadow" on Sunday afternoons. I remember listening to the Orson Welles thing "War of the Worlds"—we went outside to look around and the moon was shining and everything else.[9] The invasion! I remember listening to the bombing of Pearl Harbor, in '41. My father and I sat up two, three days listening to that, day and night, because we had a short wave band too. And President Roosevelt's speeches and all the boxing—Jack Dempsey.

The Depression years—food, we raised our own. We had a lot of vegetables, you know. We used to go picking berries—the whole family would go out there and spend days picking blueberries, June berries, strawberries, blackberries. Canning them. Canning. Oh boy, canned deer meat and everything. We'd go hunting; we had a lot of wild game. Hunting partridge, hunting

---

[9] "War of the Worlds" was a radio play produced by Orson Welles in 1938, about a Martian invasion of United States, beginning with New York City. Welles wrote and performed the play so that it sounded like a news broadcast, and many listeners panicked and even fled their homes, the play was so convincing in its portrayal of the alien invasion.

ducks. So a big source of our meat supply was all wild game. Beaver, muskrat, fish. I remember I'd go fishing, and sometimes if I didn't get any fish, my brothers and sisters didn't eat. I'd catch fish. Hunt. Go hunting, walk. Sometimes if I didn't get a deer, we didn't eat. I had my own snare line in the wintertime, and I used to freeze, I'd go from our house all the way up to through town all the way to the other end of Pokegama, used to be a swamp over there, at the end of Pokegama. A cedar swamp. I'd snare over there, after school, after I got my wood in. I'd have to go do that. I would set lines out on Long Lake, and I'd chisel them out, rebait the hooks, come in and clean all the fish. Yes, those were Depression years.

So it was hard, but I don't remember missing a meal. I remember sometimes we'd only have boiled potatoes and salt pork. But we had enough of it, and we always ate. We had venison, beaver, muskrat, fish, all our own canned vegetables. Canned berries. Canned deer meat. My mother used to do the canning when she was alive, but she died when I was young. Then my stepmother, she had a big pressure cooker. That thing was huge! It used to hold twenty-four quarts or something like that. And a wood kitchen stove and a wood heater; that's how we heated the house. I remember I used to have to carry in, chop up, and split and carry in a face cord of wood a day to supply both of those stoves when I was young. Beside all my other chores I had to do.

*   *   *

Not much [to do for recreation]. Most of us would get out and play in the snow. And ice skating was a big thing here. Weather changed, it's different now from what it used to be. I remember the ice would freeze up, in November, around hunting season. It would freeze, and it would stay clear way up until Christmastime at least, or a month and a half sometimes. It would be clear and we used to skate all over, and there'd be bonfires on every lake where kids used to skate. You could skate all over! Because there was no snow on the ice. Big thing down on the hot pond,[10] it was downtown, and they had a big bonfire there. And at Mills Point and out there on the island and on Pokegama and out to the village, we'd skate out there. I remember when I was young I used to go play out to the village. I'd leave my house over there, swim across Long Lake to what they call Pigpen Point, swim from there to the islands, walk around Strawberry Island, swim from there to the rock, and swim over there to Pouparts' house. I'd play all day over there in the village, then I'd swim back again! Then when I got a boat, of course, I rowed around.

I used to row; my father he got me a boat because I was the original ninety-pound weakling. When I was about ten years old, I acquired double pneumonia. Put me in the hospital, I was in there a couple months I guess, in the hospital in Rhinelander. Saved my life I guess. . . . Came out of there the original ninety-pound weakling. So he got me a boat, spend all day on the lake, leave in the morning, come back at night, row the boat all day. Stay on the lakes and fish. I used to

---

[10] The "hot pond" is the bay where logs where floated at the base of the sawmill on Long Interlaken Lake in downtown Lac du Flambeau. Currently it is the site of the Museum and Indian Bowl.

even take a frying pan with me and fry up on the shore. Fry the fish up and eat. I was all over the place—fishing, rowing the boat.

*   *   *

Strawberry Island never was specifically a sacred place. It acquired that because of all the Indians that died there in the last great war or uprising or whatever it was when we moved back into this area. See this area changed hands many times between the Sioux and the Ojibwe. They drove the Sioux out of here a long time ago, they drove the Sioux out of here, and a lot of people died in that battle. They drove the Sioux westward, to the Minneapolis area. They drove them west into Minnesota anyway, and I guess from there they drove them further, drove a lot of them into the Dakotas. But anyway a lot of our people died there, a lot of Sioux died there. So it acquired the religious significance at that point in time, because of that. We consider it kind of a sacred ground because of that.

Whitefeathers, I guess they sold that. I know they sold that allotment. In fact that bay right next to Strawberry Island is known as Whitefeather Bay yet, in Flambeau Lake. So that has a religious significance to us because of that, all our people that died there, and all the Sioux that died there.

I do know that it should remain as it is. It should not be developed because of the environment change that would exist too. Because if they're going to put a lot of homes there, they're going to have to put a sewer system there too. And that would set the sewer system right on the water table and pollute that lake, pollute the system. We have enough pollution as it is! So I think it should remain in the state that it's in right now, that's the way it should be. And we should fight for that, so it stays that way. Because it's sacred ground to us now. . . .

*   *   *

When I was young, vast prairies existed on this reservation. No trees, just a lot of second growth and brush. Big prairies, it isn't like it is now, now it's all grown up with popple and hardwood and stuff. But this was all pine country originally. My father told me in order to hunt they used to have to go to the Wausau area, the hunters would go south of here because there was no deer here. They killed all the deer off, what there were. So they had to go down there, and they'd hunt in the fall until the snows came, then they made toboggans, and they hauled all the meat back here from around the Wausau-Merrill area. They hunted there because there was nothing here. Deer didn't come until after the logging, when there was no big timber. Because there was nothing but timber here.

I went down and saw some virgin timber down in Keshena once, and I understood it more then. Because under that timber—the trees grow straight up—all there is under there is moss and pine needles. Moss some places two feet thick, just like a big carpet, no brush even was growing there because there was no sunlight got down there to grow food for the deer. So they didn't exist here, and what they were here, they hunted them. They used to chase buck for a week, or deer for a week, just to get them. Chase them for a week just to get the deer. Run!

In fact my father, when I was young, he outran me. And I thought I was a good runner too. But he outran me; he took off after the deer; we had moccasins on. I quit about three o'clock that afternoon. And he was still chasing them, running, because that's the way they used to do it. Run a deer down! Get after them, shoot them, run them right down.

The snow we used to have, too, was something in those days. Like last winter they said we had a very bad winter. But this winter was just a normal winter for us in the thirties. Because that's the way it was—six, eight feet of snow on the ground. And we used to use snowshoes all the time. Snowshoe out, and I remember my father and I would go out in December. We'd go hunting, and we'd take a hatchet with us, or an axe! We'd get these deer that were going to die anyway, that were going to starve to death.

So we used to run them down in snowshoes, till they couldn't run, walk right up to them in showshoes, they'd be in the deep snow. Just used the hatchet to kill them, then put them on the toboggan. We used to get deer that way. Snow was so deep. And a lot of them starved to death, you know. So those winters we used to have a lot of snow. And cold, too—we used to have blizzards that would last a week, forty below. I remember one time we had it blown up all the way alongside the house, all the way up to the roof. We used to go out the kitchen door, back of the house, and we used to shovel our way out. To get out of the house even. Tremendous snows. A lot of snow, a lot of cold.

But they used to spear, too, a lot. Every lake had half a dozen teepees on it. They'd spear for muskies in the wintertime so they could feed their kids during the Depression years. A lot of them. I remember I used to go out on Big Crawling Stone. I used to like to go over there in March especially. They'd be spearing there. Big Ed Christensen, he used to spear over there, and I'd skate over there, but I'd stay away from him. He used to use a long spear, spring spear they used to call it, it'd be two tines strapped to a spear pole. And they used to use that; I remember I used to see that big spear go up in the air, then go down. Then I'd wait, and I'd skate over close, and then he'd come out. He had a big stand-up teepee.

"Hey young Ben," [shouts loudly]. "You come to see the fish?" I'd say, "Yeah." "Pretty soon, he'll be dead pretty soon." He'd hold him on the bottom of the lake until he died, then pull the fish up. With a spring spear. I remember the first iron spear I ever seen, my dad had it. There were no iron spears, just chisels were made mostly out of used springs, car springs. They'd make a chisel out of that and wire it and bolt it to a hardwood handle. That's the way they'd make a chisel.

So those days were hard, but those were some of the recreational activities, fishing and hunting. They used to have dances; there used to be a place around by Catfish's, now over where

Ben Chosa spearing through the ice

Wolfes stay, used to be a place called Woodman Hall.[11] I remember we used to go over there; they'd have dances in there. . . . I remember they used to show movies here too, those were showed up at the old Agency. They used to have movies up there. They used to have movies at the town hall, too, I remember, in the forties. You used to be able to go down there and go to movies for ten cents. They'd show movies at the grade school here too.

The older boys and girls, there was a lot of drinking going on here, even then. Although you weren't supposed to be able to buy it, they would drink. Big recreational activity [laughs], drinking. I did my share of it, no doubt it.

*   *   *

Words of wisdom from this old codger, huh? Well I would say probably one of the things they [young people] should do is don't use alcohol or any other drugs. That is the biggest thing—I think it's prolonged my life right now, because I believe I would have been dead fifteen, twenty years ago had I prolonged my use of alcohol. That has killed more of our people than anything. Don't use alcohol or drugs. Be careful of what you eat, try and stick with more natural types of food. See if you can plant a garden with vegetables and things like that. Intake of chemicals, although it won't kill you right now if you eat it, it's going to kill you, because you'll get cancer from those chemicals. Preservatives especially. Chemical preservatives are really bad. Commodities have a lot of that preservative in them. A lot of chemicals in foods. . . .

---

[11] Woodman Hall was a large wooden building constructed in the 1920s during the lumber era, used for both social events and religious ceremonies (see also Joe Chosa and Georgian Kinstedt interviews). It is alternately called "Woodman's" or "Woodmen's" Hall.

You should really be careful of what you eat. Make sure there's not preservatives in it or any chemicals. Those types of additives are death to Indian people. Death to everybody I believe, but more so to Indian people.

I related an instance to one of my teachers, Giiwedinokwe.[12] I told her about an instance where Louise and I had left our house here and went to Chicago for a week to visit friends. We had left about a half pound of commodity butter on a saucer on the kitchen table. I told her about it: "Boy it's really warm, eighty degrees. That's going to spoil, melt all over the table, be little crawly things all over it and everything else." So when I got back, first thing I did was go look at that butter. And there it sat on the saucer, with nothing the matter, looked perfect! And seventy-five, eighty degrees out. So I took a knife and tried it, and it was all right! So I told her, "Throw all the butter out, we don't want anything to do with that! There must be preservatives in there."

So I related this to my teacher Giiwedinokwe; she said it was interesting I asked about that, because they were interested too in what was being fed our Indian people. And they had to invoke the Freedom of Information Act to get what was in those commodity foods. She told me that they found out through the farm subsidy program that they took all the food they bought from the farmers, processed it, and put it in warehouses where it stayed about seven years. At that point it was shipped to poor countries, school programs, and reservations, under the food program for needy people. She said she found out the commodity foods were just laced with preservatives, and that was why the butter on my table didn't spoil. The other foods, too, are prepared that way to keep them for a long time in case of a nuclear war or something, that was the reason behind that. But now they're taking it and feeding it to reservation food programs and schools.

I think one of the big reasons why our people are being sick with cancer and everything else like that is because of these food additives and preservatives and chemicals that are in food. All the insecticides and stuff like that that they spray on the food to kill off the insects. So they can raise big crops and have big profits. So that's why they have to watch what they eat, be very careful of what they eat.

Go back to the religion of our people. That is another thing should be done by young people. The religion of our people was a very good religion, still is. Have religion. That's about it. Listening to your elders comes with religion. In the Indian religion the first thing they teach you is to respect your elders. If somebody older than you is talking, don't interrupt them. That comes with the religion: You respect your elders. Respect the old people for their knowledge. Ask them if you want to know, ask them. They won't tell you if you don't ask them. You have to ask—about religion especially, about anything. If they see that you want to learn, they'll teach you. A lot of the old ways are being lost because of that, nobody asks. Nobody asks!

---

[12] Giiwedinokwe means "North Woman" or "North Wind Woman."

One of the things about religion specifically is any religious person will not tell you about religion unless you ask. But you have to ask. And whatever the person knows, he'll tell you.

*   *   *

One thing I wanted to say, too, to young people especially is it seems to me, when I turned to the religion of our ancestors, and I quit drinking, from then on I've never been without things. I acquired all I have now since that time, since I quit drinking, since I turned to my religion. So for what it's worth, I think people would find that to be true that the Great Spirit sees that you always have enough to live. You won't be a millionaire, I never wanted to be a millionaire. If that's the way you want to go I suppose that's it, but I've lived comfortably and acquired everything, but only after I turned to my religion. I've always been able to acquire what I needed to survive.

I am Bear Clan. An interesting story about that is I didn't really know when I was young that I was Bear Clan. I had killed a bear—I think it was with my brother Mike—I shot the bear early in the morning, and my brother finished it off. I'd taken it out to the village to show friends of mine out there, and some old fellow came up to me. In his broken English he asked if that was my bear in the trunk of that car, and I said yes. He was smoking a pipe. He went away, and when he came back, there were two old ladies with him. He motioned to me to come over there. And we were drinking beer. So I got three cans of beer, and I took it over to them and they put it in their pocket. Thanked me for it and then he told me, he said that I was Bear Clan. "You're not to shoot the bear. You can't do that. You cannot kill a bear. You cannot eat the meat from the bear, because of who you are." (I still don't know who I am.) And because of my station in life and who I am, he says I was allowed to wear the bear claw necklace. That's what they told me. Since then I have never hunted a bear or killed a bear. Because I'm Bear Clan.

When I was young, Pete Christensen and my dad, they found a bear den. Pete Christensen reached in there and got two cubs out of there. He raised them. . . . I used to take them on a leash and take them uptown, Main Street. People would take pictures of me and everything else. Oh boy, that was something, trying to handle two bears on a leash. And they were strong too! I'd be fighting with them [pulls back as if pulling two leashes]. I'd have to keep them from biting people and this and that. They'd tangle up in the leashes and squall; people would be taking pictures of me. . . . I don't know what happened to those bears, what he ever did with them. . . . So that was fun, taking those little bears up there. One would run one way, and one would run the other way, and everything else!

Joe Chosa

Joseph Chosa was born on July 6, 1921, in the town of Lac du Flambeau. He was raised by his grandparents after his mother passed away when he was two years old. After his grandfather died, his grandmother raised him by herself, relying on Joe to cut wood, shovel snow, and help her with all the household chores. For this reason he did not attend the boarding school but was allowed to stay at home to assist her, going to the public school instead. He credits this as the reason he has remained fluent in the Ojibwe language: Unlike those of his generation forced to attend the boarding school, he was never punished for speaking his language and was encouraged by his grandparents to speak it.

After graduating from Minocqua High School Joe enlisted in the Army and served for thirty-seven months in the Foreign Service during World War II, participating in the Sicilian,

Naples Foggia, Rome Arno, Tunisian, Algerian, and French Moroccan campaigns. Returning in 1945, he moved to Milwaukee to join his wife Billi. After a year and a half, they moved back to Lac du Flambeau, raising a family of five children, and have lived here ever since. Joe worked for many years as manager of Simpson Electric Company, and in this position he traveled to all the Simpson branches in the region. He continues to serve on the board of directors of Simpson's Electric Company.

After retiring he began teaching the Ojibwe language, with fellow Elders Resource Council members Reva Chapman and Cecilia Defoe, in the Family Circles Program. He has taught Ojibwemowin for many years and is a dedicated and tireless advocate of language preservation and revitalization in the community. Today he directs the Lac du Flambeau Ojibwe Language Program, and has made many Ojibwe language translations, lessons, tapes, videos, and manuals. He has given many Indian names and said countless prayers in Ojibwe for the community. Joe held the position of rice chief for many years, as his extensive knowledge of wild rice is widely recognized. He traveled around to check the wild rice beds, determining when they will be ripe for harvesting, and worked closely with the Department of Natural Resources to post the openings of the rice lakes in Vilas and Oneida counties. In recent years he has trained young men to take over in this position.

In his interview Joe remembers many pleasant events: going to the rice camp with his grandparents in the late summer; making maple sugar in the springtime, staying in a wigwam; pow-wows; seeing herds of wild ponies running through town; and skating across the Flambeau lakes. He also talks about fishing, hunting, and making rice today. He remarks that we live in a beautiful country, and need to appreciate that more: the natural beauty, clean air, and the clean water. He ends the interview saying that Indian people should be proud of their heritage, and he hopes they will be interested in preserving their language for future generations.

Interview with Joe Chosa

This interview was conducted by Beth Tornes.

My name is Joe Chosa and my Indian name is Ozaawaabik. That means "Gold Metal." [I got my Indian name] a year and a half ago. I probably had an Indian name when I was with my grandmother because she called me a couple different names. But I never really remember any ceremony or anything that was performed; it might have been done when I was a baby or real small. She usually was very thorough about everything, so I just assume that—she never told me that this is your name or anything like that. She called me Giiwedin—that's one name. It has to do with the north wind. I think that's what it is. Reva's the one that named me Ozaawaabik. I became concerned about it because I never paid much attention to it, and I wasn't sure, and since you can have more than one Indian name—you can have several—I thought that it would be an appropriate time to get somebody to give me a name. I respect Reva very highly, I think she's a knowledgeable person, and she's used to the naming ceremony, things that are done traditionally. So I asked her if she would give me a name. We had a feast here [at his home], and she gave me a name.

Reva, I think, does a pretty good job at things that pertain to Indian customs, Indian traditions, things that she has lived with all her life. They were from the Indian village, her dad was one of the leaders there. He was a member of their drum. Probably the Big Drum,[1] I would imagine. You know, that drum was here a long time back. It was active for a good many years until the owner died. Then younger—keeper, I guess, would be the word—the son, was only a very early teen at that time. In fact I think he was thirteen when he inherited the drum. . . . Bill Ackley. And it wasn't until just the last few years that he reactivated that drum again. When people asked him about it, they found that they kept it at somebody else's house somewhere. They knew it belonged to his—Bill Ackley's—father. He inherited that drum. . . . His brother was gone; he had an older brother. He started that drum up again. He asked me if I'd be a member. He did that with some of the others. . . . There are certain positions that you hold on the drum. Mine is the wounded warrior. I felt honored that he asked me.

My father's name was Joe Chosa, Senior, and my mother was Martha Bell. My grandfather on my father's side's name was Henry Chosa. My mother's father was Jim Bell. They lived over at the Old Village. Originally, when I lived with my mother and father I lived right adjacent to where Louie St. Germaine lived, big Louie St. Germaine, right across the road from him. Remember the old Woodman Hall? I don't suppose you remember that. Well it was right next door to the Woodman Hall. They used to have Indian dances, and regular square dances, all kinds of things

---

[1] The Big Drum refers to an Anishinaabe religion that has been in practice for a very long time in Lac du Flambeau and throughout Anishinaabe territory. (See Introduction.) Big Drum ceremonies or "dances" are traditionally held at the beginning of every season. In Lac du Flambeau they are also held weekly. The Round House, a round log building, is home to the Big Drum ceremonies, located in the Old Village, where they have taken place for many years.

Jim Bell

of things going on like that. It was almost like a smaller version of the community building, and they had all different kinds of things that went on at that place, mostly pow-wows. . . . It was right across from what is now that park, right next to the (old) casino, Thunderbird Park. It was just up the hill, next to the road over there.

I went to public school here for my elementary schooling. I never did get to go to the boarding school. I went to that school because at the time I was growing up my grandfather passed away. My grandmother[2] had no one to help her, so she kept me home, and I went there. And I used to have to come home and cut wood; I learned how to cut wood and work with a saw when I was very young. I was real young when I used to cut wood. And I did that religiously, because that's the only way we ever had to keep warm. We didn't have the type of heat that you have now. . . . I had to saw the wood up, that's what I did mostly. And split it and stack it. In those days we used to have to have two kinds of wood; you had to have kindling to start a fire, and then after the fire's going, then you had the other wood to burn. I did a lot of that when I was a youngster.

*   *   *

My mother died when I was two years old, and my grandmother, who was a very spiritual woman, took me, and she kept me from that point on. She took care of me. I was raised for a long

[2] Joe's grandmother's name was Angeline St. Germaine.

Harry and Angeline St. Germaine, Joe's grandparents, with Joe's sister Bernice Chosa on left

time by my grandfather and my grandmother. In those days—you didn't have the work like you have nowadays, jobs were scarce, and we ate a lot of rabbits, a lot of deer, deer meat, wild rice, and things of that sort. My grandmother made additional money a lot of times by making beadwork. In fact I still have some moccasins and some gloves and some of the beadwork she did, with all Chippewa designs that's put onto buckskin. I still have those because I've kept them through the years.

And my grandfather did a lot of hunting.[3] He worked also; he worked in the woods—driving teams. They did a lot of logging and things like that. He was a teamster. And when he passed away, that's when I really started finding things kind of difficult, because he did a lot to take care of us when he was alive.

We also had a garden, a big garden that we kept. My grandmother had that garden, she kept it up religiously. We had all fresh vegetables and things like that all summer long. Potatoes and things that were stored for winter. She grew a lot of things like squash, pumpkins, all different kinds of vegetables, carrots, beans, things that are staples. That's how we survived; that's how we lived. And we lived good. Then you just had to buy things to add to the regular meal: You had to have something to make gravy, something to make bread. I've often thought about how my grandmother used to make bread. That's what they called lugalate—you've probably heard of that. That's the most delicious bread I ever tasted.

And we went out making wild rice. I used to make wild rice too. I had a job to do when I was real young—five, six, years old. I used to have to stomp rice; I used to have to get wood to keep the fire going, things of that sort. We also made sugar, maple sugar and syrup, in the spring of the year. And we lived right out there. We lived in that, it's like a wigwam . . . with cedar bark that

---

[3] His grandfather's name was Jim Bell, Niigaanaash, which Joe says means "Something that Comes ahead in the Wind."

they put on the edges around the outside. We slept on mattresses made out of cedar boughs. Yeah, I remember that really clear.

And also, things I remember about my grandmother. . . . She was a knowledgeable woman when it came to medications about different types of ailments. She saved a lot of plants for different kinds of ailments. She had things for sore throat, for congestion, headaches, for sinus problems, oh gosh, I could go on and on . . . for dysentery and a lot of other things. Pain remedies, things of that sort. Fortunately, I remember some of it. In fact I was taught one of the things that I value today. I've showed that to everybody I know, that's when a person catches poison ivy. There's a certain type of plant that grows along the water's edge; it looks like it's almost transparent. You can pick that and squeeze that juice out of there over the infected parts, the poison ivy, and it'll miraculously clear it up almost immediately.

I know one time I first started working at the plant. . . . Old Man Simpson, I'll always remember him as a good teacher, he's the one who started Simpson Electric Plant[4] up here; he owned the company. And he became infected with poison ivy just terrible, he had it all over his stomach, both arms. . . . He was kind of impatient when it came to something like that. He went to I don't know how many different doctors, one after the other, and my uncle went out there one day. He used to visit, he used to fish with the old man. I remember—old man Simpson told me this himself—he said, "I was so miserable, that bandage was covering the poison ivy, and it was bleeding through the bandage it was so bad," he said. "And your uncle came out there and I was complaining to him, I told him I've been to seven different doctors, they kept giving me the pink stuff, and it didn't do me any good. And I got to the point where I was almost cussing those doctors out because they never helped me." And Ben told him, "I can help you . . . there's something to remedy it my grandmother had." He said, "I'll go along the lakeshore, it might be awhile before I can find it." So he started walking, came back. Mr. Simpson said he came back after about an hour and a half or so, and he had a whole bunch of this plant. And he told him what to do with it. He said, "crush it up and put the juice on top of your infected parts, and do that two, three times a day. . . ." He said you know, immediately the itching stopped. And the second day, it was a day and a half almost, when you could take the bandages off and there was no more draining of it. And that was the end of the poison ivy, he just put it on there, and it healed right up, almost like a miraculous cure.

My grandmother had medication like that for sore throats and for headaches and for sinus conditions, chest congestion, that sort of thing. I suppose in those days you didn't have the doctors that were ready to come. In those days doctors used to make house calls, too, after those doctors came. But before that, people had to know something about curing themselves, or know something about things they could do to help themselves.

---

[4] Simpson's Electric Plant is located in downtown Lac du Flambeau. The plant is still in operation today and is a major employer in the area.

I'll always remember that about my grandmother. I have a great respect for her. She was a knowledgeable woman, she could read, she could write in the Chippewa language, she was pretty well educated in that respect. She had real good common sense all the time. I'll always remember her, I'll always feel. . . . I don't know how to explain it, when you really care about somebody, learn to care about them. That's how I felt about her. Because I didn't have my father, he was up in Minnesota, my mother was gone, and my grandfather was gone. So all I had was my grandmother to take care of me. And I had to work from the time I was a kid. I did a lot of snow shoveling and a lot of cutting wood for other people, and we got along.

*   *   *

I had trouble speaking the English language in school [because I was brought up with the Indian language]. I'll never forget the time I told my grandfather, I was having a little trouble with some of the words, and I told my grandfather one day, "Why is grandma always talking Indian to me?" You know, I talked to him in Indian. I told him, "You know, I have a hard time in school and she knows she can help me." And he said, "Well, she'll help you. You sit down, I'm going to tell you something. If you're going to keep wondering about why you learned to talk the Indian language. "Someday"—he said it in Indian—"*Ingoding giga-waabamaa inini biidaasimosed, da anishinaabe wonaagozi. Gaawiin dash oga-gashkitoosiin da anishinaabemo.*" What that means is: You'll see the day when you'll see a young Indian man walking towards you. He will have all the features of an Indian person, you won't mistake him for anybody else. But he won't be able to talk the language. He said, "And that's why your grandmother wants you to learn the language, that you will always know the language." So I felt better about that.

She was a person that kept talking Indian to me constantly. Of course I made a lot of mistakes. And I think . . . you learn by making mistakes. I remember we were out making sugar one time, and she wanted me to go after an awl, to make some baskets. They used to use baskets to catch the sap. She had that, and she used to sew them on the very top. . . . They put that sap in the basket, from the maple tree. She wanted that awl, they call that a *magoos*. She said "*Naadin i'iw magoos.*"[5] An old man, Charlie Starr, lived nearby, and she said go over there and get a *magoos* from him. And she told me that in Indian. She used to kind of smile to herself, because I didn't call it *magoos*, I called it *my* goose." So I went over there and asked, there was a whole bunch of people visiting this old man, I think Reva's father[6] was there, and some of the other Indians were visiting this old man out near the sugarbush. And they all started laughing when I said "my goose." But he knew what I meant! [laughs] I brought that back, and I said, gee, they were laughing at me. And she said, what did you tell them? And I told her what I said, and she said, "Well the word is

---

[5] Naadin i'iw magoos means "Go after the awl."

[6] Reva Chapman's father, Jim Sagasunk.

magoos." So I never forgot that. I mean you make mistakes like that, but she always did it in a way where you learned a lesson, and you remembered afterwards. Because I remember people laughing at me, and I kind of vowed that they were never going laugh at me again for that pronunciation. She was really something.

You know, they talk about single parenthood, that parents should do this, and parents should do that. I didn't have any parents; I just had my grandmother. And yet I feel that I learned more from her than I could've from a lot of parents, if I had three or four people teaching me. I learned more from that elderly woman.

You know when World War II first broke out—another thing I'll always remember—I was young, I was in high school. She insisted that I finish high school; I graduated from high school in Minocqua. And when I told her I wanted to go into the service, that was during the year when Hitler was invading all those little countries all along the line, I was so incensed about wanting to get into the service. Because in those days we used to talk about well, they'll probably be over here next. Flambeau didn't have many men around. There was nobody on the streets; they were all in the service. And the majority of those were volunteers, they weren't people that were drafted. In fact there might have even been a question as to whether an Indian person could be drafted, in those days. But my grandmother said, I'll never forget that, she said, "Well I suppose if you want to go, you're going to go anyways. But you want to remember, you might not come back. You might come back maimed; you might be hurt; you might be crippled. Maybe you won't come back at all. You want to think of those things." "And also, another thing I want you to think about, really think seriously about," she says, "You haven't even been off the reservation! You've been to Rhinelander, you've been to Ironwood maybe once, and that's the extent of your being off the reservation." She says, "You're going to meet all kinds of people, people from all walks of life. Some people you're going to make friends with, they'll be lasting friends. But you'll also meet some that do not like Indian people. You'll meet some of those too." And I'll always remember what she said: "Wherever you go, you try to treat other people as you would like to be treated." I never forgot that. And that makes more sense to me now as I grow older, because I think if we had more of that, we wouldn't have the ill-feeling and the conflict and the biased opinions that come out in the papers.

*   *   *

You know, there's many things that you have in this country nowadays that people can enjoy. Just walking through the woods. I ride a bike because I'm diabetic; I have to exercise. At first I resented that; I didn't like it because it was a chore for me at first. But when I started seeing all the birds in the springtime when they arrived, the woods was just full of birds that were singing. All different kinds of birds. And you see all kinds of animals. I've seen fisher, mink, and weasels, fox—I even saw a wolf on a couple of occasions. I saw bear, and lots of deer. And other animals

Honor Roll Memorial to World War II veterans in downtown Lac du Flambeau

like that. It's beautiful out there; it really is. And you don't mind riding a bike. I usually go early in the morning, before the traffic starts. And you really see the beauty of the country.

I have markers from my house out towards Powell Marsh, I have a five-mile marker, a six- and a seven-mile marker. I go sometimes twenty miles a day. It's enjoyable. And you get the fresh air. God, the fresh air is something else. You know, people don't realize how lucky we are to live up in this part of this country. There's so many places that they talk about pollution; there's so many places that they talk [about] the stench from different kinds of mills, the smokestacks, and things of that sort. And here, I think this lake is one of the last that's termed as pure, where the fish are not contaminated. I think that we live in a beautiful country.

*   *   *

I remember the first big sturgeon they caught, over there by Medicine Rock. They caught that through the ice, they speared through the ice. In fact the guy who speared it told me—well that's Reva's husband. He was telling me how to chop additional holes. And the spear was down to the bottom, but he had to make that hole oblong. And quite a bit bigger in order to get the fish out of there. It was ninety-eight pounds, almost a hundred pounds. And the other one, Butch St. Germaine killed on this lake here [Pokegama], that second sturgeon that they had.[7] So there must have been sturgeon here, and there must be sturgeon yet because they caught some smaller ones

---

[7] The world-record sturgeon that Joe describes, speared by Butch St. Germaine and Kenneth Doud, now hangs in the George W. Brown, Jr., Lac du Flambeau Chippewa Museum. It was 7 foot 1 inch long and weighed 195 pounds when they speared it in Pokegama Lake in the 1980s.

out by the dam a couple years ago. They were not the large ones, but they were thirty-six inches, something like that. Somebody caught a couple of them. So there must still be sturgeon around these waters.

*   *   *

I'll always remember, my grandfather had a boat that he used to guide with, that he used for fishing. Every once in awhile I had a chance to use it. A few of my friends were fishing panfish from that boat. We went fishing and were gone for quite awhile--we were over at Strawberry Island.[8] When I came home, it was getting late in the evening and my grandmother asked, "Where were you? Where did you go?" I said we went over to Strawberry Island. Then she said, "Don't you ever go there again." And I asked, "Why?" And she replied, "You know, there's a lot of people that lost their lives there, and that's the reason that our tribe is here now. There was a battle that went on there, a lot of people lost their lives. We should respect those people." She said, "It's almost like you don't care about other people or the things they do for you, like you don't appreciate those things. I don't think people should go over to that island; you stay away from there." I never went there again or forgot what my grandmother said.

When Archie Mosay was here, he told us things that have to do with the spirituality of Indian people pertaining to Strawberry Island.[9] It would be better to limit this knowledge to Indian people, to be held sacred, as part of their heritage and culture.

The man that owns Strawberry Island is talking about developing the island with buildings. This means landscaping, bulldozing, and so forth. Now to tell you the truth, I don't think in this whole country you'll ever see somebody bulldozing a graveyard to build homes. And you'll never see a person burn a church down without being in trouble. A place that people come to worship, or a place that they come to show respect, should never be disturbed. I think about that a lot, you know, every time I go down that road [Highway 47], and I look at that island—it's hard for me to visualize any kind of a building on the island. And I don't think it'll ever happen. I don't think it'll ever happen, because there's enough people in this community that feel the way I do.

I respect other people's beliefs. I don't care what denomination or what church they go to. That doesn't matter to me. But I think everybody should have a belief in something. And that's how I think about Strawberry Island. I don't think anybody should ever build on that island.

---

[8] Strawberry Island, in the middle of Flambeau Lake, is the site of one of the last battles between the Ojibwe and the Dakota (Sioux), possibly in 1745. The Dakotas were defeated at this battle, and as a result Lac du Flambeau became the permanent homeland of this Ojibwe band. Strawberry Island is considered to be sacred, and as Joe relates, children were warned not to set foot on the island out of respect for those who lost their lives here. (See Introduction.)

[9] Archie Mosay (Niibaa-giizhig or "Sleeping Sky") was a Mide and Big Drum spiritual leader, teacher, and medicine man who walked on in 1996 at the age of 94. He visited Lac du Flambeau in the summer of 1995 at a time when the tribe was fighting the development of Strawberry Island. While there, he talked about the sacred significance of Strawberry Island to an audience of Anishinaabe people.

The Sioux came here this summer, and they had those healing ceremonies and things of that sort.[10] We get along fine with the Sioux people. And it's going to have to be that way with everybody some day. . . .

You know a lot of times, even when I was in the service, people used to say, "Well do the Indians worship idols? What kind of worship do you have?" I said, "You know, I had a grandmother that prayed to the Creator every day. She did that religiously every day. She prayed to the Creator and gave thanks for the things that we had, everything that we owned, the food, things that were put on this earth, she would give thanks for." So I would never criticize another person, and say this is the right way, or that's the right way, as long as they believe in something. I think we all believe in the same Creator. That's the way I feel.

I pray every day. I say prayers thanking the Creator for all things put on the earth. You know, it's a good feeling, and I've had some good things happen to me. And I think it's because of prayer, I really do. I don't pray for the impossible. I pray for things that are good, things that'll help people. That's another thing my grandmother taught me—the Indian prayers don't follow a script. It's what comes out of the heart. I pray for the people that we lost just recently. I've done that almost every day for people that are gone on before us, the last couple weeks. I pray for them, that they could reach the destination where all the people, they say, will be going someday. I pray for people that are sick, for people that have problems. I pray for people that are in pain.

You know there's a lot of people that do that. And I think if we did more of that, this'd be a lot better world to live in.

Because the youngsters would learn to do that. We wouldn't have all the turmoil and all the things that are going on nowadays. A lot of bad things have happened. I can remember days when we used to get our fun out of skating; we used to do a lot of that. Go from one lake to another. You could be out all day, some days. Hunting rabbits, hunting partridge with slingshots, things of that sort. We did a lot of that when we were kids. You might come home skunked, but then again you might come home and have a few too. A lot of these guys became pretty accurate with a slingshot. I can still shoot a slingshot pretty accurately. They used to call them "plinks" in those days. I don't know why; I think because if you snap that rubber, that pad would go "plink."

I can remember when there were no jobs here; when there was very little housing in this community. When I first came out of the service, in 1945, and we moved back here, I lived with my grandmother. I had a hard time getting a place to live because there were no homes available. They didn't have the housing projects like they have now. Even now, with all the homes they have, they need more housing. So you can imagine what it was like in the old days, when you didn't have that. People lived together.

---

[10] Members of the Dakota (Sioux) Nation came to the Healing of Nations Gathering in the summer of 1995. Its purpose was to bring together in a spirit of healing and cooperation the Ojibwe Nation and the Dakota Nation for ceremonies, celebration, and in solidarity to affirm the spiritual importance of Strawberry Island and oppose any development, proposed by its current owner Walter Mills. Although recent denial of zoning permits has halted development plans, the tribe is still in the process of negotiating a purchase of the island.

And I guess a lot of people came back from the city too. There was a period there called "relocation" where they'd pay relocated Indian people to go work in the cities. Some of them stayed there, very few I think, but a lot of them, when they found out there was work on the reservation, came back. They'd get homesick. When you get a longing for your birthplace, you feel like you want to come home. I know when I lived in Milwaukee, I lived and worked there for a year and a half after World War II—I started missing the Northwoods, the fishing and hunting, and the clean fresh air. . . . I missed it to the point where I didn't want to do anything; I was just tired of the city. And Billi said, "I know what's wrong with you. What we're going to do is we're going to move back to Flambeau." I said, "Well I don't have a job back there." And she said, "You'll find something. We'll go back." That's when I decided, maybe that's what I really needed. And I was never more happy. She was raised here too—we raised our family here. . . . And I think we live in pretty good country here. I think we should appreciate that more.

*   *   *

You know they had certain places that they had pow-wows long before they started commercializing them. They used to have pow-wows back where that new casino is, in that area, there was a regular dance ground. And if you go out to Bear River, you can tell that's been there a long time, where the pow-wow is now. You go out and stand in the middle, where they put the drum and dance around—you go and stand in the middle of that and look up at those trees up there. There's an opening up there; it's perfectly round. Those trees have been there for a long, long time. I can remember when I was a kid: We'd walk out there, or run out there; they'd have pow-wows going. That's what I'll always remember . . . some of the old-timers, older men. They used to have regular good time pow-wows, and they'd get up. One man would start talking; he'd predict different things. He'd tell things that were going to happen. And they were interesting to listen to. When he got through, there'd be another guy that would get up, and he'd talk. Several of them would say different things, things that were going to happen. They told about it, and they were accurate! The things that they told about happened.

You know, I'll always remember when we were kids, we knew how to talk the language. There were several of us who did that, then we'd get away from there. We'd be walking home, and then somebody would mimic those guys that used to talk. "Akawe omaa niwii-gaagiigid," I'm going to talk.[11] Just like those guys used to do. Then he'd go on. And somebody else would say, "Gosha gaa-giiwanim," nobody wants to listen to you because you tell lies. [laughs] We'd have more fun when we were kids. We used to mimic the guys that would talk in front of the group up there. I used to enjoy that.

---

[11] According to Joe, "Akawe omaa niwii-gaagiigid" means: "Just a moment, I would like to say a few words here."

Bear River pow-wow. Drum and dancers

They had regular dances at the good-time pow-wows. They used to have a lot of that. The one that used to intrigue me all the time was the feather dance. And that feather was only about that long [holds his thumb and forefinger apart three inches], and those guys would really have to get down there and keep in time with the drum, and they'd pick up that feather. There was no booze or drinking, they didn't need that to have a good time. And they had a ball! I remember those days, the good old days.

You know when Reva was young, she was telling me that there was a trail by the big curve, that way, right back to the pow-wow ground. It was narrow, like a logging road almost—a person could drive a team through there. I don't know how it ever came about. Reva used to ride horses when she was young. She was on this horse, and she was riding around, and they had a big pow-wow out there. I laughed when she told me about that. She said something spooked that horse and scared it, and it started running out to where that pow-wow ground is, and it just ran. That thing was going, and she said, I could just feel that breeze blowing through my hair. And she couldn't stop the horse, it just kept on running till it got to the pow-wow ground. She was afraid it was going to run right out there where the dancers were! She said she could just see herself falling off that horse somewhere. [laughs]

There used to be a lot of the Indian ponies around here, too, at one time. They used to live out on the prairie, by the Old Prairie Road. There were a lot of them, they were wild. I'll always remember when Flambeau had dirt streets, almost like gravel. And I remember when those horses used to come through town, they'd run, just like a whole herd of them would be running down the street, and that old dust would be flying, and they'd go from one end to the other. We used to corral them out there, what they call Brown's field, and they had a little corral where they'd put those horses through, and somebody'd be announcing "So and so's coming out of the chute!" And they'd ride those old bucking horses. A lot of times you'd land on your butt before two jumps, but you'd be on it doing it again anyways.

I remember one time Shkwegin was riding a horse, and he was doing real good, and that horse was bucking like this, and he was hanging on there, sticking to him. That horse didn't buck him off, but he ran under a tree branch, and it just scraped him off the horse. And he went, ah, darn, and he went and stood right out back. [laughs] Shkwegin, his name was William Peterson. He's the one that walked down with me to join the service together. His real name was Bashkwegin, that means "buckskin. . . ."

A lot of things happened in the years when people used to enjoy themselves. You know how I was telling you about how people used to skate from one lake to another? Along the shore, if you ever look when you're traveling in a boat, you'll see dried trees that have died, and the wood is dry and would make a good fire in a hurry. We used to go along, and we'd skate from one place to another, and we'd make a bonfire right on the shore. Everybody'd come sailing in there to get warm, a lot of times someone would bring some hot dogs or marshmallows or something, and the kids would sit there and share, everybody'd have some.

Those were times that we used to enjoy. I remember I used to have to cut wood. I'd be there cutting wood long into the night. At twelve o'clock I'd be sawing wood yet. Those kids'd be out there, and you could hear them laughing and just having a good time. Playing crack the whip and all kinds of things they did on the ice. Or somebody'd be pulling a sled with skates or pushing them around, and you could hear them spinning out there on that clear ice. We used to have a lot of fun. . . . We used to go all over. We went all the way to Fence Lake, all the way over there and all the way back. We used to crawl over the road by second bridge, out there by Long Lake, come on this side over here. Those skates that we had were mostly those strap-on skates, that had clamps that clamped on the sole of your shoe. They used to give us those old Army shoes that they had to give away every once in awhile, with leather soles and leather heels. We'd clamp those skates on top, there was a strap that held the back part on. A lot of times you had skates that were two sizes too small or two sizes too big, but we'd go! We had a lot of fun.

We used to do a lot of fishing too. In those days you could catch walleyes right over there next to the hatchery. Catch a lot of walleyes through the ice.

I'll never forget the time I was out there, I had set six lines. A guy by the name of Clarence Graveen came out there; he was quite a fisherman. I'll never forget; he did that for fun. He used to have long willow sticks out there. He'd embed one end in the ice; it'd probably stick up five feet on the ice. He had that minnow down into the hole, and he'd have a loop there; it'd come off, just like a slipknot almost. He'd stand in the middle with all these poles around him, and all he did was look around. He'd be jigging, then he'd look around. All of a sudden he'd get a bite on one, then he'd drop that rod and run over to that thing and turn up that old pole. He'd snap that thing off and let that fish have line, then he'd set the hook, bring him up, reset it. We used to have a lot of fun like that. I'd never fished that way, but he was having a ball out there. There was enough of a breeze that that thing would go up and down, I suppose to keep the minnow active. It was fun.

*   *   *

I learned ricing[12] from the time I was five years old. I used to go out in the rice camps with my grandmother and grandfather. I think the most important lesson I ever learned from the old man was that you would not pick rice until the rice was ripe. We were out there a week early, or sometimes almost ten days early, and he'd just watch that rice. Every day he'd look at it, go out and test it. I know towards the end of the season, when it was getting close to picking time, my grandmother would say, "Well I think we should be harvesting now." He'd say, nope. A few more days. Then I asked about that too. He said if you go out and knock rice now, before it's ready, it will not reseed. Your rice beds, someday, will be gone. He was a great believer in that. My grandmother would say, a lot of that rice is ready now. And it was ready. He'd say now, we're going to have to wait. And she'd say, you're going to lose it. A good wind will come along and you're going to lose that rice. They'd talk back and forth like that, I remember that.

I never forgot it. When they say you have good rice, your rice looks good, it tastes good, a lot of times that has to do with picking it when it's ripe. Because when you pick it when it's not ripe, it's like a needle: it's thin, it breaks up in small pieces, sometimes it'll break up almost like cornmeal if you pick it too soon. Sure, you can get rice, but it's not the real good rice.

I think after you do that, you have to learn how to do the processing in order to make rice taste the way it should.

That's another thing. My grandmother used to insist on taking the rice off the lake the first time we went out. She'd take it and start roasting it almost immediately. That made the green rice. And as it became more mature, in the latter part of the season, the rice was quite a bit darker. Of course the kernels were big; it was good rice. I used to save it. I think I've got one bag somewhere yet that I've saved. Each year I made some [of] that green rice. It's almost the color of the vegetation in that fish tank over there.

I had a lot of rice like that. My grandma used to call it Christmas rice, because that's what she cooked at Christmas.

I had different jobs. I started out doing what they call threshing. I'd get new moccasins every year, every time I had to thresh rice. Your legs would get so that the little ends of the hulls on the inside, it'd get real itchy, you'd be scratching your legs all the time. No matter how much

---

[12] Ricing refers to the process of making wild rice, or *anishinaabe manoomin*. This process includes harvesting the rice by knocking it into a canoe with ricing sticks and then drying, roasting, threshing, and finishing the rice. Traditionally, Anishinaabe families would move to rice camps in the early fall when the rice ripened and spend several weeks there gathering and processing the wild rice. Rice was, and is, an important staple in the Flambeau diet. Depending on growing conditions and the amount of the harvest, the roasted rice can last until the next year's ricing season comes around.

you washed yourself afterwards you could still feel that picky feeling on your legs. I did that and learned how to do all the other stuff. The fanning, the roasting, and all that. I know how to roast it without burning it or making popcorn out of it—I learned that real early. You do not overheat it. We used to use those big kettles. In fact I've still got two of those copper kettles. They're solid copper, and they're huge, almost like a washtub. And then you put those on the fire, but you use coals, and you stir—I would say it takes almost a half an hour to get five or six pounds of green rice roasted proper, because when it gets too hot you have to pull the kettle off, put it back on, stir some more. You have to keep watching it because otherwise it gets to the point where it gets brittle, and it doesn't taste right to me when you do it any other way. That's something I was taught too.

I don't mind doing it. It's hard work if you've never made rice before. . . . I get a lot of rice. It takes a lot of hard work, and it takes a lot of hours. And you're working all the time because you're only going to get what you work for. It's not going to fall in the boat by itself.

I use machines now, to save some of the work. I used to do it the other way. I still do some of that traditionally, but there's some that I do with the machines. And it tastes awful good, because you can control the heat; you can control the threshing of it. With the threshing it does a real good job.

I enjoy making it, I enjoy eating it. In fact there's a kettle of rice in there now. I like mine like a soup. I have that pretty often. I think I know quite a bit about wild rice—how it has to be picked, how it has to be handled. Plus there's a lot that you have to teach. I teach the young folks different ways—how they should pole the boat; how they should handle the boat. Things that I learned from my uncle—I'll never forget, I used to pole him all day long. Ben Chosa, old Ben. I used to go out with him. He used to get after me. If you were going up and downwind, if you were going into the rice bed out towards the open side of the water. He used to get after me because I couldn't turn the boat fast enough to get back into the rice bed. "Why do you spend all day out there drifting around?" he'd say. "We're not fishing," he'd say. Stuff like that. He showed me how to turn that boat so I could turn it right on the spot and go right back to the rice bed. Those guys that I rice with are a lot younger, and I taught them that too. A lot of them appreciate learning something like that. There's a lot to ricing—you don't just go out and knock rice. There's a lot of tricks of the trade when it comes to picking rice, and I try to teach the people that I go with the things that I was taught. I've riced with Wayne Valliere, Brian Poupart, Tommy Wayman, and Kelly Thompson. . . . I've had several different ricing partners through the years.

*   *   *

I know how to short life can be. I found that out in the service, how quick it can be—like here today and gone tomorrow. When I first came back from overseas, I had a feeling that I didn't want to see a dead person; I didn't want to see anything like that. I don't want to look at them. I just felt that life was so darn cheap. You could be here now and gone just like that, a snap of your fingers.

I guess I was wrong. I think that you should show respect for other people . . . but I think that war warps your thinking sometimes. I lost some of the best friends I ever had. You just have to accept the fact that it's something that happened, and something you can't do anything about.

Nowadays when people go, I feel sorry for the families. I hope that the Creator will accept them with open arms. And I know that's what happens. Because we're here for such a short time. There's going to be a time when we'll all have to face that. I feel sorry for the people that have to suffer first, because there's a lot of that too.

So people I think should live and love the life they have. When they wake up in the morning, they should be thankful for that. Appreciate that when you go outside, when it's cold or whatever, breathe the fresh air, really feel good about it. Because at least you're able to breathe it. Able to get around; able to do things. Those are the things we should be thankful for. Because when you stop to think about it, life is pretty short. A lot of people would like to live forever, but we never will.

I feel kind of an urgency in myself—I'd hoped that more people would carry on our language. We're reaching that stage now where people are interested enough they're going to want to carry it on. Do you realize how many people we have on the reservation that can talk the language; how few there are? I would like to see that carried on, and I wish it could be. I don't care who carries it on, who the person is, as long as they continue to maintain it. Because you'll see the day when more and more young people are going to want that.

*   *   *

If you're trying to lead a good life, don't always think of what the other person is doing. If somebody tries to take you off the good path, just think of yourself and the things that are enjoyable to you. Think of your surroundings. There's a lot of things to be thankful for, a lot of things you can enjoy. A lot of good things. And we don't need the other things—a long time ago, I remember the days when it was forbidden to have alcohol on this reservation. We weren't supposed to have it. It was against the law for Indian people to drink booze. There were taverns within the boundaries of the reservation, but they wouldn't let the Indian people drink. And people got along. They had fun.

I think a person can realize not only that, but if a person is tempted to go on to the bad life, to go on to the drinking or dope or whatever, just think of what it's going to do to you. It's going to ruin your family life, ruin your health. That's an important thing, because I think a lot of heart trouble, liver trouble, kidney diseases, and all kinds of things could happen to people that are living the fast life. It's just no good for anybody.

Years ago, we got along without alcohol, without marijuana or drugs, and it was a good life. And in this day and age, people who deal drugs should realize the heartaches they cause. You can make a living without doing something like that. Think of the hardship it causes. It causes illness, heartbreak; it causes all kinds of problems within the families. You know, a lot of stuff that happens nowadays is because of that, and drinking. I'm not going to say that I never drank because I did that too. When I was in the service, I could drink with the best of them. It doesn't make me any better than anybody, but it gives me enough insight to say, "I don't want any part of that."

I think if a person would think about those things, it wouldn't be that hard to stay on the straight and narrow. Think about that's what I'm doing to myself, to my family. And if you really put your mind to it, you can do anything. You can do anything with your life that you want to. If you can keep that in mind, you'll always be happy. You'll always wake up happy, and you'll always feel that there's something to live for. You don't have to get drunk to pray to the Creator. You don't have to be on dope to be able to tell Him how you feel, or how you feel about other people. To appreciate the things that are good in life. You don't need it. That's my belief, and that's what I'd tell someone if they ever asked me.

It's not that a person is better than anybody else, it's just common sense. If you can talk people into using their common sense. God gave everybody common sense. If you learn to use it, and use it in the right channel, you'll always be a happy person.

*   *   *

I think being an Indian person that people should be proud of their culture, be proud of their heritage, be proud of the fact that they are Indian people. And I think that there's no reason in the world why a person shouldn't be holding their head up high and show people that. I don't mean they should get out of line, or do it in a manner where people aren't going to like you for it, but just be proud of the things that you do. I mean you as an individual. I used to tell my children that, when somebody'd tease them—they can come up with all kinds of derogatory names for Indian people, and some of them get pretty mean about it. They're something that could be taken to heart, and it kind of makes you feel—I guess some people try to make you feel inferior because of your Indian heritage. I feel that if you're proud of who you are, they can call you all the names in the world, and they won't bother you. I think that sometimes, that some kids going to school, if they hear enough of those negative things, it could discourage them from going to school. Because I know I felt that way because I went to Minocqua High School, I graduated from there. When somebody would say things to me, they hurt. But you can't let that get you down. You can say, "I'm proud. I don't care where you're coming from. We are all individuals. I'm proud of my heritage, and I'm proud of the fact that I'm an Indian person."

And I still feel that way. That's why I try to help people with the language. I'm proud of the fact that I talk the Indian language, and I hope people will be interested in preserving their language.

Wilhemina Mae Chosa

"Billi Mae" Chosa was born Wilhemina Mae Shelefo on June 12, 1925, in Pawhuska,
Oklahoma. Her father was a Santee Sioux, who passed away when she was a young child, and her
mother was Irene Beard. When her mother was a girl, she had moved to Lac du Flambeau with
her father, who had married Lac du Flambeau tribal member, a matron in an Oklahoma boarding
school. Irene married a tribal member, Herbert Ackley, who became Billi's stepfather. In her
interview she shares many memories of her childhood growing up on the Ackley farm: canning
corn, tomatoes, and berries with her mother, and speaking Ojibwe with her Grandpa Wesho, who
was also a great influence.

As a child, she also spent several years living in small towns in the Midwest, as her father
worked with a small Flambeau crew on defense construction, building small airports in towns

throughout the Midwest. He also worked as a printer in Kansas, at a lumberyard, and as a school bus driver, when Billi was in high school.

She attended Minocqua High School, where she tutored many of her classmates in English. World War II began soon after she graduated. She moved to Milwaukee and worked in a defense plant as there was little work in Flambeau then. Her fiancé, Joe Chosa, joined her in Milwaukee after returning from the war in 1945, and they married that same year. The couple later returned to Flambeau where they raised five children. Billi and Joe were "childhood sweethearts," and have been married fifty-seven years. After their children had grown up Billi worked at the "old casino," as a hostess, and then as tour and travel assistant at the present-day casino for five years. She now spends time at home visiting with her children and grandchildren and playing with their white cockapoo Waabishkaanakwad ("White Cloud").

In her interview she recalls many vivid memories: the "Indian dances"; the band concerts of the 30s; the plays, singing, and dancing held at the old Agency gym; playing tennis in summer; and in winter, ice skating on the lakes. She also recalls the prejudice she and Joe experienced at Minocqua High School. By contrast, she remembers how well the Indian people were treated in the South, where people shared what little they had, leaving watermelons, chickens, and eggs on their doorstep. She ends her interview saying, "The spirit (of Lac du Flambeau) has ingrained itself in my soul. . . . I've been a lot of places since I grew up, but I'm never happy until I get back here."

Interview with Wilhemina Mae Chosa

This interview was conducted by Verdaine Farmilant.

My name is Wilhemina Mae—I'm otherwise known as Billi by everyone mostly. My name last name is Chosa, née Shelefo. I don't have an Ojibwe name, but I do have a Sioux name, seeing as how I was enrolled on a Sioux reservation. My Sioux name is Diikamebidesii.[1] It means "A Little Bird on the Ground." I do not know who gave it to me, I was very small when it was given to me. They say my grandmother did, my father's mother, in Pawhuska, Oklahoma.

My father's name is William Edmond Shelefo. I had a stepfather who was a full-blooded Chippewa from this reservation. His name was Herbert Ackley. My mother's maiden name was Irene Beard. She was married three times twice to full-blooded Indians and once to a Greek man, her last husband. My mother had no Indian blood at all. . . . My grandfather's name was Charlie Beard. We lived with him here on the reservation; that's how we came to be here. We came here when my dad died—I was four years old. He had married an Indian woman from here, after my grandmother died. He came here and he had married an Indian woman that he met out in Oklahoma. She was an Indian matron out in one of the boarding schools out there. And when the school closed down, she came back. My grandfather had married her, and they came back here together. When my father died, they sent for my mother and me to come live with them. I was a child then, and I've been here ever since.

*   *   *

For a long time, I didn't even know [Herbert] wasn't my father. I have a great many recollections. In fact, all of my recollections are of my stepfather's family, whom I considered to be my own family. I still do. I'm very close with Bill Ackley yet, who would actually be my uncle, and he's younger than I! [laughs] He's my dad's youngest brother.

They had eleven children in their family. My father was the oldest, and Bill was the youngest. He always lived here, but he went away to school, and he went away for different trainings and things, but he was here for as long as I can remember—he always came back here. He lived in Ashland for a good long time. Ashland and Odanah, he was going to school there.

After my mother came here, she met my stepfather and married him. And he raised me until he died; I was grown up when he died. He died in his forties. He had something to do with blood poisoning from an abscessed tooth. We didn't have those things [penicillin and antibiotics] in those days. I'm an only child. Herbert had no other children that I know of.

---

[1] Billi told me at a later time that she also has an Ojibwe name, Binesiikwe, which she says means "Bird Lady." She also told me she is enrolled in the Santee Sioux Tribe in Winnebago, Nebraska.

I lived here since I was four years old. Went away during the war, worked in the city, in Milwaukee in a defense plant. While I was growing up during the war, I went to many, many different high schools all over the Middle West.

[My father] worked in construction. He drove big heavy equipment for building. We traveled with a big group from Lac du Flambeau who went down to the South, and we built small airports all over the place down there. What they were trying to do was to be able to have a place to move airplanes out of the city and land them in these small airports in case of an air raid. And that's why they were being put in these little towns. I went to school in Oak Town, Indiana. I went to school in Owensburg, Kentucky. I went to school in Madison. When we went to Madison, the airport that's there now was a big hay field, Truax Field. And they built that.

Going to school in Minocqua, I always felt a little put down by the Minocqua people in those days. But there were some very good people too. I had a very dear friend, Eloise DuBois, whose father had the local drugstore there, and I stayed overnight at her house. And Mary O'Keefe, who's now LeFrenier. Stayed with her many a night, at their house, when we had class plays and things that I had to practice for. And we had a very good relationship.

But there were those who put us down. Especially Joe, he was put down. He did not have the good clothes to wear; his grammy used to patch his overalls. She wanted so bad for him to finish school that she did everything to keep him in that she could. She tried very hard to keep him in school by keeping his clothes clean and nice. But he still didn't have the things that the other kids had, you know. He didn't even have enough money to have photos taken at the end of the year, like all the other kids.

And I remember staying home from school because we had to take a dime in to buy a gift for Mrs. Ames because it was her birthday. And I didn't have the dime to take in! [laughs] That's how hard it was in those days. Ten cents came hard in those days. Ten cents could buy a pound of hamburger in those days!

[In the small towns where the Flambeau construction crew lived] they had never seen Indians before, and they were literally fascinated by us, and by my father. They had my dad put on some shows for them; my dad was a great horseman. He trained horses for Ethel Mars in those days, and she had some beautiful ponies. And he could ride like the wind. They used to have him—they put stuff on the ground and have him pick it up while he was in the saddle, lean down and get it. And then he would bounce from one side of the horse to the other side of the horse. My dad, he was wonderful on a horse. He was really good.

The people there, they put down the black people there, but they did not put down the Indians. We had some of the best treatment of our lives over there. Every morning we'd wake up, and there'd be some gift on the front porch. Somebody'd bring two great big watermelons; someone else would bring two big packages of frozen chicken that they had gotten out of their locker. Pretty soon there would be a dozen eggs there. Just every morning, it was something different.

We lived in a small house, and it belonged to one of the farmers there. And every morning she brought us fresh milk and fresh eggs. And they had fruit trees, and we were allowed to go and help ourselves to the fruit. Everyone had watermelon fields. It was about '42, '43. It was the first taste we had of outside the state of Wisconsin, and I think we were all kind of surprised at the treatment we got down there.

George Christensen could tell you. He was with us down there, and he's my age. He knows what fun we had down there, because his mother and dad were with us, too, there. And the Spencer Smith family, Donald Smith's mother and dad were down there. The Tom Stark family went part way with us, not all the way. Jim Grey and Frances were with us.

They were heavy equipment drivers, and this one company hired all the heavy equipment people that were working on this Highway 47. There was no Highway 47 when we were kids; we had to go [Highway] 70, you know. They rehired them when they finished this job, to do some other highways. Then when the defense plant came the highways stopped, along came the defense work. For building they hired all these Indians who were very good and very faithful to this company. The little airports that grew up while we were there were really something. But we moved an awful lot. . . .

We did not do the actual building of the airports, we did the groundwork. The flattening and the leveling and the moving of the dirt and things. And then we moved on. But when we would come back through the airports with barracks and training centers—like Truax Field had a training field there—the barracks had grown there, and the army had already moved in when we came back.

We were a private sector so we lived in regular houses. They always found us nice places to live, the townspeople. In Owensburg, Kentucky, I went to school. The people were very poor there, and they were—when I went to school, it was warm there but not real warm all winter. It snowed a little now and then, but not heavy snow. It was kind of in the mountains of Kentucky.

When I went the first day of my high school in Owensburg, Kentucky, I saw all these big high school boys going to school barefooted. I couldn't figure it out, and I asked one of the teachers, how come they don't wear shoes? I thought maybe because it was just very warm or something, or there was some reason for it. He said they can't afford shoes, they only wear them on Sunday. [laughs] This is no lie; this is the truth. And yet the kids were smart—they were very smart—they just didn't have any money, you know.

And they didn't know how to make money because there were no jobs or anything. In fact, in the town there was only five places that had electricity in that whole town. And one of them was a grocery store, one was a morgue, and one was the house we lived in. We had a half of a house, she rented the downstairs and kept the top for herself. She had electricity. It was a little old lady. And then there were another couple, one of the teacher's homes, and then one of the town officer's homes. And that was all there was in the whole town, no other electricity.

At first I did [feel threatened by the Japanese and Germans during World War II] because—nowadays it's even worse, nowadays they could reach this country. We thought that those planes could make it over here; some could come off an aircraft carrier and destroy your airports at any time. [I remember] having air raid drills, wherever we went, even the very smallest town, they had air raid warnings and air raid practice. As to what you should do if something happened, if a bomb should fall. And then of course we had all the people who watched the skies.

*   *   *

My children? One of my children's names, the oldest one, is Jody. The second one is Bill, William, named after me and his Uncle Bill. His uncle Bill Bayliss, whose house we live in now. And the first girl is Leanna Rae, she now lives in New Mexico, Albuquerque. And she has an Indian crafts store, it's called "The Indian Way" in Albuquerque. Bertha was out there, she's one of our hostesses, and she visited the place. I told her to stop to see her. My fourth one is Cheryl, and she lives here on the reservation. And then Kathy Sue is the baby. She lives in Wisconsin Rapids, and she works for the Nekoosa Ho-Chunk Tribe as a nutritionist.

I have many, many grandchildren. I'm not going to name them, there are far too many! [laughs] I have great-grandchildren, many of those too. . . .

None of us knew [we were poor] because everybody else was in the same shape we were in. And we felt pretty rich, I think. I remember about my childhood, one thing that still sticks in my memory, is that I loved to go to my Grandma Ackley's house. Because outside they always had this great big teepee built. And she would sit out there and do her beadwork in the afternoon. And in the evening we loved to sleep out there. And there were mosquitoes at that time. But we always slept out there, and we always had a smudge going out in the front. And on this smudge they would lay these cedar boughs. I used to lay there and smell that! I can still smell it in my sleep sometimes. You know, the way that smells so good and refreshing.

[She] lived right about over in here [points to the pine trees behind the Elderly Center]. She had a little tiny house there, her and her husband. The kids were little then, Bill and Rosemarie, his sister. And they lived there, and the teepee was outside right beside it. They always had that out in the summer; they practically moved out into it. There were always mats laying there, and it was nice and soft. When my mother and dad wanted to go someplace, I was always dumped over there by them. And then I'd stay there overnight or sleep there. I remember sleeping in that teepee—it was, you know, like camping out. It was such fun. And we didn't have electricity in our home until I was in the eighth grade. We existed all that time, and we never did have running water, I remember. We had to carry our water.

[They used to have pow-wows] right there by their house. They just got together and had a pow-wow. It wasn't necessarily a pow-wow, it was called a dance. It was all Indian dancing. [Tourists] were welcome to come, but nobody was in costume. This was done for fun. Where they charged for them, and where the tourists came was over by Bill Jackson's house. They had a pow-wow circle built there. And that's where they had the tourist pow-wows where they dressed in costume for those. But these were the Indians, the true Indians, who had their dance. They danced for fun over there. The dances were held like once a week, at least once a week. Sometimes even more, if they had something to celebrate.

And it's so funny because with the Indians, when it's your celebration, like your birthday, you don't receive gifts, you give gifts on your birthday. Everybody gives away to somebody. And they give whatever they do, on their birthdays, on their anniversaries, on their name days, they give away. They give, not receive. It's the opposite of the white man. It's a giveaway.

*   *   *

Old Boodoo was Celia's[2] stepfather, but he was very much like my stepfather. He raised her, and he was good to her. And she calls him her dad too. I think his name was William, Bill Catfish, but everyone knew him by Boodoo.[3] That was his Indian name.

My grandfather, his name was Frank Ackley, went to school at Haskell. And he was a great musician. He learned to play the French horn. He was so good at it that when Sousa brought his band to the Haskell Institute, Frank Ackley was asked to travel with him for the summer. And he did! He was just a young boy then. And then when I grew up, I took the French horn as my musical instrument because I knew I could get a lot of help from Frank. And I did! [laughs]

My dad was no kind of a musician at all, but Frank was, he could. . . . He was a drummer also. He drummed on the town drum, the Indian drum. And then he also was a musician by the white man's way too. [laughs]

[I remember the band concerts] in the '30s. It had to be the '30s because I went away in '41. So it was in the late '30s. It was all Indian people—there were a couple of white people in there, Mike [Aschenbrenner], and I think there was a couple that stayed here only in the summertime, who came and joined the band too. There was just a little podium out there, right up here, in front of the Indian bowl.[4] At that time the Indian bowl wasn't there. We used to have our fireworks on Fourth of July from down in that bend there. And they had a pow-wow ground down there, but not the seats built in concrete like they are now. And when the band concerts were there, a lot of us played in them from the schools; we had learned to play the instruments. There was Wanda

---

[2] Celia refers to Cecilia Defoe, a contemporary of Billi's, who is also interviewed in this collection.

[3] *Boodoo* means 'tadpole' in the Ojibwe language. Boodoo Catfish's name in English was William, or Bill Catfish.

[4] The Indian Bowl, built in the early 1950s, is an amphitheater used as a dance arena, as well as a pageant arena during the 1950s and 1960s, on Long Lake at the site of the old Flambeau Sawmill. In the summertime tourists come to the Indian Bowl to watch the weekly pow-wows, with singers on the drum singing traditional Lac du Flambeau songs, and dancers wearing their regalia and performing traditional dances. When it was first built, at the height of the resort period, its 2,500 seats were always filled, and the local dancers and singers were well-paid to perform twice a week, not only traditional songs and dances, but also the plays and popular music of the time.

Lac du Flambeau Indian School Band

Brown,[5] and Violet Brown and her brother George and her brother—I don't think Jimmy played, but Leonard played—and Harry St. Germaine. He was a great trombonist! Old George Brown played trumpet. And Cobbie LaCasse played. Injun [Peterson] played drums. Most of the old Indian men. Bill Skye even played an instrument. They learned it in the old government school. They were forced to play them, you know. That was one thing they took to heart because they loved it. They're music lovers! [laughs] Yeah, they were music lovers.

I think Dorothy Stewart [started the concerts], I'm pretty sure. I don't know if she organized it, but I know she got George Brown interested in starting the band. She said, "There are so many musicians. Why don't you get them together?" And so he did, and I'm pretty sure that's how it got going. And there were very many people that played on the reservation. You would never have known who could play until they started hauling their instruments in.

*   *   *

It seems like we all got along with each other so well. I remember family picnics as a kid, when we had these picnics with her family [Verdaine's, the interviewer], your Aunt Bess's family.

---

[5] Wanda Brown Hunt is also interviewed in this collection.

Jeannie and Harry . . . Harry and Bess, they had big bonfires. And you know what they did? They would sit around and sing. They all sang afterwards, the songs of the day. And we had no TV. Her dad [Verdaine's] had the most beautiful voice. He had a gorgeous voice. He was asked to sing at all [events]—I don't know if you remember, but I remember.

Do you remember an old minstrel show they had? Up at the old school? It was something else. I was maybe ten years old at that time. But I remember your mother was a chorus girl. My mother was a—what do you call, a chanteuse? She would sing, she had one of these little flat hats on her head, and an evening gown. And then they had all the young Indian ladies, all married ladies, as the chorus girls. And they did all their little kicks and everything, you know, and it was so cute! They had it where the Niijii building[6] is now; we had a big gym there. And it was in, I think it was the building right next to the Niijii. It was such fun. It was all Indian people.

And Grandpa Ed Anderson, he played the part of an old-fashioned minister. He got up, and he was reading from his book, you know. You know how prim he always was. And he got up, and he was reading from his book [looks primly down her nose as if reading a book], and then he'd tell a little joke to the side, and they would all, just kind of roaring, you know. He was a comedian. And it was really something. And everybody in town had a little part in it. Dolly Gurnoe did a little song and dance. And Hiram Valliere recited the Gettysburg address. [laughs] [Very dramatically, voice rising] "Four score and seven years ago, our forefathers brought to this country a new nation!" with all the expression. [laughs] They always had him do it because he was so good at it. And he was just little.

* * *

When I first started school, in first grade, we had an old red schoolhouse over here [points towards the Bingo Hall]. A one-room schoolhouse. It was right where Clyde Chapman's house is now, near Bob Chapman's old house. [Then there was a school] right in front of the Flame Cottages; it was a brown one then. And the fifth through eighth grade was there. But the first through fourth was over here in that one room. And we had an outdoor toilet, and we had a pump inside. A woodstove but it burned coal, in those days they had coal. And then we had outside, wood piled up for kindling in the little porch outside. And we had our pump out there, and every day one student was assigned to pump the pail of water, and go out and bring it in to the school, put it in there. People had to raise their hand if they wanted to go and get a dipperful of water and put it in a glass and drink it. [laughs]

We went to school our first year, it was in 1932. 1931. We broke for Christmas vacation in '31, and when we came back in January of '32, we went to this school. And it was like heaven! We

---

[6] The Niijii Building or Niijii Center is one of the few buildings still standing of government boarding school complex. In the 1980s it was used to house offices and classrooms for the Family Circles/AODA Prevention Program, a curriculum based on traditional values that included Ojibwe language instruction. The word *niijii* means 'friend' in Ojibwe.

had indoor toilets, and we had running water, and we had a gymnasium. And all the school was together, the first four grades in one room. We still had one room, but we were all together, and the other four were in the upper grades, we called them.

This was a public school. Where the plant[7] is now, that was it, that was our school. They still had the government school at the same time as this one. You could go to either one. Because at that time government school was not mandatory then. But at our school, the public school did not give free lunches, free meals. And they did over at the other one. So many of them still went over there, because they did have free meals at noon. And we didn't. They also gave to their students coats, shoes, long johns, hats, stockings. Gave them a lot of things you know. Plus they were able to take a pail of milk home every day to their family; they got fresh milk. The kids from our school, the Indian kids, also could go up there and get a pail of milk once a week if they wanted to. I often did! [laughs] And cod liver oil. Little footballs! [laughs] But we lived through it. I remember Nan Anderson was on the school board, I think, all my grade school life. She was the chairman of the school board. [To Verdaine] She was your grandma right? Yeah. Nanny Anderson.

From the eighth grade I went to Minocqua High School, and I went there through my junior year. I had wanted to do anything to do with writing or with English. See my father was a printer for the *Tulsa Tribune* and also for the *Kansas City Star* when we moved to Kansas City. And then my mother was a proofreader for both papers, so I had dreams of being in. . . .

I had a teacher named Louise Ames, and I think everybody in the world had her as a teacher. Because she stayed there for many, many, many years. In fact she retired from there, and she could hardly move or walk, she was so old. But she was so good at her job they kept her on for just about forever. And she said she saw my potential as being an English teacher, and even wanted me to help me through school if I would keep on going, to realize my potential as an English teacher.

Of course I didn't go on. [laughs] I got married instead. And the war came. But she had me tutoring about half of the Minocqua students that I went to school with, who were not very pleased at being tutored by a Lac du Flambeau child! [laughs] But I still see some of the kids I went to school with that I tutored as a child. One of them was Bobby Yeschek. And George Roberts, he comes here all the time with Peggy Oldenburg? Her husband. I tutored him too.

*   *   *

Now I think there are less stores. There used to be more. We used to have a five and dime, a Pamida-type thing, only it was smaller.

We had three or four grocery stores going at one time, so you could take your choice of the prices, you know. We had a bakery; we had a furniture store; we had several gift shops going at the same time. Of course, we didn't have any casino in those days. But we had a good time.

---

[7] "The plant" refers to Simpson Electric Plant in downtown Lac du Flambeau.

Most of our time as teenagers was taken in—what we did was skate. We did a lot of ice skating. And in the summertime we played tennis a lot, up on the old courts at the old government school. We all learned to play tennis through the old government school, which wasn't a government school at the time. But we still had an Indian agent here, and we still had the courts up there. We always used them, they were always free to use.

There were various kinds of jobs. . . . I remember your [Verdaine's] dad. He started a restaurant here, and he did really well with it. Your mother and Bessie cooked for him. I don't remember what it was called. I waitress there, so I should know, shouldn't I? I think it was just "Dick and Louise's."

My dad, he drove a bus for the school. He drove us to Minocqua to school. Elmer Graveen drove a bus too. And then my dad, in the summertime, we worked the farm. My dad had a big farm. We had lots of horses, and we had a couple of real heavy dray horses. And they looked almost like the Clydesdale horses, you know, they were so big! They were really huge animals. And we had a cow, so I had a lot of milk. And we raised our own corn, our own tomatoes. Our root cellar was always full of squash and potatoes.

I think my dad wasn't the great farmer, but my great-grandfather, I should say step great-grandfather Grandpa Wesho, was the great farmer. And he had all this equipment. It was all pulled by pony, nothing was mechanized. But he had a disk, and he had a harrow, and he had the reaper to roll the hay up. We raised all our own hay for our horses. And we raised fields and fields of corn, which we fed to the stock in the wintertime. Right out where Bill Ackley's house is now. We had forty acres there to plow.

That was their own land, and it still is. Yep. That house we lived in has long been gone, but Bill has built another one since. It's nice.

We dried, because there was no refrigeration in those days, but my mother did lots of canning. And whenever she gave gifts, most of the time that's what she gave, was something she canned. She canned blueberries, blackberries, Juneberries, venison, tomatoes, anything that she could put away. She cut corn off and put it into pints. Our shelves were lined with. . . . We didn't have a pressure canner like I have.

My husband won't eat tomatoes that are bought in a store. I have to can them. To this day I'm still canning tomatoes! [laughs] We survived through Mother's ingenuity along with my dad's, I think.

We had the manure because we had the stock, see. And every year Grandpa would go out and spread this. And where he learned these things, because he could hardly speak English. Very few words of English could Grandpa speak. And he and I communicated very well because he taught me the language when I was very little. I talked with all these little old men in their old tongue, and I could just go forever with it. But I lost it as I got older because I never talked it. But Joe kept his, because he was raised by his grandma, and Grandpa Wesho died.

We lived with Grandpa Wesho, my mother and father and I, and Grandpa Wesho taught me so many things. I believe he was the greatest influence on me as a child. And then he would have his little friends come in to play cards. They loved to play cards. They would come in to play cards, and he would say, he would call me and say to me—he would call me by the Indian name for great grandchild, and then he would say [whispers], "Niibiish!"[8] which meant that he would like a cup of tea. And then he would say, "Ziinsibaakwad"[9] which meant that he wanted sugar with it. And all along he would tell me the different things. And then "Bakwezhigan."[10] And he was just showing me off to these men that he had playing cards. He wanted them to see how much I understood. And every time I would bring him what he had asked for. Those old Indian men would shake their heads and laugh. Because I was really light-headed as a child, they really couldn't believe that I could understand. [laughs]

*   *   *

For the turn of every season, there was always a dance. And there was a dance for something going on. And those that belonged to anything like a drum or a Midewin,[11] theirs comes on a certain date, but ours, those that didn't belong, we still had the celebrations. Like my mother would always, our fall one was always Thanksgiving. And we always had all the great big celebration out at our house. Because we had all the, I'll tell you—we raised chickens.

And I'm telling you that that was the Sunday dinner all the time, was chicken. And I got a little sick of chicken after a while. Joe still loves chicken. I myself, I can hardly look at it in the face any more! [laughs] But he loves it, because his family didn't raise chickens. But I did. I remember we used to gather eggs; we always had eggs.

And Bess was a great, one of the best cake makers I've ever known in my life. Her aunt [Verdaine's] Bess. And my mother's best friend, by the way. She could always furnish the flour and the rest of it, and my mother always would send her eggs, so that she could make cakes for the big celebrations. We always had cakes, and then Bess made great pies too. She was a good cook; she was a baker. And cookies. Remember her big sugar cookies? They were always like that [shows a six-inch cookie]. Geez, they were good cookies.

What I remember [about the Depression] is the WPA[12] when Franklin Roosevelt came in, and he started these, like the CCC camps here. Life started getting a little better after that. It wasn't

---

[8] *Niibiish* is a shortened form of the Ojibwe word *aniibiishaaboo*, meaning 'tea' (literally, 'leaf water').

[9] *Ziinsibaakwad* means 'sugar' in Ojibwe.

[10] *Bakwezhigan* means 'bread.'

[11] "Drum or Midewin" refers to the Big Drum Society and the Midewin Society, the two primary Native religions in Lac du Flambeau. (See Introduction.)

[12] Works Progress Administration (WPA) was a federal agency (1935–1943) begun by Franklin D. Roosevelt to institute and administer public works projects in order to relieve national unemployment following the Great Depression.

Fire tower with observation post

a great big bunch of money, but at least it was some money that you could depend on being there every week, you know. Or every two weeks, whenever the payday was. And it helped here a lot in Flambeau at that time. All the young men were in it. And some of the people had regular jobs, like the people who were in civil service up at the BIA,[13] they had regular income all the time. But people like my dad, he had a regular job but only in the wintertime.

And then Harry St. Germaine. . . . He was one of the few people in town who had a year-round job, because he janitored for the public school, and in the summertime he was the fire tower. He was Joe's uncle and her [Verdaine's] uncle. He always had a good income, and we considered

---

[13] BIA refers to the Bureau of Indian Affairs. The BIA established an agency office as part of the Boarding School complex in 1895. In 1922 they conducted a survey of all the households in Lac du Flambeau. The BIA office employed several civilian employees from Lac du Flambeau. For example, Gilbert Chapman was a BIA policeman as well as a tribal policeman.

him to be one of the more well-to-do people on the reservation because he had a job all year round, where the rest of us kind of eked it out the rest of the year.

Our years ahead of the Depression were bad, so they didn't change [during the Depression]. We didn't know it; we had plenty. Rice was part of our mainstay. My grandmother and grandfather, we all went out as a family and camped at Star Lake. Because the old Escanabas[14] were the great-grandparents up there. They camped right on their grounds up there. And we always went up there to make our rice on—I forget the name of that lake now, where Andrew Johnson comes from, Marguerite Johnson's husband?

* * *

We never had a bus. All the years I went through the eighth grade, we never had a bus running. I walked from home. One day I froze my face; I froze both feet, and my hands. It was fifty-five below, but I didn't know it, and I started out. And my mother didn't know the temperature. She just got me ready for school, and I left. I had the lunch in my bag, and it was frozen solid. When I got there, I had frostbite and I was hurting, and Harry St. Germaine quickly went and got a tub of water and put ice in it, and he went out, and he got snow, and he put my feet in it. And then he rubbed my hands, made me put them in the water, rubbed my hands, rubbed my face. And to this day I can feel a little of it, when it gets cold I feel it here [points to her cheek]. But he saved my hands and feet. It was a mile and three quarters.

It wasn't so bad when I went to high school, I just had to travel down to [Highway] 47. So it was half the distance, you know. And I'd catch the bus right there, when Elmer drove it. When my dad drove it—we had one of the few cars on the reservation—and my dad would drive us in, after we got a car, to pick up the bus, and I would ride the bus to Minocqua with him then. Because he drove the Minocqua bus in my later years. But when I was in grade school we didn't have a car. And then my dad sometimes, before he drove the bus, he had to go out into Michigan to work, in the lumberyards. Used to go up into Michigan proper, not the peninsula.

* * *

I suppose you've already heard these [stories about Strawberry Island] from all the others, but we were always told, "Don't bother that island because it's a sacred place. There are many spirits there. Don't disturb them. Leave them rest." And we never did go out there as children. Some of the kids, it was always going to be a dare. "I dare you to go to Strawberry Island," you know. And if you were a man, you were going to show your manhood by going out to Strawberry Island and proving them that you weren't afraid.

---

[14] The Escanabas were a Potawatomi family who lived in the area. Andrew Johnson, their grandson, was from Star Lake, and Marguerite ("Maggie") Johnson was from Lac du Flambeau, where she lived until her death in 2002.

But I don't think anybody ever did it. When we were kids, nobody ever did. We'd go to Ant Island over there, but we never would go to Strawberry Island. Pigpen Point, but we never went to Strawberry Island. And we did go past it, but we always made a wide circle around it, on skates, you know. We used to start from Moss Lake—Mud Lake in those days—and then we would skate out, skate over to Long Lake and then skate over to Flambeau Lake and skate over all the way out to the village.

And we'd pick up a few kids out there, maybe five or six, and we'd all skate back from Flambeau and we'd go up to Pokegama. [laughs] And then all along were bonfires. You could stop by all these different bonfires and get warm. Thaw out before you started again. But we used to skate for miles and miles and miles.

Medicine Rock wasn't so scary, but we were always taught that that was a great-grandfather in that rock, and that he was watching over everyone. And that he was going to see that you were doing the right thing. That's the way I was told by my grandfather. Kind of like a conscience, I would say. But you always knew that there was someone there watching.

And so you didn't swear or say anything bad when you went near that rock, because that person could hear you. Because there was a spirit in that rock. I believe that yet today.

Well I'll tell you, that spirit [of the reservation, which Verdaine mentioned] has ingrained itself in my soul. Because I can't be happy for too long away from here. I've been a lot of places since I grew up, but I'm never happy until I get back here. The most I can stay away at a time is two months, and I've got to be back.

Cecilia Defoe

Cecilia Frances Defoe (pictured at left above) was born January 27, 1916, on the Bad River Reservation. Her family moved to Lac du Flambeau soon after she was born. She was taken from her parents at age five and like so many other Native children, was forced to attend the Lac du Flambeau boarding school. After boarding school she contracted tuberculosis and spent several years at a sanatorium in Bayfield. She had a son, Milton Peterson, with Henry Peterson and later married Vernon Defoe, Sr., from the Red Cliff reservation. They lived in Lac du Flambeau, where they had two sons, Vernon and Lawrence, and one daughter, Jackie. Celia's husband was struck and killed by lightning while working at a construction site when he was only twenty-seven, and afterwards Celia raised her children on her own with help from her family.

All these incidents show the resilience and strength of Celia's spirit, for she was a survivor, like so many of her generation. She raised her own children and several grandchildren, living at different times in her life in Bayfield, Red Cliff, and Lac du Flambeau. She worked for many years as a cook at Holy Family School in Bayfield, and in her later years she was a foster grandparent in both the Lac du Flambeau and Red Cliff public schools, where she taught Ojibwe language and told traditional Ojibwe stories to the children, which delighted her. There everyone knew her as "Grandma Cel." Her grandchildren, great-grandchildren, and her "adoptive" grandchildren were very close to her, and she shared her teachings and stories with them at every opportunity.

Beginning in 1988 with the Family Circles Program, Celia worked as an Ojibwe Language teacher along with Reva Chapman and Joe Chosa, sharing her extensive knowledge of Ojibwe language and traditional ways with her students and others who wanted to learn about their culture. People often approached Celia not only with questions about Ojibwe language and traditional ways, but also to ask about their family history, as she was an unofficial tribal historian in Lac du Flambeau and could tell just about everyone who their relations were. She had a very clear memory and could recall with amazing detail events from childhood, as her narrative demonstrates. Her days at the boarding school are recollected vividly here. Celia immersed herself in Ojibwe traditions and history, always asking questions of other elders and reading every book she could find on Ojibwe history and culture.

Celia taught in the schools and in the Ojibwe Language Program until the last years of her life. Even then she participated in traditional doings and ceremonies, and her last words were spoken at a ghost feast, "Make sure you follow the Indian way. Don't lose it the way it was taken from us. Everything goes back to the Creator. Make sure to say your prayers every day and teach your children these ways. Make sure you don't lose what the Creator has given us." She spoke these words the day she walked on: May 9, 2000.

Interview with Cecilia Defoe

This interview was conducted by Marilyn Conto.

My Indian name is Waabanongagokwe. It means "Morning Star." My clan is Awaasii. It means Fish Clan.[1] My aunt [gave me those names], I was just a baby I guess. At that time they gave you two names. My other name is Wiishkii. It means "woodland buffalo." My other aunt gave me that name—I have two namesakes. That's the way they used to do. They were still doing that when they gave my son a name. My family gave him a name, and then his dad's family gave him a name; Petersons, from here, his people, they gave him a name. Milton. Lawrence, he has an Indian name too. He forgot his Indian name—he came and asked me one day. "Red Cloud," Mishaakwad. He laughed, he said, "I didn't know that! I forgot my Indian name, I thought I didn't have any." I said, "No, your people gave you a name." He's related to the LaBarges. They gave him a name.

My mother's name was Susan Menominee. She was an Ojibwe from Brimley, Michigan. It might have been "Rice," Manoomin, originally. My father's name was George Smart. But he died when we were small, my brother and I. . . . And my mother married a man from here.[2] I think I was about five, my brother was not quite a year old. There was just my brother and me. We've lived here ever since. And he raised us. And he was good to us. He was very good to us. Sometimes we lived in the village; sometimes we lived in town. We were like nomads, eh? [laughs] Then when I was about six, one day the police came and said I got to go to school. So they took me to the government school.[3] She cried, she didn't want me to go. She thought I was too young. But they said no, you have to go. I was six. I went to school there until I was eleven. Then I graduated, I guess they call it nowadays. It only was as far as sixth grade, government school.

And then I went to Flandreau.[4] I was there four years—I couldn't even come home. Because they were having hard times you know, they couldn't—they didn't pay your way.[5] They took you

---

[1] The clan system was a form of social and political governance whereby each clan had its function in the community and their special place in ceremonies. (See the footnotes of the Reva Chapman interview for a description of the clan functions.)

[2] The man her mother married was "Boodoo" (William) Catfish, Celia's stepfather, whom she considered her father.

[3] The government boarding school in Lac du Flambeau. It was a common practice for the police to forcibly remove children as young as five and six years old from their homes to attend boarding school. In the second part of this interview Celia describes how Aniwabi, a medicine man and their next-door neighbor, hid her under a bed when the policeman came for her. Later that day the policeman returned, found her swinging in a backyard swing, and took her to the school. According to Celia, the Indian policeman who took her away from her home was murdered several years later, and the suspect was never found.

[4] Flandreau Indian Boarding School in Flandreau, South Dakota, which many children attended after graduating from the Lac du Flambeau Boarding School. (See also the Reva Chapman interview.)

[5] Most government boarding schools were free. As Celia states, however, Flandreau charged a tuition of $36 a year, which was a hardship for many families. Many sent their children there during the Depression years, because it was seen as a haven for their children at that time, as they received housing, clothing, and regular meals as well as an education and job training.

over there, but you had to pay your way. You have to serve four years when you made out your application to go. You had to sign for four years, and then you could come home. And they'd send you back again. But you had to pay your own way. We couldn't afford that. I think it was only about thirty-six dollars, but gee that was hard. It was hard times, during the Depression. So you stayed over there. I came home.

I couldn't talk English. Boy I had a hard time. I was telling Reva.[6] Gee, I said, we think back now, you know. And then you'd go home in the summer. You'd be there all winter, in school learning English. You're having a hard time, you're being punished: "You got to do that." Then you go home. And my grandma—she was my step-grandma, but we'd call her grandma—you know, she wouldn't answer you when you talk English. Just quiet. She wouldn't even look at you. Then finally it dawned on me. Geesh! I tried her out, answer her in Chippewa, she started talking to me. She said to me, "When're you gonna wake up? Talk. You want to talk to me, you talk the way you were taught to talk." So I continued talking Indian.

I used to like to follow her all the time. She used to do different things, you know. What I was really interested in was, she used to make mats in the prettiest designs. I liked colors then. I used to watch her. I'd go with her on the boat; we'd go up the river. She'd go and get those reeds, and it was just like she was in a store, you'd say now. She'd look them over, look at them, and "somebody's been here," and we'd go to a different place again.

We had to row, I had to row her in a rowboat, flat-bottomed. We'd go down, and after awhile she'd take out our lunch, and she'd have tea and bread. Sometimes we'd have grease on it with onions. We'd have our little lunch and drink our tea. Then we'd come back again. The boys would have to take her reeds uptown. And she'd set them up, and she had a place there by town. It was on a table. She'd set them up there and dry them. Then she'd dye them different colors.

That's when I remember. One time I rebelled. I was a little afraid of rowing that old boat, you know. She wanted me to go with her to that rock.[7] It was in the spring, I guess. We were going to go make sugar. That's what we all ready for, getting ready, but she wanted to go over there first. So while they were loading up, her and I went. I was mad going there. I was sulking I suppose. So while we were over there she started talking to me. She told me, "You're offering tobacco right there. It's not nice to be like that." The way I was. She knew, you know. So I asked her, "How did you know I was mad?" She said, "I can tell. The way you act." She said, "That's not nice, don't act like that any more. You knew we were coming over here." She said, "We're going way out in the woods." She said, "We have to ask for protection, you know, to have a good sugar." You know, what we were going after. And she said, "We're going to be on the water; we have to put our tobacco down."

_____

[6] Reva Chapman, her "chum" as she always called her, was Celia's best friend ever since they attended boarding school together as young children. They also taught together in the Ojibwe Language Program for many years along with Joe Chosa.

Ruth Bell (Jim Bell's second wife) holding dyed reed mat, unidentified man on right

I told my mom when I come back, she said, "Good for her." Then she'd take my hand. She told me she was glad. After that I used to like to go with grandma. Because my mother told me, "She's teaching you. She's not being mean to you." I thought she was trying to be mean to me. But she wasn't; she was teaching me. So that's why I give credit to her, [for] a lot of things that I do now, you know.

I wish, oh many times, I wish I would've paid more attention. Because there's other things I remember seeing her do. Like when she'd tan hides. I'd hold my nose, and I'd run through that shed, you know. Ho! Because that's where she'd have them, in pails. Then she'd want me to go and pick that rope up for her, and I'd take off. Go across the bridge and see those girls. We'd always play outside, go swimming. I'd run away I guess. But I wish I would've stayed and seen what she did in between that time, because when I'd come back she'd have it all laced and on a frame.

She'd say, "Do you want to do this or that?" I'd say, "Show me how," and she'd show me. But in between I lost what she did. Different things, you know. That knowledge you know, you think about it. There isn't many people that can do that. In a few years it'll be lost. Because I know a lot of people in Milwaukee; they take deer hides, maybe two, three sacks, and take it to Milwaukee.

Take it to a tannery so they're done. Because nobody does that anymore. That's going to be a lost art. Hopefully. . . . I know someone who does that, I'd like just to watch them. There's a lady up near Cloquet, she still does that. I'd like to see her, go up there. When they have their pow-wow, maybe I'll go and see.

Do you know? That last night those kids were here. I've got pretty near . . . thirteen great-grandchildren. The boys, they come here, there's about nine of them. But the girls, the little girls, came, they were in there eating cake and ice cream. I got some stuff for them. I wanted to take a picture of all of them. And I said, "My goodness where did you all come from?" I didn't even pay attention to them! I'd see them, but I never counted them. I knew they were all there, you know. Then that little kid said, "Come on and sleep in with us! You can do your puzzles, your jigsaw puzzles." So I said OK. I was telling Joe:[8] "My gosh, I said, I didn't think there was that many!" That's why I said, I hope I can do a little more teaching. . . . That's what I want, somebody, anyway, to learn. Because jeez, I'm in my eighties now, so—I won't live forever. Figure that out.

I was telling Joe that. "Yeah," he said. "We've got to do something." That's why we're disappointed we didn't get that school [referendum passed].[9] We were wishing they would because the kids have no room of their own there, to drum and dance. And they're doing their culture there. They have to go way in the dining room and do their stuff there, right on the tables. They have no place to put their things, you know—you could go over there and see their drawings, their pictures, who's doing the best, things that like, listen to them sing. But they have no place for that now. They had a room, but it had to be taken from them because they didn't have enough classrooms. So that's what Joe, Reva, and I were talking about, we sure want that for their kids. Because you could see in the future they should have a place of their own. That was kind of a disappointment.

*   *   *

What we need is funding. We need it for the culture; we need it for the dance and drum outfit, for the Indian language too. They could've had storytelling there, legends. There isn't any kids that know legends. My kids, the little boys, they always sit in the room, you know, and I tell them legends. The other night I scared the heck out them! I told them about Esiban; that's Raccoon. And the crawfish. He let all them little ones, the crawfish, eat him, you know, pinch him. He was waiting for the big ones; he didn't want those little bitty ones. He wanted those great big ones.

_____

[7] "That rock" refers to Medicine Rock, a sacred site in Flambeau Lake, where tobacco is traditionally offered in the spring and fall. (See Introduction.) Celia notes later in the interview that the year her grandmother did not make this offering was the year that four boys drowned, including her grandson.

[8] Joe Chosa, Celia's friend and fellow Ojibwe language teacher, who currently directs the Ojibwe Language Program. (He is also interviewed in this collection.)

[9] This referendum to increase property taxes in order to expand the Lac du Flambeau Public School would also provide a classroom for the teaching of Ojibwe language and culture. It was eventually passed.

He let them pinch him. And those kids would go [shrugs her shoulders], you know, shake their shoulders. [laughs] They know things.

Then I tell them about things they used to tell us when they're making maple sugar. They had a Birchbark Lady and an Owl,[10] come and take you, snatch you, if you don't behave. A big one, in that wigwam out there. When we were making sugar, we had to be quiet. And I told them, "It wasn't only that long time ago, even before grandma's time, my time, we had to be quiet. Babies couldn't cry; they had to learn to be quiet. Because there was some people that were after us."

And I told them they're called the Sioux. In Indian we'd call them Bwaanag. They're an Indian tribe to the west of us. Past Minnesota. Stayed there. Some of them were in Minnesota, and we fought them, and they went back. That's where they are now. In them days, they'd try to sneak up. Kids had to be quiet, because the kids were crying like they are now and running wild like you kids do, I said, they'd have found us. Cut your heads off. [laughs] Bwaan, that's Sioux.

I had a lot of friends when I went to Manitoba. I was sitting there you know; they were dancing. You know Chippewas, we go clockwise.[11] This one guy, I was sitting there looking at him, he was going the other way. So I said to Reva, "Look there's Sioux." She said, "Oh!" We were sitting close to him. So when he was coming, I hollered. I put my fan up and I hollered, "Wuh! Bwaan!" And he looked up at me, he started laughing, and he started dancing in front of us, you know, showing off. After that he come, and he said, "You know that's the first time Chippewa ever said that to me." I said, "I noticed you, you're the only one out there going the wrong way!" He said, "How about you people, you're going the wrong way!" [laughs] You know there's little things like that. We had a lot of fun with that.

*   *   *

My mother came from Sault [Ste. Marie], Canada Sault. My dad's people came from LaPointe. That's where they all came from, I guess. They sent a delegation up to Canada, and from there they must have met. He must have been with Chief Buffalo. I was just reading it there; boy they had a hard time.[12] They got stuck in Detroit. They had to put on a little show to make money to get further. See, they went from LaPointe right down the lake to the Sault; they picked up more delegates there. And they went on. They ran out of money in Detroit, and they put on a show or

---

[10] These stories about Owl and Birchbark Lady were traditionally told by parents to their children at bedtime in the wigwam at sugarbush and later in homes to encourage them to be quiet. As Celia says, long ago the Sioux were in the region and might attack Ojibwe encampments if they were discovered, hence the importance of children being quiet. We see how Celia was teaching the children not only traditional Ojibwe stories, but Ojibwe history as well. She loved telling stories to children, both as a parent, grandparent, and a teacher of Ojibwe language and culture.

[11] At a pow-wow or ceremonial dances Ojibwe people (Chippewa is another term for Ojibwe, which Celia uses here) traditionally dance clockwise around the circle, while Sioux people (Bwaanag in Ojibwe) dance counterclockwise.

[12] See footnote six in the Ben Chosa, Jr., interview for more information on the Chief Buffalo mission.

Celia Defoe, left, with friend and fellow resident Hazel Ellickson at Bayfield sanatorium

something. That's when they were trying to move us out of Wisconsin. Chippewas. We wouldn't be here now. We'd be maybe in the west or in Canada. But Chief Buffalo went and pleaded and promised—I don't know what he promised. And they let us stay! That's in a book. That's not a lie; that's the truth.

*   *   *

It's nice when you have family right here. I don't think I could go any other place. I was married and lived in Bayfield, you know. But I took sick, I had TB, and I was in a sanatorium,[13] in and out for about nine years. I'd go home, my kids were small, and I'd go home. I know what happened. I'd be carrying water. You know those things you put on, you carry two pails? Then I had to wash my hands; I'd have to heat my water on the stove, or heat it outside on the big kettle, you know. Then wash clothes. It was too much, it was my breakdown. First thing I know, I'd see that nurse coming; I'd say oh-oh. They'd take the kids again. My two oldest boys would just go in Pipestone. But the young ones, they'd stay with their family in Bayfield. Finally that's when I had surgery. I had my upper lung taken out. It would heal, and as soon as I'd start working again it would break out.

---

[13] At this time it was not unusual for Native and non-Native people to contract tuberculosis as there was no vaccine available until Jonas Salk developed one in the 1950s. Because it was a highly contagious disease, those who contracted it were confined to a sanatorium, like Celia, who stayed in the Bayfield sanatorium off and on for nine years, as she states.

Just think, nowadays you don't have to go through that, you just get a vaccine. They don't even bother. They say it's coming back, that people that have that AIDS, they catch that so quick. Us, they put us in a sanatorium in Bayfield. There was a lot of people from Flambeau there that were sent there too. A lot of them died there. Once one that I know that was there was Eddie Poupart. One day I got a call, I was working at the school, and he said he wanted to see me out at the sanatorium. I always used to get a scared feeling, you know.

So I went out there, and there he was. I'd look at him, I'd say, "What are you doing here?" He'd say, "What do you think!" [laughs] He said, "I called you, I want you to bring me some snuff, you know, tobacco." I said, "You've got to be careful with it; you've got to spit in your spit bag." "Yeah, I know. Because they live in Milwaukee, my people. It's too far for them to come see me. It's closer here." So I said, "Yeah, OK."

He said, "And make some bread, some lugalate, and put a lot of grease, salt, pepper, and onions. And bring it! I'm so hungry." So the next evening I went out and laughed. I got some soft bread, and I fried it, and I took it out to him, that lugalate. And he laughed! "Oh my gosh," he said. "I'll buy you some flour, you come again. Come every Sunday and bring me that." So the next Sunday I went, his aunt was there. No, that was his mother, Josephine. I told her. "Yeah," she said. "He was telling me." She said, "He wouldn't tell me that!" She said, "I could've brought some." He said, "Well Celia brings it, it's nice and warm, you have to come all the way from Flambeau!" he said. [laughs] You know things like that. I laughed. Yeah, there was quite a few there from here.

And you know, at that time I must've had that when I was younger, and then when I was having kids, that's when I broke down. See that pushes your lungs up. And after your baby's born it goes down, that's why it opened up. That's the way they thought I had it the first time. I must've had a scar. I must've caught it from somebody and didn't know, hina? Never got it X-rayed. That's what the doctor thought. How we had it! And then when I had the babies, it pushed up, and my lungs were opened. Then working hard. . . .

*   *   *

I was born in 1916 in Ashland. I lived here until I was eighteen and then I got married. And I must have lived there for about ten years. My husband died; I was married about five years when my husband died. And then I was there five years, and I started having trouble with TB. And then I got well. I came back here because my mother was here. She was still living. She said, "You've got to learn to stay by yourself, you know that?" I said, "Yeah, I know that." Because like now, they'd be out camping. They'd be trapping and making sugar. And she thought I couldn't do that, because I had those five kids. "No," I said. "I can do it." And then when she died, I broke down again. I had to go back. Then I got out, that's when I went to Milwaukee. I was there about ten years. Then my friend wrote to me and told me, come back to Bayfield. And she said, go to school. So I went back to school. And I finished cooking. And I applied for the job and got it—cooking. I cooked nine years then. For Holy Family.[14]

Every summer I went to school in Stevens Point, Eau Claire, and Rice Lake. I had to go to school every summer, take me up to different—what you call cooking [school]. I cooked for 175 kids. And I had just one woman. She was on some kind of assistance; she had to work for that and she worked with me. Just her and I. We had to cook for them sisters, you know. That's why when I go back to Bayfield, I see all those guys and girls, they're all grown up. Married and kids, you know. But then I quit.

I retired, and we got along. When I was sixty-two I retired, that was in '79. I was getting along real good, you know. Then this time I had two heart attacks. So Jackie went and got me. I come back here, and I've been here ever since. . . . I like it. It gets kind of lonesome sometimes though. Even Reva says . . . the ones we grew up [with] that are our age, they're all gone. There isn't very many left. There's Reva and Maxine [Decota], she's younger than us, and Josephine Jack [Doud], she's younger than us. And of course there's Dorothy Poupart, she was a teacher when we were in school. She used to be years older than us. She wanted to start that Nokomis Club again.[15] She said, "Why did we quit?" I said, "We all got sick!" Reva got sick, she had that ulcer taken out. And I had a triple bypass and different ones. And it just fell away. We used to meet on a certain day; we'd all be together. We'd take turns, we'd have it at my house or Reva's, different places we'd go. Then we quit that, and we went out to the Elk's Point. We went out there, and out there, a couple of the women that had belonged to our club, they died too. They got sick and died. The rest of us, we could never do like we used to.

*   *   *

There's Milton,[16] Lawrence, Jackie, and Vernon, the youngest.

*   *   *

---

[14] Holy Family is a Catholic grade school and church in Bayfield near the Red Cliff reservation.

[15] The Nokomis Club (*nokomis* means 'grandmother' in Ojibwe) was a club formed by elderly women who got together regularly at each others' houses to work on crafts such as beadwork, crocheting scarves and afghans, knitting mittens, and sewing quilts, shirts, and outfits. They often donated the items they made such as lap afghans to elderly people, outfits to dancers, and baby blankets to expectant families, or sold their crafts and baked goods to raise money for different projects. One Nokomis Club project was to raise funds for building a nursing home on the reservation, a project that was still in progress when the club disbanded. (See also the Josephine Doud and Georgian Kinstedt interviews.)

[16] Milton Peterson, Celia's eldest child, was born in 1932 and passed away in January 2000, just four months before his mother's death.

Celia Defoe and her children Vernon, Jr., Jackie, and Eddie

I remember the government school there, and then summertime they'd let us out. Sounds like we were in prison! [laughs] We went home for vacation, and I lived right in town. I was just thinking, you could see across the lake, you now. Kids'd be standing by the tree looking . . . thinking, you know. They tried running away, you know, and they'd get caught. In ways, now when I look back, the discipline was harsh. But we learned things too. That's where we learned to fix bread and keep our house clean, keep your clothes clean. And when we were sick, we were taken care of. We all had children's sicknesses, there were not just one or two but sixty or seventy kids who all had mumps or the measles. I remember one time we were all in the gym, I was right under that basket thing. Those kids would make a big ball, you know. The first time I got mad because they hit me. I was laying there, I was still sore, I had a rag around my head—I must've had mumps. I got mad, I was chasing them kids. We never tried to hurt each other. We'd hit each other, but we wouldn't try to do you in, you know, anything like that. It got so you were like all sisters. That's the way it was, you know. It still was like that after we left. I felt a great loss when Vangeline[17] died, you know. She laughed, she said, "You know Celia, I know when it's somebody I went to school with," she said. "They never call me Girlie, they call me Vangeline!" "Yeah, we got used to that," I said. And that's the way we'd say—"Oh Vangeline!" And she'd look. "I knew that was you," she'd say.

---

[17] Evangeline Valliere, who attended boarding school with Celia. In later years her nickname was "Girlie." Celia also talks about her in the second part of this interview.

When May died I felt the same way, May Thompson. And Marie. And when what's his name died here not too long ago, that Tittle, Stanley? Joe said he misses all them guys. They're all gone. You look around, you get kind of. . . .

We were laughing. Sometimes we think about things, you know, we talk about—especially at night we used to walk around Flambeau. There was no lights. You'd see lanterns, you know, kerosene lanterns. When somebody had a flashlight, oh they'd show it off, you know. That's something. [laughs] You were rich! My stepfather had one because he trapped, you know, and sometimes he'd go on along and look at his traps during the night, and he'd reset them. He had to do that, maybe two or three—especially if they'd go out and stay. Then on moonlight nights you could see good. But you never heard of anybody fighting, or raising heck or anything, you know.

Then we'd all go back to school. I remember one time, I must have been in fifth grade or so There was three of us, we took ourselves back to school. My mother was so mad at me. She said, "You were supposed to watch your brother." I said, "I watched him." I said, "I put him to sleep." I said, "You said we had to get back to school, and youse weren't here. So I went back to school." She got there later in the evening—I knew she was going to get there.

They took us to church, you know, we had to go to church. Some would one way, and the others'd go the other way [to the Protestant or Catholic church]. We'd march to church like little soldiers. They had two different rows. The next year you may be going to the other, you may be going that way! You didn't choose where you wanted to go, you went where they told you. That's why I say, it's pretty hard to, that's why a lot of them—you weren't like, when you once went that way, to keep going that way. Some were lucky, they did.

It was nice not to show your emotion. I think that's why a lot of them older ones are like that. They don't show what they're thinking. You could be talking your head off, and they ain't even listening to you. I used to say that, that's the way we were brought up at the school. Because if you showed your emotion, they were going to do the opposite from what you want to do. So that's why we learned that. Then when you're at home, what you learn, the teaching—you keep that to yourself. And when you get to be a woman, you teach only your family. You don't go out telling everybody. That's why a lot of people, when they go around, they don't say anything. You're supposed to save the culture.

But Joe talked to us, me and Reva. He said, "You know, if you don't tell everything, there's things if you don't want to tell, it's too sacred, you just keep it in your family. But there's some things you have to tell because who's going to know after we're gone? Because the people now," he said. "There's a lot of them who say well, why should my kids learn to talk Indian? Because they're not going to use it. They're not going to make use of it, why should they learn?" After I heard that, that's when I started to think, you know. Might as well tell something, you know.

I got a big picture like that of the government school. My granddaughter [Sharon] has it. The one that lives in Glidden. I have my little head circled. She said, "When'd you do that?" I said,

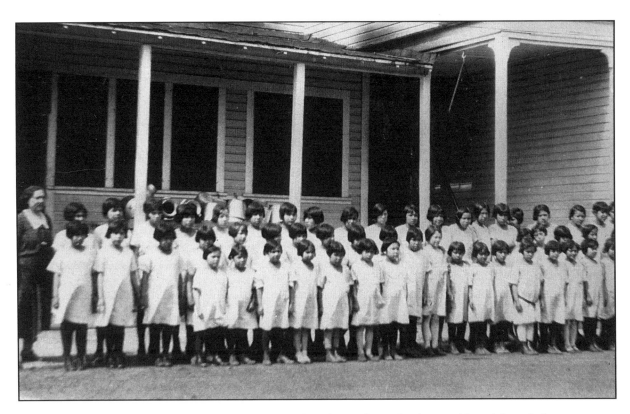

Girls at government boarding school, Celia Defoe in back row, 6th girl from left

"I used to do that a long time ago." See it was just this one little picture, you know, and then they had it enlarged. I told her different ones that I knew in there, so she marked them, put the names on the other side. It's none of those they've got over here.

My aunt used to take pictures, my Aunt Sophie. She cooked here for the school for a long time. She was married to Milton St. Germaine, Big Louie's brother. And the boys are good to me, the sons of Milton's. And then his daughters are living, Koosie, Jeri Kay. So I've got quite a little family, a lot of little ties I've got. She cooked here for thirteen years. She cooked first up at that other school, you know, where Niijii was? Then when they got that building, what they tore down, she cooked there. Sophie, she passed on in '63, someplace around there. Her name was Cartwright. She married a guy from Baraga; she lived there for a long time. Then when he died she came here, and she married Milton St. Germaine. That's how come Milton's got that name Milton. She wanted me to name him that. So her children are stepchildren. But they're like hers, because their mother died when they were little kids, and the little boys were in a foster home. And when her and Milton got married, they let them come back home. And she had the boys. That's Jimmy, and one boy got killed, Bobby. He got killed in Germany when they were making that—that [Autobahn] drive. Bobby Bullet [St. Germaine] says that's his dad, he told me. I said, "I don't know, I wasn't around here." He told me that, he come up to me one time. He asked me, you know, if that was my aunt. I said, "Oh yeah." He said, "Bobby was my dad." I said, "Oh." I said, "When I left here, I got sick, he was going with Dorothy Thoms." He said, "Oh, yeah?" I said, "Yeah, but I wasn't here. I was just telling you that; I was just teasing you." I said, "I wasn't here." So he gave me tapes, you know. Bobby St. Germaine always comes here, and he brings me deer meat and stuff. He packages it, you know. The other day he came and brought me deer meat. I thought it was tenderloin; he must have butterflied it. I said, "You know I'm all alone, nobody wants to eat deer meat." I said, "Give me small portions. I don't like to waste it." What I do is I give it away, like if they're going to have something going on, I'll donate. I'll donate a roast.

*   *   *

Do you know women hunted too? There was a bunch of women hunters around here. They'd go hunting. And they were all good sharpshooters too. They were all pretty near the same age. Good friends. They'd clean their deer and everything. One was Celia Boniash. Another was Josephine Burgess. We'd call her Bebiichii—that means "putting on shoes." Another one was Mary King. There was two others, I can't think of their names. Sometimes they'd go with horses. That's when back in the old Indian village—it's all grown up now—they used to call those "prairies." There was wild horses out there too. And I think that's where they used to go hunting. And they'd go down the river in canoes. Sometimes they'd go to McCord, or to Mole Lake; they'd walk all the way.

It was like an expedition, eh? Because when they'd come back, they'd have not only deer meat, they'd have other game. Beaver, zhigaag.[18] They'd skin them, you know, and then burn them. Not burn them, you know, singe them. The ducks, too, all the feathers, you know, they'd put them in one place, and they'd clean them. Then they'd, pretty near all of them did beadwork. Jose lived over here on Fence Lake, right across, further from where Yukon Tom's is. Josephine Burgess, her name was Josephine Peterson. And they'd all clean them up; they'd all have enough for each of them. Gee, I used to love duck.

They were married; some of them were married to baseball players. You know at one time Flambeau had a beautiful park, a baseball park?[19] Every Sunday there was a big time, baseball. You wouldn't think it. That old ballpark was just torn down not too long ago. It was right around back of the mall, the Ojibwe Mall is there, Jerry's. There was a ballpark there, with a big fence. I remember those guys used to make knotholes, and they'd watch. You had to pay to go in. You've seen the pictures of those guys, that's what I'm talking about.

---

[18] *Zhigaag*, which can also be spelled *chicog*, as in Chicog Street in Lac du Flambeau, means 'skunk' in Ojibwe.

[19] At the boarding school children learned to play baseball, basketball, and other sports. They continued to play the sports as adults, and they even taught them to younger people. The Flambeau Indians baseball team played in the 1920s and 1930s in a ballpark with covered wooden bleachers located in the field between the Ojibwe Mall (the tribal grocery) and Jerry's Pizza, a restaurant owned by Jerry Maulson. The baseball park was formerly the site of a planing mill during the logging era in the early 1900s. There are photos of the baseball and basketball team in the William Wildcat Tribal Center.

The Flambeau Indians baseball team

Lac du Flambeau basketball team

Same way with basketball teams.[20] From young kids to older men, they all played basketball. They were good. Those colored teams came here a couple times. What's that one now, the Harlem Globetrotters, they came here. And the Ethiopians. That's how those guys learned all them moves, you know. They used to say, "Make it swish!" They'd [makes a swishing sound] shoot from way long ways; they were good at it. Circling that, rolling that ball all over, they learned all that from them guys.

* * *

My brother served [in the military] in the same place that Joe served.[21] That's what Joe talks about, my brother. He met him overseas, and they used to talk Chippewa. He said, "We would've been like them code talkers." Where they were that guy was either too lazy or he didn't like Indians or something. It never materialized. That one guy wanted it, you know. Joe just laughs.

* * *

You know at one time you knew everybody. Oh, there couldn't have been very many people. If there was three or four hundred people, that was a lot of people. But now—holy cow!—there's lots of people. You knew everybody, you knew when somebody was, you know—we knew when somebody died, because they'd toll the bells. Churches would—we knew the different sounds, Catholic church bell would be tolling, if they were Catholic. If that Protestant church bell tolled, they were Protestant Indian, or Indian that didn't have a religion. They buried them over there though. Catholics were the only ones—well you know what they do, they bless their ground.

I was Catholic. I haven't been to church for—I didn't get no ride. I just quit. I'd go Easter, Christmas. But it don't bother me anymore because I figure I do my praying too. It counts just as much. Sometimes the kids get mad at me, but I tell them, well let's just leave it if we can.

The changes I've really seen, and it isn't just me—the housing has improved, and people are interested in dressing. You know, they dress nice. More drinking. In our day there was no taverns on the reservation. And then people were always helping each other. It always seemed like, like they used to say, we're related to everybody on the reservation. They used to say that you know. They wasn't literally, what they meant was I've got friends all over the reservation. And those friends were just like family, extended family, that's what they meant.

---

[20] The Lac du Flambeau community basketball team was a popular team begun in the 1950s by local businessman and promoter Mike Aschenbrenner. As a team they did quite well, often scoring over a hundred points in a game, and they played many national teams including the Harlem Globetrotters.

[21] Joe Smart, Celia's brother, served in the Army with Joe Chosa, also interviewed in this book.

Because anybody I talk to [says] be good to the older people. Because they came a long way, you know. They were on a long road. You don't answer them back. If you want to answer them back, keep it to yourself. It's always good advice. I don't care what you say, or what anybody else says. I think Flambeau has come a long ways. Like they're teaching the young now, respect. If you can catch all of them, kids I think will get along better in school too. Teach them to respect, no matter who they are, teachers, anybody, they're older than you. Respect them. I think they'd get along better.

But we can't do that all at one time. It's got to be gradual, you know. We're trying to teach them. It's nice that they respect people. They do, you know, respect older people. There's a lot of them, like when they have pow-wows, those kids want to wait on you right away. I always tell them, "No," because I don't want everything that they got. "Thank you," I said. "I like that, really. But it's just the idea. I can't eat everything, and I don't know what's up there." I said, "I'll go get it myself." "Oh OK. That's good."

But you've got to explain. I notice that, if you just said no, they get kind of . . . you know. And I don't blame them. I told Reva one time, I don't blame them. They think that you don't want them to do that, or that you're being disrespectful to them. So you tell them, nice, "I can't eat everything, I'll go up." "OK, OK, that's alright." And then they go on to somebody else. But otherwise, they look at you. [laughs] But lots of times, there is people that will have somebody go. But lots of times they tell you you've got to eat everything on your plate. But if they've got a place where they can put that stuff, well that's something else, eh? Because that's already blessed. You're supposed to eat everything you've got on your plate.[22]

*   *   *

People worked in resorts. Then people had gardens, and they hunted. And they say, "Well how did you keep your meat?" This was a big guy I was talking to him. I said, "You know when we lived in the village? We lived by Charlie Sunn then. And there was a big well. It was real deep. And halfway was like a cover. And under there they clean their deer, wash it good. Do you know that it kept cold down there and didn't spoil?" It was in the pump. And he looked at me and said, "You know Celia, I can't say you're lying. Because you know what? We did that just not too long, long ago." I said, "Yeah?" That's the way they kept their fish, too, you know. And then lots of times they dried and salted it. Sometimes they'd hang it; they'd be in there. They'd take that down and soak it in water, two or three times, get the salt out. Then they'd cook it, it was good. Same way with meat— they dried their meat outside. They'd make these. . . . Some had shelves and some had ladders above, some flat. Then they hung some way up high. This fire was going down below.

---

[22] At ceremonial feasts it is customary to eat everything on your plate, hence Celia does not want the children to give her too much, so that she will not have leftovers.

Thay'd dry that meat, like jerky, beef jerky. And then they'd store it. That had like, what do you call those . . . root cellars. They'd have berries; they'd make them in big jugs, and they'd put paraffin on top. If they didn't have paraffin, they'd put like a deerskin then tie it tight. Then they'd put it in that place. And they had potatoes down there, rutabagies, squash, all their stuff down there. It was nice.

But I was telling you about that deer. And I said, oh my dad would go hunting. He'd say, "All I need is one bullet." And he'd go hunting on Bear River. Pretty soon you'd see him coming; he'd have that deer on his shoulders. He must've been a strong guy, eh? We'd see him coming, and he'd hang it up. He'd have a place in the back, and he'd hang it up and you could hear that go [makes a ripping sound]. You could really hear him when he took that skin off. Then he'd cut the head off. Everything had pails there. Then he'd come in and ask what they wanted, you know. My gosh, I said, he never even cured that. We used to eat that, and he'd just killed it. I said, "I don't remember that we ever had a bellyache or anything, but we used to eat to beat heck."

That's one thing too. We'd eat great big meals in the morning. That's because they had to walk clear around the lake, like that Tower[23] up there? Rogers Creek. Then they'd go to Squirrel Lake, walk around. Then they'd sit and make a fire someplace and eat their lunch. While he's going after the traps, she'd start skinning them. Muskrats and beaver, whatever it was. And when he'd come, he'd starting putting them on—they'd have these boards they'd nail them on, stretch them. They'd turn the fur inside, and they'd tack them on these boards. And then they'd put them in great big bags, you know, like gunnysacks. That's what we ate. When they'd come home, she'd put maybe six, seven, maybe eight of them, wash them, put them in the oven, onions. We never bought onions either, we had those wild onions. Those are strong. And she'd put carrots in there. It was a good meal. That's the way they got along.

*   *   *

Indians never had Thanksgiving. But when we were going to school they had Christmas for us. We didn't even know what Halloween was. I was surprised when I came back and saw kids dressed for Halloween. When we were growing up we didn't know what Halloween was.

When somebody was named, or had their first kill [that was our celebration]. The naming ceremony. Then you'd have a spring dance, summer, fall, and winter. They'd celebrate those. Then when they'd have their Big Drum, and they had the Midewin. They had one in the village, and they had one in town.[24] It would be someplace there, you know where the nutrition center is? There was

---

[23] The tower refers to the former fire tower on Squirrel Hill, located off Highway 70 just south of the reservation line near Squirrel Lake. Rogers Creek is the creek below Squirrel Hill. Winterpark Ski Resort is now located on this site.

[24] "Big Drum" and "Midewin" were the two primary Indian religions in Lac du Flambeau (see Introduction). Celia refers to a Midewin lodge previously located in the village and also one in town, near the Elderly (Nutrition) Center.

a field there. That's where they had it. In the village; it's all overgrown now with trees. It used to be kind of a field, you know where Pouparts live there? Got trees all around their house, never used to be any in there. That's where they had that.

*   *   *

I didn't even know [when the Depression was]. I asked Reva. "I don't either," she said. "We were never hungry." Because we lived off the land. Only thing they bought was sugar, once in a while, lard. Flour. That's all, I guess.

*   *   *

Frank Sinatra was singing at that time, Dorsey Brothers, big bands, Glen Miller. The dance we all learned was the Charleston at school. Somebody came, I think that girl came from Carter, must have been Potawatomi. Showed us kids all how to do the Charleston. Wow, we used to do the Charleston to beat heck on the pavement by the school. We learned how to waltz. [laughs] Now I laugh! The boys had to learn how to dance too, you know. Just go right even with the room, turn over there and go way down that way, then turn over there, and go. . . . [laughs] Just make us squeal. I remember dancing . . . had a little band; we had to learn to dance. I suppose they wanted us to forget how to do that Indian dance, you know, the teachings that go with that.

*   *   *

I was told to stay away from there, that's all. And I got a pretty good licking one time. We lived in the village, a big bunch of us kids swam out there, to Strawberry Island. You know that's a long ways. We swam, and we'd touch a certain tree over there. Oh what we'd do! I'd swim just as close as I could. We'd touch that, and then we'd go back. Swim again. I'd dive waaay down and come up waaay past them. And one time we did that, and a snake chased us. You'd just see him coming. That's when I had to tell my mother. Boy, did I get it. "Don't you ever go there," she told me in Indian. "You disturbed those spirits." She said, "Don't go out there. You stay away from there." That's all she ever said to me: "Don't go out there. Stay away from there. Because you'll disturb them."

And then one time, I heard that's where they had a fight, out there. I wondered who was there, who was buried there. That was no older person that told me, it was a girl in school. She told me that's where they fought. "Had a big fight there," she said. "They chased those Indians way out. Had to send people there to bury them." A lot of women used to do the burying, because the men would keep going. They must be buried there. They ain't going to swim with a dead body way over to. . . . That's what I said, "They must have buried them there. They ain't going to have somebody roll them up in a canoe."

*   *   *

[Then there's] that stone, crawling stone. That's what they used to hear them call it, hina?[25] Now they call it something else. When we lived across there, sometimes it changes. You know, seems like it does crawl. But I think that's the water, goes down. But you look, and you point; that one tree is right back there. That's where that one is. No, now it's the other way. Could never figure that out. It seemed like it crawled. My mother said, "The water. It drops, and it looks like it's crawling. Then the water goes up again; it looks like it's. . . . " But I know that place was. . . . Went with Grandma there, and she went and put tobacco. For the water. Every spring she went—and every fall. And the year that she didn't go, she felt bad because that was the year her grandson drowned. She felt bad. It might've been that, you know. That's what she thought. Four boys, I think, drowned.

*   *   *

We were taught to respect older people. No matter what you had, share with them. Share with people that haven't got anything. They're not going to ask you for anything. If you know, share. Especially somebody that lost their parent or lost their child. You had to be good to them, you know. Share what you have, because what you have will be given back to you. More than what you gave.

Another thing was, listen to what your older people are telling you. Listen to what they have to say. Because they've come a long way. What they meant was, they've lived a long life. Some of them old people, they lived to be a hundred and four. Older! They came a long way, lived a long life.

*   *   *

I think they [human remains and sacred objects] should be brought back. Because it won't be too long that a lot of people are going to forget what went with that. Which ones they can tell for sure they've seen. You know that Sawyer? Their drum was taken.[26] They think the Creator took

---

[25] "Hina" is a form of the Ojibwe word "ina" which indicates a question is being asked. Variations of "ina" have been borrowed into regional English speech, and loosely translate to "isn't that so?"

[26] Sawyer, Wisconsin, is west of the Lac Courte Oreilles reservation (LCO).

their drum—they didn't listen. It was left in a gym. How was it left in a gym? It was left in a gym. It was locked up. They don't know how they got in.

Milton went, and he said they don't know who could've took it. They were here; they came here and asked for prayers. They're scared. I thought it was LCO, you know, and I asked, I didn't know just which one it was. You know why he got me mixed up; he said, "That boy was killed, and they did nothing about it." He said, "They're afraid to do anything, hurt somebody's feelings. They should've did what's right. They didn't." That's why I thought it was LCO. Then when Milton called I asked him. "No," he said. "It happened in Sawyer."

*   *   *

Pray to the Creator. And be good to your neighbor. And try and lead a good life. That's the main thing. Everybody has to believe in a god, the Creator, that's what we call him. That's the main thing. Because everything comes from there. And everything goes back there.

Not too long ago, I was talking to this old woman. I don't know where we were. I don't know if it was in St. Croix or over here in Watersmeet. I said, "What do you think of this cremating? Indians are being cremated. It's a cheap way. . . . " She said, "Well, I don't know about you, but I'll tell you something. You go back, and you look, read," she said, "the way we were told. We came from the earth, Mother Earth, and it says back to Mother Earth you go. We didn't say burn up your ashes. I don't believe in that," she said.

I thought about that before, that's why I asked her. She's an older woman; she's older than me. And I just wanted to know, because it's happening, you know. She said, "No, even if they have to get the cheapest thing there was, you know." She said, "Long ago, you can't do it now," she said, "but long ago, Indians were just wrapped, either in birchbark or a blanket. And a lot of them were buried here like that." Even me, when I was growing up, I've seen them. They'd wrap them, they'd prepare them, fix them. Dress them real nice in their Indian outfit. And then they'd wrap them up in a blanket and bury them.

In town, it's right near where the Niijii is there,[27] on the other side of that house, there's a building there, still stands, it's gray, near the bridge. That's where they started making boxes, for people that were buried. And a lot of people were buried. My mother said, "I'd rather be buried in that one." Old George Brown, he's the one that used to make those. They'd put a sheet in there, and a pillow. She said, "I'd rather be buried in that, because that's made so strong. You know, real hard wood." She said, "Them old caskets they got, they're just nothing but a little cardboard painted gray." She used to say that! [laughs] Because they'd help, like when somebody died, the ladies

---

[27] The Niijii Center, formerly the boys' dormitory in the old boarding school complex. The gray house Celia mentions here still stands next to the bridge across from the fish hatchery.

would go there and bathe that person and dress them. And they'd dance, you know.[28] Sometimes they'd dance all night! And they'd bury them first thing in the morning. It all depends on when that person died. If they died in the morning, they had to bury them before the evening. Before the sun goes down. Gee, he made beautiful boxes. He'd measure you. She'd say, "Those are good, and strong!" By the time it broke down, I suppose she meant there was nothing more of you left! [laughs]

Yep, that's all I've got to say to you.

*   *   *

Cecilia Defoe Interview, Part II

Editor's Note: The following interview was conducted at a later time by Beth Tornes. Celia had said that she wanted to talk more about the boarding school, so I went to her house one day with the tape recorder, and she talked for a very long time. These are some of the stories she told.

I remember that time, there was three of us, there was another girl, she was from Manistique,[29] I think. Her name was Pearl Nettle. And we were all pretty near the same size anyways, and she told us, she said, "Feel my head," she said. And her head was burning hot, and she said, "I can't breathe sometimes," she said. "Can you see if you can try and get someone to come and see me? You know, see if the matron will come." So them girls, they said, "Celia, why don't you try? You know, try, you can outtalk them." I said, "Well, I don't know. Remember, if I do go, you're going to get punished right along with me." They said, "That's OK."

So went to that door and I knocked and knocked and knocked, and pretty soon there was that matron. She was the head matron, but she was old, older, Mrs. Lee. . . . Everybody knows her. She came to that door and she said, "Now what's the matter? Who is this?" And I told her my name. I said, "Grace is sick. She said her head is just hot, and she can't hardly breathe." I said, "And she's making funny noises in her chest." She said [in a harsh voice], "What kind of noises?" I said, "It sounds like it's gurgling, and . . . making an awful noise, and she can't see us any more." Jeez that door fell open just fast. She had her flashlight, and she went flying down there, where that girl was. A little while after she went out, and after a little while the lights came on and this guy, they used to call him the night watchman, pretty soon I seen him. I was so. . . . I ran and jumped in my bed, you know, but I was peeking at him, first time I seen him pushing her bed out. Pushed all

---

[28] Traditionally, before a funeral the women wash and dress the body of the deceased in their best traditional clothing and beadwork, and a new pair of moccasins, to prepare them for their journey to the spirit world. The wake often goes on through the night, as she describes.

[29] Manistique is a small town on Lake Michigan in the Upper Peninsula of Michigan about 170 miles due east of Lac du Flambeau.

Older girls at boarding school, 1915, several years before Celia attended

the beds over this way and then they pushed her bed out. Then another girl, her name was Nancy McCulley, I guess, she was a cousin to that girl. She started crying. She says, "You know what I think?" I said, "What?" She come back and she was by me, you know. They locked that door and put a padlock on it again, locked us in. She said, "I think Grace is dying. I heard that noise once before," she said. I never heard, you know, I never come in contact with anybody like that. And I said, "Couldn't be." You know. So that same night they took her, and I think they even took her cot along, and they put it on a train. They met that train and it went clear to Ashland.[30] On the way to Ashland she died.

They said it was me, and my mother—it was just awful—she come flying up there, you know, started raising Cain with everybody, and they said, "No, she's in there." She made them open that door so she could see me. I just grabbed her, and I start crying. I said, "That was my friend they took, where'd they take her? She said, "They took her to Ashland, she's real sick." She didn't tell me she died. And she said, "You better go to sleep now," she said. I said, "Gee. What happened to that little girl?" She said, "I don't know." I said, "We woke up, she was calling us." And I told her, "You know, she was making funny noises in her chest," I said, "Just gurgling, like water, you know . . . like it's bubbling, you know? Like a funny noise." And I said, "And her head was just hot, and then she couldn't see us," I said. "Then just forget about it," she said. And she left, and

---

[30] Ashland, Wisconsin, about ninety miles northeast of Lac du Flambeau on Lake Superior, was the location of the closest hospital at the time.

they locked us back up again. And a couple days later I heard that girl had died. She must have had pneumonia! They just never took care of anybody. They didn't have no hospital in them days. They had one later on, when I came back from Flandreau; they had a hospital, the first Indian hospital. Right across from the Niijii there? There used to be a building across there. Upstairs is where they had like a hospital. But that was way later, it was about ten years after that. But when we were going to school . . . jai, wonder if that building ever caught fire, how would we ever get out of there? Over a hundred girls sleeping. That dormitory, it was about from here to the lake I guess long [she nods towards Fence Lake, about 150 feet away]. Just one stairway. Supposed to have a fire escape, but I never seen it. That was terrible.

But there was one guy, he was from Red Cliff, his name was Mr. Gurnoe.[31] And he was good to us kids. He'd talk Indian, while we were eating? He'd tell us, "Hurry up! Wewiibit'aan, wiisinin!" he'd say. He was a disciplinarian for the boys. And there was another girl—she must have been a young girl, she must have been only about eighteen. Her name was Miss Boyd. She wasn't there very long; she got sick. They said she had TB, and she disappeared. But we used to have a lot of fun with her. In the morning, they'd open that door. She'd come flying, she'd be all dressed, and she'd say [in a loud, lively voice], "Come on, come on, you Indians, hit the deck, hit the deck! Come on, come on, [starts clapping] let me see them little brown feet going!" We'd have a lot of fun, we'd giggle and laugh. She made our day I guess, you might as well say. You got up with a nice . . . you know. They could have all done that! Then poor thing, she got sick. They said she had TB. She just come from, she came about the same time that a lot of them teachers came, and secretaries. Like there was one, her name was Dorothy Yellow Calf. She married a Stuart, later on, I guess, here. And that girl, she was real nice. I don't know if she was studying to be a nurse, or something, must have been, she came to us when we were sick. We'd line up you know, and she'd give us all cough syrup. Or you'd get in another line if you had, if you were constipated. And you'd get Castoria![32] [laughs] A lot of kids just used to like to get in that line so they'd get Castoria, give you the runs! [laughs some more] Then another line, we all had to go through, they'd give us— what's that stuff that tastes like fish?—cod liver oil! Some kids could drink that just like. . . . They just loved that! I suppose that fish taste, you know. They'd take a whole, ugh, I'd just hold my nose! She'd say "Take it, take it, you won't catch cold, you won't be sick." That's the only reason that I took it.

Yeah, there was many a time that . . . and then you had to make your bed. You had to roll your blankets just so; they had to be perfect. Your undersheet, it had to be pulled just tight. And you had to have your corners, square corners. Didn't have no pillow. That old red blanket and then a sheet, they had to be just fixed just so, and then you roll them, in a square, at the foot. Then they lined up your, straight, those beds had to be even lined, like when you got through making your bed

[31] Red Cliff Chippewa reservation, 115 miles northeast of Lac du Flambeau on Lake Superior.

[32] Castoria was a popular laxative, so named for its key ingredient, castor oil.

you had to line it up with the next bed. Had to be just straight, otherwise they'd come along; they'd tear the whole thing apart; you had to do it all over again. Then you had to make it to the line! They didn't give you time, what they tore up. . . . Boy, I learned to make my bed good, boy. I made sure that everything was good. Some of those kids, I used to feel sorry for them. Get their bed all torn up, then they'd get punished.

That's another thing they used to make us do, make us kneel in the hall. One time, just for laughing! [exasperated sigh] I didn't laugh! That's what I'd say, "I didn't laugh, I was just smiling!" Oh. . . . Those kids used to tell jokes in Indian, under their breath, you know. It sounds funny. Crazy, and you'd smile. And you'd get punished for that! And you'd say, "I wasn't laughing, I was just smiling." That didn't go either, you was laughing, that was laughing. Had to kneel in the hall with your hands up in the air like that [lifts her arms straight up] and kneel . . . for hours! Sometimes your hands, they'd just go to the wall. . . . [in a harsh voice] "Up straight, up straight!" And I'd just think, how in the world can she see out here? But she just [laughs] just must have figured, time, time they must be getting tired, yay, their arms would be going down again, yeah, put 'em all up again. Oh. It was just, just terrible.

One time those kids were telling us, too, three of them came from Bad River, Odanah?[33] They came to our school, and they said, "Oh boy, you got it made here. This isn't like it is at the Catholic school. The sisters' school? That's where they were going; that's where they were stuck. In Bad River, and Bayfield, they were put in convents, and they said the sisters, they said were just mean. They said, "We'd rather be here!" I thought it was terrible where I was! And when they could say it was worse yet! They'd tell you the awfullest things, you know. "Sure, because your grandpa or your uncle killed somebody for nothing, you're gonna burn too." Things like that you know. The nuns, they'd tell—how do they know [angrily] if that girl or that little boy's ancestors killed somebody? They don't know! And to tell somebody that, henh . . . that's foolish. That's what they said though. There was quite a few little girls and boys came from Bad River; they went to school here, the Wesleys and the Sharlows. There's still Sharlows, they stayed here and intermarried, they were all from Bad River. But they came here, and they went to school. And oh, that was . . . another time too. We weren't supposed to be outside, and them trucks came in? I don't know where I come from. I might have came from the laundry; I think I was over at the laundry. I worked in the laundry for about a month, and we had to hang baskets and baskets of clothes. That would be, you know where the Niijii is, this way, over where that building is. They've got some kind of plastics building,[34] back over there further there used to be a laundry. They had lines and lines back there going towards the lake. We had to fold them all up. And I was coming, and just as I got right in

[33] Odanah, on the Bad River reservation ninety miles northeast of Lac du Flambeau. The Ojibwe word *odanah* means 'town.'

[34] Here she describes the Simpson Plastics plant on Highway 47 and also the Niijii Center, both on the grounds of the former BIA agency and boarding school.

the front of where that road now turns to the road where it goes back. . . . That's where the girls' building was, in the front there, and in the back there was a big building, a meat house. On the side there was a building where they had steam and electricity. Anyway, I was just getting there, and them trucks, a big truck and a great big wagon, it stopped. So I stopped too. I was afraid of them horses; they were great big things. And the kids were getting all. . . . So I was watching them; they lined them up you know. That's the time I seen that, they lined them up and said, "You go on this side, and you go over here. You're Catholics and you're Protestant."

In the dining room you had to sit, eat, and get done. So this one girl. . . . We had prunes, you know we used to have prunes. I was eating. I liked mine, so I was eating mine. My friend sat at a different table than I did; we were good friends. And she had those, you know, those prune seeds? I must have been sitting like that, you know, and she was gonna get me right between the eyes. I must have moved, and I [laughs] . . . that matron just happened to be coming around, she got her on the forehead. And she looked at me, and I was busy eating, I wasn't. . . . And she looked over there, and she could see that girl was just all flustered, you know. She made her quit eating and stand up in the chair. She didn't bother me . . . but we had peanut butter, so I thought, "Oh gee, I'm gonna take some of that peanut butter, she's gonna be hungry." So I put it in my hand, and I was wishing I could get some bread. How in the world am I gonna get bread? I tried, couldn't get it, couldn't get no bread. Well I had that peanut butter anyway. So we, I waited. We all lined up anyway, going to march. So just as I was getting to where they were, you know the matrons, they pushed me aside. I thought, Uh-oh, what did I do know? She said, "Put your hands up." I don't know how that happened. Did she see me? So I had to put my hands up, and there was my peanut butter! [laughs] I had to scrape it all off and throw it in. . . . I don't know where I threw it, someplace, they told me where. And boy, we got a good licking that time. Both of us, she did, too, and I did too. But I was just trying to help her, you know. I figured she was going to be hungry because they took her before she could eat; she was playing with her prunes. She didn't get to eat. We just sat down, you know, and I started eating— I ate two or three prunes. You had to eat fast, otherwise you were gonna be darn good and hungry. That's why I thought, well I'll take her some; she'll have peanut butter anyways, and I didn't know how I was going to get bread.

Good thing I didn't take any, gosh. . . . Wow, did we get a good licking. I can just hear her screaming at Girlie; she got hers twice on the back. Just strapping her, strapping me too. But I, I didn't try to stand up or anything. I just let them hit me on the back. But her, she'd try to stand up, and she'd scream, because it hurt, you know. And she's crying just hard. And then later on, she told me, she said, "That's ok," she said. "I'm gonna tell my dad. And he said they'll just do this once more, and that's it." We were sitting way outside against the fence, you know, where nobody could hear us. It got so that there was some kids that would tell on you, because they figured they'd get in good with the people, you know? But you learned to, to kind of watch out, you know. You'd like—I don't know what it would be—and when you once made a friend, you stuck to that friend, because you figured, you know. . . . But boy, that's the thing, I never got a good licking like that again. But she said I was stealing, that's how come I got a good licking, because I was stealing. I told her, "I wasn't stealing." I said, "My friend didn't have anything to eat. She's gonna be hungry." "That's her business. She has no business playing with food. She's not supposed to be playing with food." You know they wanted to be so correct, too, you know. "God don't want you to be playing with food," you know. "You're not supposed to be playing with food." And yet, why are they holding that food back, you know? As small as I was, I used to wonder. You know, I couldn't get over that.

They brought that girl back. The one I told you that died? And I remember we went to her funeral. She's buried back of that Protestant church, in that graveyard? I don't know where that fence is now, but she wasn't too far from that fence. About two, maybe the second row, but it's all mixed up, and I wouldn't know now. That's where she was buried. I remember that so good. It was getting dark, and I was thinking, she shouldn't be afraid, because we were always in the dark anyway. You know? And I remember they were singing that song, what the heck was it, something about "Abide with me. . . . Fast bows the eventide, or evening. . . . I remember I was standing there listening. They let about ten of us little girls go to that funeral. But I always thought about that, you know. That was something that happened, that shouldn't have happened, you know? If we'd have had the right care, the right matrons taking care of us.

And a lot of people don't believe that they'd lock you up like that at night. . . . One woman, I was telling her that. She's from Germantown. And I was telling her—she asked me about government school. She said, "Did you have dormitories?" "Yeah," I said. "We had dormitories, but it was just one great big room. Then they locked you in there at night." And I said, "There was no heat! There wasn't any. And all you had was one blanket and a sheet." Yeah, that was a big dormitory. There must have been about seventy kids, seventy-five kids sleeping in there. I remember in the middle; those beds were just about that far apart. I remember one night I was sleeping just good, you know, and those kids must have been playing. I don't know what, I suppose they. . . . I woke up, and I kept saying, "Cut it out!" I was telling them. And they'd be quiet for a little while, and they'd start playing again. And they said [gasps], "There's somebody playing with us that shouldn't be here," she said. "Who is it?" They were trying to scare me, too, you know, or something. I wouldn't pay any attention to them. Finally the lights came on. They were sitting all under the bed! [laughs] I don't know what happened to them. I didn't want to know. Boy those . . . you know you can't help it, little kids going to bed so early. It's different when you work, you know, you work hard. Because we had to work. But they were a little younger than us. Company A was big girls, real big, then Company B. We were in Company C. There would be like Reva, Marian Sunn, and I. We were all pretty much the same size and the same age. We were all in that one group. Then there was younger ones yet. There was one little girl. We had to take care of one little girl in that first line. There was this one little girl; she was the smallest girl in the school, her name was Naomi . . . Van Zile. She died here not too long ago; she was married to Charlie Ackley. She used to come see me every now and then. I used to meet her at Foster Grandparents. For a long time she told me, "You know," she said. "For a long time I thought that was Celia Sunn that used to take care of me." I said, "No, that was me." "Really?" I said, "Yeah, you was the littlest girl in school. When you'd march way up ahead, I used to watch you. You used to lead them." You know, she'd be the first one marching. "I used to watch you," I said. "I had a hard time teaching you how to keep step." [in an excited voice] "I remember that!" she said. "I remember that, when yous were teaching me that!" I said, "And we'd sneak stuff for you?" "Yeah," she said. Crackers and little cookies, you know. We wouldn't eat it; we'd save it for her. She said, "Yeah, my mother died, and that's how come I had to go to school." She must have been only about three or four years old. I was five [when they took me away]. She said, "She's too young, she's just a baby yet." They said, "No, she's got to go to school." I was old enough to go to school.

*   *   *

That old man, Aniwabi. . . .[35] He's the one that tried to protect me when that cop came there, tried to take me to school? My mother wasn't home. He made me crawl under the bed and stay there. Oh, and I just sweat under there. After a while I peeked out and said, "Is he gone?" And he went outside and looked, and he come back. "You can go outside and play," he said to me, "On that swing. And if they come there, you come and tell me," he said. That cop, he must have been pretty darn sneaky, just grabbed me off of that swing and took me. My mother, when she got home, she went up to the school and tried to get me out of school. She said, "She's too young. She's just a baby yet." Huh-uh, she couldn't get me out. If they took me out of school, those people wouldn't get their rations, they wouldn't get their money, the little money that they got. That's how they did. That's terrible. Took the kids right off the roads. The kids were playing, and the first thing you knew they were at school.

 I remember that first night I was there, all night long, I'd sit up, and I had a sheet around my head. And I sat there pretty near all night. The next day all I wanted to do was sleep. Because you know, that was the first time I'd ever been away. I was just shaking, oh. . . . They cut your hair, first thing, then they took your clothes and put government clothes on you. Might as well say they . . . they told you you couldn't talk your language; they didn't want you to talk. . . . If you do, you're gonna get punished. "Talk English, that's the language you're gonna learn, that's what you're gonna do." Half of the stuff they told you, you couldn't understand. Why, you know, why is this happening? Why? And you know, my stepfather he was good to us, very good to us. He was more like my dad. That's the only one I did know. He came up there and boy, he bawled them people out. He said, "You had no business to do that. That little girl has never been away from her mother.

---

[35] Aniwabi, a medicine man mentioned earlier in her interview, who lived next to Celia's family and was an important influence in her life. She tells more stories about him on the tape of her interview, but they are not included here for reasons of length.

Aniwabi holding a feather

Aniwabi with bow and arrows

Why don't you pick up all them kids around here that got no place to stay? Those are the ones you should pick up, not those that have a home." But they wouldn't listen. Had to have a "good reason."

*   *   *

But I'll tell you one thing though. . . . I hope and dream, if anything happens to me, I hope my little ones never have to see that. But they keep taking things, taking things, you know. The world isn't that small anymore. It don't take long to get from one place to the other. That's why I always think, like that little boy that came in here? [her great-grandson] He was telling me; he was sitting there the other day, I was mad. Eez. He said that teacher took all his stuff, what he had on his desk. He was putting it all together and he was getting ready to go home, because they said, "Hurry up, the buses are lining up!" She got mad at something, and she took all his stuff and threw it in the wastebasket. And he wasn't gonna tell! But his friend told Jackie [Celia's daughter], and Jackie ran back, and she, she was gonna make that teacher dig all that stuff out. And oh, I was mad. I said to him, "Don't you ever do that again, hold anything back. You tell! If anybody's being mean to you. Don't be like I was." I said, "They taught me to keep my mouth shut. Don't do that," I said. "You tell! Let people know what's going on. I don't want you to go through what I went through. . . . I'll be watching out for you. As long as I'm here. After I'm walking on the red road, and you can't get me back, well that'll be something else!" [laughs hard] "As long as I'm around, I'll be there fighting for yous."

That's what I don't want to happen. I just don't want that to happen. I don't care what they do, everything else, but they shouldn't do that to the kids. Why can't those kids have something nice, you know? What we had was. . . . They stole our childhood, you might as well say, they took our . . . our innocence. They took that all away from us! We weren't no little soldiers! We were young children! You know? We should have been treated like young children. We were treated worse than big people. Like hostages. Look at all the spankings, and lickings, and dragging people by the hair. . . . That's no good! That shouldn't be done now in this day and age. I don't care what they say. It's time those young couples woke up and listened to what their kids have to say. That's what I keep telling my granddaughters, "When your kid says something to you, listen to them. Listen to what they have to say. They're saying something. They're telling you something. You should be interested."

Josephine Doud

Josephine Doud was born in Lac du Flambeau on June 16, 1917, to Joe Jack and Ida Ackley and lived here all her life. Her father was Prairie Band Potawatomi, from Kansas, and her mother was Lac du Flambeau Chippewa. She grew up living the traditional life with her family, hunting, trapping, fishing, making maple sugar in the spring, tanning hides, braiding rugs, and making beadwork. She learned many of these skills from her father and also from Mary Potts, her aunt, who raised her. Mary was blind, but very adept at Native arts and crafts and cooking, which she taught Josephine, herself a talented artist and a good cook. Josephine attended the Lac du Flambeau Boarding School and public school until she was seventeen, when she got married and started a family. She had thirteen children, seven of whom survived into adulthood. She was a fluent speaker of Ojibwe and often spoke it when teasing friends and relatives, which was a favorite pastime. She was a great kidder, and always made people laugh wherever she went. She was a founding member of the Nokomis Club, a group of ladies in the community who made beadwork, crafts, and baked goods. They gave them away or sold them to raise money for charitable purposes.

Josephine was famous in Lac du Flambeau for her beadwork, especially her moccasins, and she taught many in the community to make them. People would come to her continually with requests for a pair of moccasins, especially if they needed them for a family member's "final journey," as she called it, to the spirit world. It is traditional for a deceased person to have a new pair of moccasins for this journey. She stayed up many a night beading and sewing moccasins, often helped by her daughter "Wause" (Loretta St. Germaine). She continued making moccasins, "jiibik" charms, and tobacco pouches throughout the last years of her life, although it was increasingly difficult for her. She would always joke, "If they want moccasins after I'm gone, they're going to have to sit me up in my grave!" Josephine passed away on September 18, 1999.

Interview with Josephine Doud

This interview was conducted by Mildred Tinker Schuman.

My Ojibwe name is Naawakamig. That means "Level Ground." Bearskin gave that to me. I have two names. The other one is Endasogaabo.[1] I think old man Wesho, my grandfather on my uncle's side, gave me that name. It was when I was younger. So I'd know I was an Indian.

My father's name was Joe Jack. My mother's name was Ida Ackley. She was from here, one of the Ackleys. My dad was from Kansas. All my brothers and sisters are gone. I was born June 16, 1917, here in Flambeau over by Stearns Lake. When I was a child, I also lived with my aunt, Mary Potts. I've lived here all my life. I moved into this house in 1979.

My children are Loretta St. Germaine, James Williams—they're the ones in Flambeau. Chuck Burns lives in Minneapolis. Anthony Williams and Delores Williams are in Chicago. Ron Williams lives in Siren, Wisconsin.[2] And Edna Williams—she used to live with me. I lost her last summer; she was sixty. I still miss her. I would've had thirteen—the others passed away.

When I was a child I used to go help my dad. He used to go out and set traps for rabbits in the winter. I used to have to follow him, so I could know where they are. Then I'd have to go the next day and check up on his snares. He used to go hunting too.

I used to help him train his horses. My sister and brother were scared of them, too. They'd just cry when they were around those horses.

I'd help my dad pour sap, make trails. I used to watch him make the sugar, and stir it up, boil it, and stir it with those cedar boughs so it wouldn't boil over.

I used to watch my blind aunt scrape deer hides. Once in a while I'd help her scrape it. After, she'd stretch it out and let it dry, after she was done scraping it. I'd sit there and watch her make moccasins. She used to braid rugs. I used to help her tear rags. She'd ask me what color they were, and she'd roll them up in a ball and set them out just so. She'd know which was which—to keep track of the colors.

That was Mary Potts, Jerry [Maulson] and Tom's grandma.[3] That's where Jerry learned how to make those baskets. I'd help her cut moccasins. I'd cut them out, and she'd sew them. She'd tell

---

[1] Josephine's first name, Naawakamig, is short for Naawakamigogkwe, she told me at a later time. According to fluent elder Joe Chosa, this name literally means "In the Middle of the Earth Woman." She told me it was given to her by Bearskin (Makwayaan), a medicine man. This is the name she called herself as an adult. Her other name, Endasogaabo, means "Forever Standing," according to Joe Chosa. Her grandfather, "Old Man Wesho," who gave her this name, is also Billi Mae Chosa's grandfather, as she tells us in her interview.

[2] Her son Ron Williams, of whom she speaks, passed away in 1999.

[3] Jerry and Tom Maulson, Josephine's twin nephews. Their mother was Hannah Maulson, Josephine's cousin, who taught Ojibwe language at the grade school, and participated in the Wisconsin Indian Language Preservation Project from 1973–1975. Jerry was a well-known artist and birch bark basket maker, as well as an avid supporter of education and the arts in Lac du Flambeau. He passed away in 1998. Tom Maulson was Tribal Chairman of Lac du Flambeau from 1986 until 2000. One of the original "Walleye Warriors," for many years he has been a leader in treaty rights and tribal sovereignty throughout the Great Lakes region.

Bearskin, Josephine's namesake (awen'enh)

*Jack family. Josephine is at far left, her mother Ida Ackley third from left
and her father Joe Jack at far right*

me what kind of cedar to get. You know that wiigoob? She'd tell me what kind of bark to get. She dyed that wiigoob, to sew with. She'd tell me how to cook foods. . . . She was like a mother to me.

I attended the government school until seventh grade. [I didn't go to school after that because] I fell in love then. [laughs] I got married when I was seventeen. I didn't like school. I used to stay in the kitchen, do laundry, make food. [I remember my classmates] Lou Thompson, Lavanne John. . . . It was all right. Of course you had to mind. They'd make those kids behave themselves.

My parents used to pick potatoes, work on a farm. They got along, stuff wasn't so high then. We'd go out and pick berries and stuff. We used to go out to Powell Marsh, pick blueberries. We used to go fishing by Gresham Lake. I used to go over there with my aunt. I used to enjoy that. We'd catch panfish. Pick berries, those big blackberries. We'd carry that big pail. . . . We'd get home; she'd ask, "Do you want pie or sauce?" "Sauce!"

One time I made a cherry pie. I put that on a chair to cool off, and my aunt comes in and sits right on it. "You're going to sit on my pie!" I said, and she sat right down. She was just all full of cherries! She said, "I'm going to eat it anyways. Nothing wrong with it!" [laughs] And she ate it.

She liked her fish—those little panfish. I'd fry them. She used to eat that fish faster than us! She'd have a big stack of bones there on her plate. She sure liked her fish. After, I went and got a hold of her hand, held her hand up and said, "The winner!" She looked like she could see me, where I was standing. Finally, she caught on—she had more bones, so she champed us all! We'd sit there and laugh at her—she'd laugh too.

[There have been] lots of changes. We used to enjoy ourselves. Nowadays you can't! Some of those kids, whenever you go down the road in a car, they throw snowballs at you.

They used to have a lot of dances. They used to have a dance hall by the pines where that school was. By the field there. We used to have one by the village. We used to have big pow-wows. People from all over would come. They were good. We used to have good costumes. Lots of beadwork on them, not like nowadays. The pow-wows were bigger than Bear River is now.[4]

We used to celebrate Christmas, have a big feast. Those old Indians would have glass dishes. They would have a feast and have all the dishes tied up and laid out. Christmas time they'd get them down, fill them up with candy, have a big feast.

During the Depression years, we used to have to skimp. It was hard to get food. Really hard. But they managed to feed us. My daddy always planted a garden.

My sewing? I picked it up here and there. Watching my auntie, my mother-in-law, my daughter. Stood watching, and I'd ask them, "How did you do this one? How'd you make this one?" Finally I tried to make moccasins. Of course they were funny, my first ones. I kept on from that point.

---

[4] Bear River refers to the Bear River Pow-Wow, Lac du Flambeau's traditional annual pow-wow held in the Old Village.

Now I say, when people ask me, "Can you make me a pair of moccasins?" I say, "I'll try." Later if they want moccasins, they'll have to come dig me out of my grave, sit me up! [laughs] I've taught that to other people, too, my husband, my daughter. I used to make beadwork for the children, beaded shirts, dresses for the girls, moccasins. For the pow-wows.

We had a club going, us elderly ladies, the Nokomis Club. We used to make beaded costumes for the kids to dance at the [Indian] bowl. Bake sales up by the library to raise money to donate for Christmas, for the school, for baseball, different doings. At Christmas we'd make those afghans for the lap. We used to make those little quilts too. Me and Dorothy Wayman, and Dorothy Poupart, she was the head of the club. We'd make moccasins, make medallions, beaded shirts, to raise money, help this one and that one. I miss that. . . . Nowadays some people smoke pot, go out drinking. They need to do something. I'd tell them to get out! Keep your mind busy! Just keep busy, I say.

Rose Anne Fee

Rose Ann was born on August 15, 1921, in Lac du Flambeau. Her parents were Robert McArthur and Matilda LaCass, and she had two half-brothers and four sisters. She was first cousin to Gib Chapman, also interviewed for this book. Rose Ann attended both the boarding school and the public school in Lac du Flambeau. She went to Flandreau, South Dakota, for high school, returning to Flambeau every spring.

Rose Ann lived in Lac du Flambeau until 1943 when she moved to Vancouver, Washington, where her father worked at the Alcoa aluminum plant. From Vancouver she moved up to Alaska, following her husband there, who worked as a mechanic. They lived first in Kodiak, then Homer, and eventually in Fairbanks, where they raised seven children. She returned to Lac du Flambeau in 1991, as she says, because "she just got lonesome being up there all those years."

In her interview she recalls the busy downtown of Lac du Flambeau, not only its shops but also the cows, pigs, and even the bands of wild horses. She also remembers the vegetable gardens everyone had and recalls the day when she returned from Alaska in 1950 to find that everyone had electricity in their houses—they no longer burned kerosene lamps, but just flipped on a switch. She also remembers making sugar at the sugarbush with her Grandma McArthur where they stayed in a wigwam, the Indian dances at Woodman Hall, baking bread and picking berries, and skating and sledding in winter using sleds they made from boxes. She also recalls with fondness her life in Alaska, hunting moose and caribou, fishing and smoking salmon, making drums and mukluks out of sealskin. Rose Ann went blind in her later years, due to glaucoma. She always dreamed of going back to Alaska. She passed away on November 22, 1998.

Interview with Rose Ann Fee

This interview was conducted by Beth Tornes.

My name is Rose Ann Fee. I was just known as Rose McArthur. But in Alaska they called me Rose Ann. My father's name was Robert McArthur; [my mother was] Matilda LaCass. She was a LaCass after she married my [step] dad. I never stayed with my dad; I always stayed with my mother. She kept her name LaCass by her marriage name.

[My grandmother was] Sophie McArthur. He [Gib Chapman] was my first cousin. I was related to Gib through my mother. My grandfather's name [on my mother's side] was Joseph Chapman, I think. I just called him Grandpa when I was small.

The McArthurs came from Ireland; the Chapmans on my mother's side came from England or Canada or someplace. They had lived here a long time. [My parents] must have met on the reservation here.

My half-brothers were Harry Austin and Freddy LaCass. My sisters were Evangeline Austin, Juanita McArthur, and Fain LaCass. Then I had one little sister that died, Isabelle.

I was born August 15, 1921. I think I was born here in Flambeau. I lived here until 1943. I moved back here in 1991. [I left Flambeau] because I was going out to Vancouver where my mother and stepdad were working . . . in the state of Washington. He was working in aluminum, an Alcoa plant. We went after my parents. I left Vancouver in '46 or '47, went up to Alaska. My husband [was why I went there]. He was from Ogden, Utah. He went up ahead of me for a job. He was a mechanic.

I came back here a couple of times, for a visit, like when my mother died. I loved it up there, I still plan on going back. I lived in Kodiak, then we moved to Homer, finally settled in Fairbanks. I loved everything. People were friendly all over, the Eskimos and the Indians up there. They had some of the same beliefs we have. Eskimos were all different though, just the Indians [had similar beliefs].

I just came back [in 1991 because] I got a little bit lonesome for. . . . I intended on going back. I just got lonesome after being up there all those years.

I had seven children. Six of them are living yet. Harold is the one that's dead, he was the oldest one. And then Teddy, then Skip, Rosemary, Roxy, Bobby, and the other one I let someone else take in. I divorced from my husband, left him years before that. I have one daughter here, Rosemary. Roxy, she moved back to West Silla, Alaska. She just moved back up there last year. Teddy, he's in Fairbanks, Bobby's in West Silla. It's down by Anchorage.

*   *   *

I remember quite a bit, but I couldn't say just exactly [what I remember about my childhood]. Lots of memories come to mind—going to government school, and back to public school. I grew up in town here. We lived across from where that old casino is. That's the last place I remember anyway.

My parents, my mother and my stepdad [influenced me most]. Just by talking to me. I had a real good stepdad, Charlie LaCass. I never stayed with my real dad. He [Charlie] was nine years younger than my mother. He was good to us. He never would whip us, left my that up for my mother to do. He was an avid hunter, and he'd go guiding in the summertime. Hunted deer mostly. In the summer he did fishing mostly, guiding tourists when they come up.

[My mom] worked in the summertime in the resorts. She was a good cook. That's where I learned my cooking, from her. She cooked the Indian way and the white man's way too. I liked the squaw bread best of all. It's just flour, regular yeast, like when you mix yeast. She'd take some, fry it in deep fat. It's good. I used to make it myself up in Alaska. They use baking powder. When I mix bread, I always use my yeast, some of the bread dough to make my fry bread.

I attended school here, then I went to Flandreau, South Dakota. I was in the ninth grade. It was all right [boarding school], then I went to the public school. Then back to the government school again. Then to Flandreau, South Dakota. I liked Flandreau. I loved the boarding school here, though. Because we stayed there, and all the kids were there, you know. When I went to Flandreau, I took up mostly cooking. I was there from tenth grade to twelfth, but I didn't finish the twelfth grade. I quit in the twelfth grade; I should have went right on and finished it. I didn't go back to Flandreau. They used to bring us home every spring.

My stepdad was the night watchman at the old government school, and he did guiding in the summertime. [He had to] check all the buildings, you know. It wasn't open, just the teachers living there, doctors. Kids used to run away, but they didn't have no place to run. They brought them back. This [the Niijii Center][1] must have been the old girls' dorm. They slept upstairs. Dining room and everything was downstairs. I don't know [what this room is] because I was blind when I came here.

I just went blind about a year and a half ago. I had glaucoma, and the doctor told me I'd go blind eventually. I got that glaucoma in 1970, '71. Been blind about a year and a half. I just woke up one morning and couldn't see.

*   *   *

[Lac du Flambeau] has changed a lot. It used to be a little bitty place. I knew everybody. Now I don't know all the people since I came back.

---

[1] The "Niijii Center," formerly a boarding school dormitory, was converted into apartments for a brief period in the 1990s. Rose Ann lived there at the time this interview was conducted.

We never had all these roads and stuff. The town grew since I left here. It's grown up a lot. Main Street—there was more stores here then. A couple taverns, two soda fountains. There was a telegram office. There was a couple restaurants then, the Dew Drop Inn and another one right in front of my mother's house. We lived right in the back of the town. Vetternecks and Thompson's, Tom Thompson's, Douds [were our neighbors]. Then Elliot's, and Schillman's gas stations. There were more stores, now they only got that one store. There was Oldenberg's, and Gauthier's, and Aschenbrenner's. We used to still go down there, to Minocqua, to shop around for clothes and stuff. Just to be going down. People had cows and pigs and everything else. We had them wild cucumbers on our windows, and the cows would come and pull them down. They had two bands of wild horses—they'd come in town, and they'd get in big fights and oh my goodness sakes! Everybody would scoot for home or run to the nearest store or something to get in. Two bands of them. They lived out on the old prairie, out by the old Indian village. I really don't know what happened to them.

My aunt had cows, and pigs, chickens. She had everything. That was my aunt Ollie. . . . We lived right across from where the old casino was, and we had a big garden back there. We grew potatoes, peas, just regular stuff, radishes, turnips, rutabagies. . . .

I know I used to pick berries quite a bit when I was young. Blueberries, blackberries, raspberries, any kind of berries that you could pick. They used to have some huge blackberries sometimes. My mom would can them and make jam. Or just can them maybe. Then eat them! [laughs] Make blackberry pie.

The town was real small then. I was surprised when I came back from Alaska in 1950, to see the changes. Everybody had electricity in their houses. When I lived here only one or two houses had electricity. Then when I come back I was surprised to see how that changed. People used lamps, coal oil lamps. That's how I used to study going to school, by lamplight. Just flip a switch now, you got lights!

In the winter especially [we went to bed early]; in the summertime it stayed light a longer time. I always got up early in the morning, mostly around five o'clock. Four, five o'clock. You'd have your bread all mixed.

We used to have to wash clothes by an old washboard then, no washing machines. I'd do them in a tub. My mother and them, they had a pump right in their yard. A lot of people used to come get water by our house.

*   *   *

I used to go out with my Grandma McArthur.[2] She had a sugarbush, but I forget where it was at. We'd gather the sap buckets from the trees. I never made it myself; we'd just gather the sap.

---

[2] Grandma McArthur was Sophie McArthur, also Gilbert Chapman's grandmother. The sugar camp is probably the same one that Gib talks about in his interview.

First electrical lines in Lac du Flambeau

I don't think they do it any more, maybe some do. . . .

They don't have so many Indian dances here any more and all that. I remember I used to go to all of them. Whether they were at the Old Woodman Hall, or wherever they'd be, I'd always be where most all the Indians were. [There'd be a lot of dances], and I used to go all of them. You'd hear them drumming, drumming. I miss them too.

In the summertime there'd be some tourists there, in the wintertime, mostly all Indians. Nothing but the Indians. I know they don't have all the Indian dances like they used to. I was gone from here so many years. It was all changed when I came back.

During the Depression, I remember everybody was kind of poor. Hungry. They used to get WPA. People used to be poorer in them days than they are now, I'll tell you that. It was hard. I know we were hungry sometimes. Most people relied on that [hunting and fishing]. My stepdad was a good hunter.

We played all kinds of different games. We used to have fun. We didn't get many toys at Christmas I know, because we were poor. Sure did [change]. We was lucky if we got one toy when we was small. I remember my doll; I got that from my Aunt Ollie. It was way different then. We mashed it all up, my cousins and I!

Oh yes, we went swimming. Skating in the wintertime. They did more skating then. I don't hardly see anybody skating nowadays. They surely don't do any of that now. We used to have big skating rinks out on the lakes, sliding hills on sled and boxes and everything else you could find. Take an old box and use the bottom, slide down the hill on that. We didn't have hardly any sleds then, so we had to be [creative] because we couldn't buy all that stuff, like they do nowadays.

When they'd go skating they had a big bonfire out there. I don't know if they do that anymore or not. We used to have lots of fun when we were kids. Had to create our own stuff though.

[In the summertime] we used to take hikes and things like that. We had to walk, walk, walk. Nobody had cars or anything. They used to walk—I know I had to walk out to my Grandma McArthur's sugar camp, but I can't remember where it was at. We used to go out to visit my Grandma McArthur, I and my sister Juanita. Gather sap for her. I used to go out there. Stay out there a couple days—because school was still going on, we'd miss a couple days. But I used to love it out there in sugar camp. She'd cook the sap on a big pot, gather wood, and all that. My cousins were there too.

*   *   *

We used to get that great big salmon up in Alaska. Smoked salmon and all that. I loved it up there, I'm still going back if I ever get up there. Fairbanks [was my favorite place]. It's real nice up there.

I worked up there. I did some cooking, cooked in a camp a couple summers. It's still easier to find a job up there than around here, and they pay a lot better. It's a little more expensive up there, but they pay you more so it comes out even.

They eat like Indians around here, but they have their seal and walrus and all that. Porcupine—well, they eat porcupine here, too. [There were] deer, bear, grizzlies, black bears, cinnamon bears. They call them cinnamon bears, like a black bear but cinnamon-colored . . . and plenty of moose. Caribou. Yeah, we used to go moose hunting, caribou hunting. I loved that.

They're in big herds you know. If you shoot you know you're going to hit one of them. Caribou, they're in big bands. In Fairbanks all around. It's got a different taste altogether [from deer meat]. I used to eat a lot of caribou and moose meat up there. They eat it like we eat deer meat around here. They make moccasins, boots [out of the hides]. [They make drums] out of sealskin. I used to make sealskin mukluks; I don't know what happened to them.

[When the 1964 earthquake hit] my kids were down in Seward going to school, and I was up in Fairbanks. Them trees up in Fairbanks were just back and forth touching the ground [waves her hand], and I knew that there was an earthquake someplace. I didn't know at that time that it had hit Valdez and Seward and all them real bad. Stuff fell and broke and everything else. I knew there was a heck of a big earthquake somewhere, but didn't know exactly where till later. My kids were going to school down there, and it was panicky for me. I got word down there, though, that the Fee children were all all right. That was my biggest worry right there. My son was down there then. Skipper, my son that's here now. I'm pretty sure he was in Seward when that hit too.

When I first went to Fairbanks there was no thunder or lightning. Few years later there was thunder and lightning and everything else. They have storms like we do now up there.

I think I'm still going back anyway, blind or not blind. A lot of my friends up there, they've died since I've been gone.

*   *   *

Some [stories about Strawberry Island] were scary. We never went over there, us. My mother told us not to go over there, bad luck. I lay awake sometimes at night, thinking way back.

*   *   *

Tell them to do as the old saying goes, don't follow the other person, just follow yourself.

Wanda Brown Hunt

Wanda Brown Hunt was born on July 16, 1923, in the Old Village, to George Brown, Sr., and Sadie Norris Brown, and lived there most of her life. She attended the Lac du Flambeau Public School soon after it opened in the 1930s, and she was in the only class to graduate from the Lac du Flambeau High School. In her interview Wanda describes in rich detail what life was like in the Old Village, where people still lived very much in the old ways and continued to practice their Indian religion. She also talks about how the Village has changed since that time.

After high school she attended business college at Haskell Institute in Lawrence, Kansas. When World War II broke out, she moved to Washington, DC, where her sister lived, and worked for various government agencies. There she met her husband Christopher Hunt on a "blind date" with another couple. They took a moonlight cruise along the Potomac, and that was the beginning of a marriage that lasted fifty-three years, until Chris passed away in 2001. The couple had two daughters, and when Wanda retired in 1980, they moved to Vero Beach, Florida. They did not like living there much, so they returned to Lac du Flambeau to live on Wayman Lane in the Old Village, not far from where she grew up.

Wanda now spends every winter visiting her daughters and six grandchildren, who live in Virginia and North Carolina. She enjoys doing needlework, working on jigsaw puzzles and crossword puzzles, playing computer games, going on the Internet, and exchanging emails and photos with her friends and relatives.

Interview with Wanda Brown Hunt

This interview was conducted by Verdaine Farmilant.

My name is Wanda Brown Hunt. My Chippewa name is Wemitigoozhiikwe. Now what that means I don't know, French Lady or something like that.[1] [laughs] I was born out in the village,[2] lived there all my life—well, until I left to go to work.

I was just a little child when I was given that name, but I don't remember who gave it to me, or whether it was a ceremony. I remember my grandfather and grandmother, they lived out in the village too.

My father's name was George Brown, and my mother's name was Sadie Norris Brown. She was from around the St. Croix area.[3] I think she was about a quarter Chippewa and Norwegian. Her father was Chippewa but her mother, in fact, her people, came over from Norway. They were all Norwegians.

My grandfather [on my father's side], I don't know if his name was John, but they went by Indian names. What I heard, they named him when the census people came and took count. They couldn't spell his name, so they gave him the name of John Brown. . . . When I was very small, I do remember my dad took me over to his house when he was dying.

We used to go over there, to my mother's grandparents,[4] and sometimes they would come to see us. They had a little farmlike place somewhere in Minnesota . . . and I remember the way they looked, but I don't remember too much about them. I think she died first, and then he did. I was very young then.

My father's family always lived here, he was born around here. I did have three brothers and one sister. My oldest brother [Jimmy] died but the others are living, George and Leonard and Violet. I was born over in the old Mitchell house. . . . At that time my dad was a carpenter, and he was building our house then when we were living over there. Then we moved to the house where we lived all our lives. That's where my two younger brothers were born.

I think it was an old shed or barn he started out with; we've got pictures of when he was building it. At that time there were over twenty houses in the village. Just think, today there's not that many. There was about twenty-some houses with about forty people, then their kids. Maybe they had two or three, some of them had more.

---

[1] Wewemitigoozhiikwe means "French Lady," as Wanda says.

[2] The Old Indian Village where Wanda grew up. (See Introduction.)

[3] St. Croix (Chippewa) reservation in western Wisconsin, which is made of five parcels of land spread across three counties near the St. Croix River, which forms the border between Wisconsin and Minnesota.

[4] Her mother's grandparents were Charles and Mary Norris.

Bearskin

When I was a kid, there were a lot of elders. I remember seeing them walking by, going to a feast with their cloth bags carrying their dishes and utensils. Because when you went to a feast, you had to carry your own. And then if there was an older person there, they'd take them on a wagon or on a sled, like Bearskin,[5] he was real old, couldn't walk. I used to watch them go by. They had feasts in different homes. I guess whatever they were going to talk about, or whoever was giving the feast, everybody would go to that house.

Sometimes they would have ceremonies up to the Hall[6] above our house. I remember in the summer they used to have ceremonies in their medicine lodges, those great big long wigwams . . . somewhere around Ben Poupart's house, I would say a couple blocks from where we lived.[7] Because when we were kids, we would go in there and lift up the bark and peek under there. Because we weren't allowed to go in, that was a real religious thing.

---

[5] Bearskin (Makwayaan in Ojibwe) was a highly respected medicine man of the time who lived to be very old. (See also the Reva Chapman and Gilbert Chapman, Sr. interviews.)

[6] The "Hall" was what they called the Round House, where traditionally the Big Drum ceremonies take place.

[7] The Midewin medicine lodge, a long wigwam made of birchbark. (See Introduction.)

When I was about six or seven, I guess, I sometimes stayed with a lady in town. One summer day she took me berry picking and that night, my knee swelled up really big, and I developed a high fever. So they drove me home to the village, and my mother and dad were so worried, they drove me to Minocqua to see a doctor there. They wanted the best care, I guess. But the doctors there wouldn't take me in, saying we have a government doctor here and I should be operated on by that doctor.[8] So we had no choice, but the doctor here did pretty good with my huge knee and red lines running up from it. I do have a big scar on my knee though.

For operations or emergencies we had to drive to the hospital in Hayward.[9] When I was ten, I had to go there to get my tonsils out. I remember the doctor was very rough and shouted at me to breathe when he put the ether cup over my face. I remember trying to hold my breath from breathing that awful smell.

*   *   *

I have two daughters and six grandchildren. The oldest one is Patricia, the youngest one is Christine. They're about eight years apart. The oldest one lives in Virginia, and the youngest lives in North Carolina.

I went to school here. In fact our class was the first graduating class in the high school they tore down. And I think that was the last one, because after that all the kids went to Lakeland.[10] But I graduated there, then I went to Haskell for a couple years, business college. Then the war came, so my sister got a job in Washington. She worked in Ashland, at the Indian office there, then she got a job in Washington. So I decided to go there, too, because during the war they were hiring all kinds of typists and secretaries, you could get a job real easy.

I worked at several departments—HEW,[11] Manpower Commission, Labor. I didn't see any [other Indians] except the boys from here, when they would come through. They were camped over there, and that's the only ones we saw. The ones we went to school with, too, we were able to see them. But it wasn't until the '50s when the Indian office from Chicago moved there, then there were a lot of Indians. They had these organizations, American Indian Society and others, after they moved out there. Then they had activities and things you could go to.

Then I retired in '80, and we went to Florida. Moved there and stayed there for a couple of years—I didn't like it there. Then we decided to move here.

---

[8] The Minocqua hospital at the time would turn away Native Americans. There was a clinic at the BIA agency complex, where the boarding school was also located. The doctor she refers to practiced there.

[9] Hayward was the location of the nearest "Indian Hospital," a hundred miles away from Flambeau on the Lac Courte Oreilles Reservation.

[10] There was a high school in Lac du Flambeau for a brief period in the 1940s in the school building that was torn down when the new casino was built.

[11] HEW is the U.S. Department of Health, Education, and Welfare.

My dad had one sister and two half-sisters. Then on my mother's side they were all in Wisconsin's western part or Minnesota, but we didn't see them too often. Once in awhile we'd go over there, or they'd come here. She had a lot of sisters and brothers and they had a lot of children, so I have a lot of cousins around somewhere! [laughs] Her oldest sister's ninety-some years old.

It was mostly my dad [who influenced me]. He was very strict with us too. I remember my sister, and I used to go out skating at night—we had a lot of fun when we were kids—and we'd slide down hills with makeshift sleds. But then at 9:00, we'd always hear the horn blow, it was almost like a fog horn. Then everybody'd say "Oh, the Brown girls have to go home!" [laughs] So we minded pretty well. Those were the good old days, we really had a lot of fun when we were kids.

We were out to the village, we never went to town. I never knew too many kids there, there were always the kids out here that I knew. They used to call me "Tommy" because I played with boys, I was a tomboy. We used to climb trees, make houses, snare rabbits, and make our own slingshots. We had a lot of fun. So I feel sorry for the kids today. Even with their TVs and their Nintendo, I think they miss a lot.

We lived across the street from the Skyes, Elsie was one and Violet was the other one. Elsie was older, and then the Sagasunks were next door from them, and then Rose Bobidosh lived way past the bridge. And then the Neganis. Reva was a little older, and Margaret was my sister's age. So there wasn't anybody my age except Rose. And then one of the Negani girls, but I never was over there that much because they lived across the bridge. And then there was Pouparts, Ben Poupart had a couple daughters. So I played with mostly boys! I had cousins, the Mitchell boys, and then my brothers. So I hung around them.

I remember my mother and dad used to have, I call it a microbrewery. They used to make home brew, and they must have had a thriving business, because boy a lot of cars would come out to the house. Then they used to make root beer for the kids, and that was delicious. Besides that [Prohibition], they wouldn't sell liquor to Indians anyway.[12] So they made their own! [laughs] But the "revenuers" I call them used to come over occasionally and smash the crocks and break the bottles.[13] We had a regular bottle capper and everything up there! They'd come out and break the crocks and dump the beer right in the snow outside.

My dad was a carpenter, and my mother was a housewife. He started making signs way back, those rustic signs.[14] He and my oldest brother carved, and my mother and I did the painting.

---

[12] It was illegal to sell liquor to Indians at the time.

[13] A "revenuer" was a U.S. Treasury agent whose job it was to search out and destroy illegal liquor stills and arrest those who operated them.

[14] Wanda's father, George Brown, Sr., was a carpenter and artist who was famous for his woodwork, including wooden "rustic" signs, totem poles, figures, carvings, and other crafts. As Wanda relates, his family would help him make these crafts.

That's what we did all summer, and he had a good business too. He did a few totem poles, and then he made lamps with little totem pole figures and birchbark shades, and she would decorate those.

Years ago when I was a kid, we used to make beadwork, she and I and my sister. And all we did was just hang them around the front porch, and the tourists would come by and see them and stop. We sold a lot. And you know, a lot of people would come out to the village, the tourists. I think they were hoping to see Indians living in wigwams. But we would direct them up to the Park,[15] they were able to go up there and look around. And I used to make money taking them out to the old cemetery, climbing that big hill. Used to be across from our house. So they wanted to see that, they'd give us money to guide them up there.

The last one burial I remember was one of the Mitchell boys. He was buried there in the late '30s. There might have been some other people buried there after. In fact they did take some people from different places and buried them on the hill.

They used to put spirit houses—wood structures, like little, long houses—over the burial.[16] Then they had a little shelf in there where they put maple sugar, rice, tobacco. I guess to help the spirits on their way.

My dad never wanted to talk Indian when we were kids, because my mother didn't speak it. But he was very fluent in it. He went to Hampton when it was an Indian school, it's mixed now. It's in Virginia. It was an Indian college and then, whites and blacks are there now. I don't think it's private. It's still a college. He took courses to teach, and he also took carpentry and music. See he was a music teacher here after he didn't get any more carpentry work, I guess. He built a lot of those homes around the lake, or he helped build. The summer people that live around here, like Essers and the Oelrich's around that way.

We had a nice bandstand right there by the lake and we used to give band concerts every Sunday.[17] I really enjoyed that. My sister and I, I don't know whether George was too young for that, but my Dad was conductor. And Harry St. Germaine and Cobbie LaCass and Schmidt, Eli, and the two girls from Fence Lake, I forget their names. Anyway we had a good time practicing, and then we'd play a march or something, and all the horn people would blow their horns. . . . [laughs] It was right near the museum. I don't remember exactly. Oldenberg's store was right around there, it was on this side of the store. Across the street from the bandstand there was an ice cream parlor. There was a big lime green building there, and there was a blind man that used to play piano. . . .

---

[15] The "Park" is where traditional dances were held in the Old Village; today it is known as the Bear River Pow-wow Grounds.

[16] A spirit house is a small, low wooden house constructed over the grave, where it is believed the spirit resides for a certain length of time before passing on to the spirit world. A spirit house has a small opening, like a window, with a ledge beneath it where relatives of the deceased placed food offerings and tobacco.

[17] The bandstand she describes was located on Long Interlaken Lake at the site of the present-day museum. (See also Wilhemina Mae Chosa interview.)

And we used to have a store in the Park. You know when they had the pow-wows, it would last for about a couple weeks. So we had a store out there, in the old Park. We used to sleep there. [We sold] convenience goods like bread, milk, and a few canned goods, and then a lot of sodas. I know every time I smell or taste strawberry soda or cream soda, it always brings me back to the store. It's funny how a smell or a taste can take you back, like deja vu.

You know as you go through the entrance to the park, it was on the left, across from the riverside. And they used to have canoe races there too. It was a whole two weeks they were there, I think, and people used to come and put up their wigwams.

You know how now they have so many drums around? They didn't have that then, they had that one drum and the singers. They didn't have groups . . . then they used to adopt somebody every year, and they'd have a big ceremony for that. And they'd have social dancing at night, everybody was out of their costume.

And oh my, there were a lot of tourists. I know we would sit out on the porch and check the license plates, oh so many states. So I think it was mostly a moneymaking thing too. It was for both [the community and the tourists]. My sister would sell tickets, and I would take the stubs. Those were big pow-wows, all kinds of activities out there, not just dancing. Races and things like that, games. Then they did have those moccasin games. And the tourists would just walk around and buy the beadwork or watch the games. Then they would have the dancing. It was a big thing.

Just my brothers [were in the military]. My dad had a disability, I don't know what it was, during the first war. George was in the Navy, and Buddy was in the Army during the Second World War. One time I was thinking I would like to go in the WACs, but my dad wouldn't let me do that.[18] I think he just thought it wasn't an occupation for a young girl [laughs].

*   *   *

I never really spent much time in town, but it's smaller. There used to be more people walking around. We had a lot more tourists in town way back. I think they mostly came to see the Indians, and they wanted to go out to the village. Most of the tourists went out there.
Less people, less houses now [in the village]. . . . My aunt Tilly used to have a little store, and she used to sell candy and cigarettes and pop right in her house. That was years and years ago. It's the only one I know of.

They didn't have cars, they had, like Sagasunk, a horse and wagon. And we had an old Model T. We'd skate and go right to town on skates. We had a lot of fun on skates, we used to go all the way to Sand Beach, and then we'd hold our coats open and the wind would take us right back to the village [laughs]. It was a lot of fun. We had an old boat; we used to go across to the rock

---

[18] WAC is the Women's Army Corps, an auxiliary branch of the U.S. Army. According to a later interview with Wanda, these women took over jobs that the men had vacated to go to war, mostly office jobs.

Dancers and tourists in downtown Lac du Flambeau

Dancers and wigwams at the Park (Big George Sky in center)

and have picnics over there. We had a lot of fun at home, just the family. We didn't socialize a lot. But being kids, they spent a lot of time with us, which people don't do today, I don't think. Parents don't spend enough time with their children. But I remember we used to sit around at night and turn the light off and listen to the radio when they had that—scary ghost stories. And then we had taffy pulls. We had a good time.

*   *   *

When I was living in the village, all the kids went to the boarding school in town. But my dad said he didn't want us to go there because we'd have to board there. So he sent us to that public school, and he said he would drive us.[19] Sometimes we'd walk, and sometimes we stayed in town if the snow was too deep. Then they built that new school where the Simpson Plant is, so we went to school there, elementary school, and we'd have to walk from there to the old boarding school for lunch and walk back. It was a long walk!

My sister and brother were in school in that brown school, across from Vetterneck's over there.[20] So after our school was out, their school was still in session, and I had to walk all the way over there and wait out there in the cold until they got out. I remember Ollie Vetterneck used to come out and call me in, I think she took pity on me out there in the cold. She used to say, "Well come on in and play with Jessie awhile, warm up!" I thought, "Oh good!" We used to have real good school programs when we were at that old school, across from Sharlows, somewhere over there. And she used to sing at Christmas, and somebody used to play the saw, you know, make music with the saw. Songs like "Silent Night." The adults really participated in those days. Then after I left Simpson's school—I must've been in the eighth grade then—we went in the new school and graduated there. My brother and sister [Jimmy and Violet] were going to that little brown school. He used to take a sandwich, they had to take their own sandwiches, cold cuts and things like that, and we never had that like the white kids used to take. He'd take wild rice sandwiches, or beans, and the kids liked it so well they'd trade their cold cut sandwiches for it.

*   *   *

We got rations from the government. I remember they gave us shoes, army blankets, coats— ugly things. And in the summer we all had gardens, and we canned. My dad [did] a lot of hunting, fishing through the ice, snaring. In fact, we had [raised] rabbits, too, little white rabbits.

---

[19] By the time Wanda went to school, the public school had opened, a day school, and students were no longer forced to live at the boarding school.

[20] The brown school was a small one room schoolhouse that served as a middle school.

Bearskin's house in the Old Village, medicine pole near house

I remember when I was in ninth or tenth grade we had victory gardens.[21] It was during the war, and before we could get a grade in school they'd come out and inspect the gardens. They gave us seeds, and told us what to do. We had pretty good gardens.

My dad used to work in Baraga for awhile.[22] And in the summer a lot of the young kids used to pick potatoes and apples, or whatever they were, like migrant workers. I don't know about anybody working, I don't know where they'd work. Then we had a CCC camp over there by Sand Beach, the young boys worked there. That was in the '30s.

* * *

---

[21] Victory gardens were vegetable gardens that families were encouraged to plant during World War II to increase food production.

[22] Baraga, on L'Anse Bay in the upper peninsula of Michigan, which along with L'Anse is a town on the L'Anse Chippewa Reservation.

I don't think many people in the village converted to Christianity. I know we always had a good Christmas celebration, but I don't think many of the others did. Although one year I remember they had a big celebration in the Hall [the Round House] up the hill, somebody dressed up like Santa Claus and gave toys to the kids. But I don't remember people having Christmas trees and trimmings in their houses, but we did. And they had a lot of programs at the schools, it was really nice there. They'd give skits and a lot of singing, like glee clubs. It was nice. Everybody participated. In the summer we had a Reverend Murray from the church up here, he used to come out every Sunday and instruct the children. And he brought an organ, I think my mother used to play, and sing. And so we got religion.

They used to all come to our house on Sunday. He'd tell a story, and then he'd hand out these things to color and give us the crayons. We didn't have that, you know. We enjoyed that. I think he came too for his glass of home brew [laughs].

In the village the Indians had their own church, longhouse, medicine lodge, whatever you call it. They had their own ceremonies. And people that didn't belong couldn't go in. When we peeked under there we could see them all walking round and round, doing something with their tobacco, or whatever. I never knew what they did. Then they would sing, chant. Their children went in there too. At every house they had a little banner or flag, a clan, like they belonged to the fish or the bear.

During the war everybody left to go work, in factories, and they went to the Army and Navy, and they got bright ideas and they came back and started to modernize everything. . . . Too when they left, a lot of them joined other churches, like we did when we left here. We had to see that our children had religion, so we went to church. You wouldn't go back to the old ways if you weren't here, you know. Which is too bad. . . .

*   *   *

I just remember being so poor [during the Depression]. Seemed like one time all we lived on was potatoes, and meat when we could get it. We never had vegetables. But other than that—no clothes. And we were always warm because we had woodstoves, and we always had a lot of wood. Oh, I guess we had enough to eat, but we just didn't have the good things. And we didn't have the things we needed, like milk, when we were kids, oranges. We had oranges at Christmas, in the stocking.

We used to go out and get berries, pick cranberries too. I remember we used to go out there [Powell Swamp] and get our feet wet. This fall we went over to the Powell Swamp[23] area where

---

[23] Manitowish Waters, about fifteen miles north of Lac du Flambeau, where many commercial cranberry bogs are located.

George Brown, Sr. in his studio

Women in medicine lodge

they sell them, Ocean Spray, up in Manitowish. We'd eat them raw, or else we'd mix them with sugar, make sauce. Nowadays we freeze them.

* * *

My dad was a singer with the drum, and we heard [the songs] so much we knew the tunes. I have the tapes. Then we always had music at home. Sometimes banjo, guitar, country music.

I played coronet, and my dad played everything. George played trombone, and Vi played coronet. I don't remember what Buddy played; he plays guitar now. We liked all kinds. Polkas.

I remember when I was very young, we had an orchestra came to town. It was a black orchestra, and he had black singers. Everybody danced. . . . I remember sitting there with my mother watching. It seems to me that these orchestras used to come to Trout Lake or some big resort. And at one time the Indians couldn't go in there. So I think they took pity on us, and they came over and played here. It was a famous orchestra. It was before the big bands, in the '30s. I was too small to dance. I remember that singer, he was a black singer. He was good looking, he had a good voice too. And everybody dancing, it was a loud band too. My mother and dad wanted to go, so they took all of us.

They did a lot of stuff like that. My dad used to sing, and Big Tom used to sing. Something like amateur hour. I remember one that was at the old, I call it a red school house. I remember we had a big program there one year.

* * *

A long time ago, my parents had their own club out there at the village, they paid dues. I forget the name of it. I came across an old record book of my dad's where he was a secretary or a treasurer, and he had the names of those that attended the meeting. And then they played cards. They did a lot of things in the village. They had a lot of people out there that used to come over and play cards and other things.

* * *

I think the best thing for young people is to stay in school, stay off drugs, drinks. Because they can always succeed in life if they put their mind to it. But it's so hard now because if their peers go to something which is not good, they don't want to be any different, so they join them. But if they put their minds to it, I think they can make it.

Georgian Kinstedt

Georgian Kinstedt was born on March 28, 1925, in Lac du Flambeau, at the Agency home of her aunt and uncle, who was the farmer at the BIA complex. Her parents were Charles N. Valliere from Lac du Flambeau and Agnes Ruth Kelly, an Oneida from the Oneida reservation near Green Bay. Georgian grew up in the town of Lac du Flambeau with five brothers and sisters, and attended the "public school." (At the time parents could choose between the BIA "government school"—the former boarding school—and the "public school," a day school.) She recalls hearing both the Oneida and Ojibwe language at her home growing up, as her parents both spoke their ancestral languages. As a young woman Georgian worked cleaning resorts to make a living. She graduated from high school at the Haskell Institute in Kansas.

Georgian married Clarence "Clank" Kinstedt, whom she met after graduation, in Chicago where she lived and worked as a secretary. They moved to Palos Heights, Illinois, and lived there for twenty-three years, raising their children John and Tiana. The couple moved back to Flambeau in 1976 and lived in their Elsie Lake home the rest of their lives. For many years Georgian worked as an accountant at the Peter Christensen Health Center, setting up many of their current accounting and billing procedures. Georgian was also a gifted seamstress, and like many women her age she donated many of her quilts and sewing projects to the Nokomis Club to provide for children's outfits and raise funds for those in need in the community. She also cared for her elderly mother Agnes in her final years, when Agnes lived at Elks Point Elderly Housing. She was a devoted grandmother and loved visiting with her grandchildren. She was also an animal lover and always had a pet dog when they lived in Flambeau. Georgian passed away February 2, 1998, one year after her beloved husband "Clank."

In her interview she remembers many events from her childhood, including berry picking, carrying ice home from the icehouse, bringing a pail of milk home from the Agency, hearing the drum, and watching the dances at Woodman Hall. She also recalls her father's interest in his children's education, and how hard he worked hunting for the family as well as building houses. She also recalls her mother's wanting her to learn piano, taking in laundry so that Georgian could have piano lessons. She ends her interview with advice to young people to listen to your parents, and to keep learning.

Interview with Georgian Kinstedt

This interview was conducted by Beth Tornes.

My name is Georgian Kinstedt. My father was Charles N. Valliere, my mother was Agnes Ruth Kelly. My grandfather was Charles Nelson Valliere, Sr. and his wife was Julia Stevens, who was my grandmother. My dad was a descendant of Chief Amour and Na-kwe-kwe-osinokwe.[1] I didn't look this up, but I knew because I had to put in an application for the tribe here. My mother's father was William Kelly, and her mother was Electa Hill, both from Oneida reservation.[2]

All I knew was the Lac du Flambeau reservation, but my mother came from Oneida, and my father's family came from around the Merrill-Wausau area. They had relatives here, so when times really got tough, then they moved to Flambeau. It must have been about early 1920s.

I was born in March 1925 in the home at the [BIA] Agency where the farmer lived.[3] My mother had come up here to help her sister with her first baby. Rather than go all the way to Hayward, which was our hospital, she was at my aunt and uncle's.[4] Did I say that this was the former Bauman home that I was born in, right near the fish hatchery in town? It's a one-story but it's built up, you know how the agency homes were built. There was no second floor, but it was a nice, comfortable, and very well kept home. Later when I was approximately three years old, my dad had built a home on Moss Lake, it was called Mud Lake at the time. He built a two-story, but they had a living room and a kitchen, and that was that. And we had three bedrooms upstairs.

And later on, of course, there was a bathroom put in. And running water. Because we just had the pump, which would be frozen in the winter. We'd have to go out to the outhouse, even if it was frozen outside, you waded through the snow. In fact, when you had to go you put on your boots and coat and got bundled up and went out. So that wasn't too great. The frozen pump had to be thawed out, it had to be primed by putting hot water in it. That's how we did it. It was cold!

We decided to make the move nineteen years ago, and we've lived here on Elsie Lake ever since. Both of my children were through college, and I worked, as well as they, to help put them through. I told them I would help if they wanted to go on, I would help all I could. But they would

---

[1] Chief George Amour (1850–1928), whose Indian name was Ma-ghe-ga-bo, was one of the last traditional chiefs of the Lac du Flambeau Ojibwe. He was married to Bah-Jajig, "One Who Travels Around." Their daughter, Na-kwe-kwe-osinokwe, was married to Gilbert Valliere, a Canadian trapper and a trader who was half Chippewa and half French. They were Georgian's great-grandparents on her father's side. (This genealogical material comes from *Black Magic and Stolen Timber*, a Valliere family history published in 1993 by Yvonne M. Madden, a family member.)

[2] According to Georgian's brothers, William Kelly, Georgian's Oneida grandfather, was given that name by a BIA agent when he was given his allotment on the Oneida reservation in Wisconsin. His real name was Kelly Webster.

[3] The farmer at the agency was her uncle, an Oneida named Murphy Baird. (She mentions him again toward the end of the interview.)

[4] Hayward, a town one hundred miles from Lac du Flambeau where the "Indian Hospital" was located, is on the Lac Courte Oreilles reservation.

have to help too. And I didn't want them quitting in the midst of the whole thing. I wanted them to complete college, and they did, both of them.

My daughter's name is Tiana Borchardt, she is a teacher, and she worked here. Her first job was here in Flambeau. I think she was trying to please me, you know, because I used to talk so much about my hometown.

[I used to live in] Palos Heights, Illinois. Our address then was 1300 South. And we lived there for twenty-three years. When the kids left, because they both had different things to do, then we decided that we were going to come back here. My husband loved it here, and of course so did I, and things were changing, and it wasn't so poor as it used to be when I lived here. Of course we went through the Depression then too.

My son John is an attorney, who went through the University of Wisconsin Law School. So he's had quite a bit of education. John lives in Ohio; he's married and has two children. My daughter Tiana lives in Fort Atkinson. She has four children. She's a teacher in the Janesville school system.

I have to admire her because on her own she obtained a master's degree in reading. All this while she taught school, took care of the home, studied, and drove a number of miles after school in order to complete her master's degree. One summer I kept the kids so that she could go the full time and get it over with. So those are my two kids, and I'm very proud of them.

[I remember] picking berries. Every summer we'd pick berries, and when we got through with that we'd have to go home and take care of them, canning them for winter. Of course we picked raspberries and blackberries and blueberries. And the other thing that I have to say is, I loved going barefoot and went barefoot practically all summer long.

I remember the icehouse in town. They used to have horses that went out on the ice. They took blocks of ice from there and put them in a big building. They covered the ice with sawdust so that it didn't melt so fast. If they needed ice, they could go there and purchase it. It wasn't very much at the time. And some had those little iceboxes that you put the ice in. I suppose they were lined, I don't know, we didn't have one. The snow made our jello and everything else! [laughs]

Then the other thing I remember in the summer, we would hear the drum. That's where the casino is now, and we'd call that "The Pines." And the Indians used to dance there, you know, and we'd run through the town, and we'd go in to watch. That was what I loved. We went to the Pines to listen to the drum and the singing and watch the dancers. I loved that. It was [beautiful], it certainly was. I don't really know if it was regular, but we always heard the drum. You could hear that, you know, because the lakes carry the sound. Sometimes they would have tourists come, but there was no charge or anything. They did this, they wanted to do this, that was part of the heritage. Part of their culture.

My mother and father influenced me the most. I'll tell you a story about what happened up here. My mother was from West Depere and was expecting my brother Corky [Carlton] at the time. And she wasn't feeling very well. So she went home for awhile to be with her parents. When she was in West Depere, my dad and Hiram and I were at home. They had put my brother Bill in government school at the Agency. At the time I was five years old, and my brother was three. We're all two years apart. My dad taught me how to read and write and do problems in arithmetic. So when I went to school and was put in the first grade, I was not there very long. They put me into second grade.

My mother knew the Oneida language because when she was going to school she knew all of that. That's the way they talked in the home. And of course you've heard different people talking about the government taking away their language, and they had to learn English. But she never forgot her Indian language, and she spoke it fluently up to the time she passed away. Artley Skenandore[5] is also Oneida, and she and he used to talk in the Oneida language and they both enjoyed it.

My father knew a lot of words because he was with the Indians. There were a lot of Indians that were relatives of his. Well anyway, my mother even though she had a lot of kids and had to do the washing by hand and the baking, my father wouldn't eat store-bought bread. I mean he'd just squish it like an accordion. And then she would have to bake, and oh was that good bread, I'll tell you. So anyway, she was active in the Dorcus Society of the Community Presbyterian Church. And these Indian ladies, they would make layettes for the expectant women, and they took care of the rummage sales at the church. Oh, they did a lot of things. And when anyone would come in that they knew could not afford hardly anything, they would let them pick out what they wanted at the church. And they'd go home with bags full of clothes, but *needed* clothes and so forth, and they would just give whatever they could afford. These ladies got together, I think it was once a week, and one would be designated to make a little dessert or a sandwich, whatever they had just to get together. And they spent practically the whole day there.

And then there was a lady, a good friend of my mother's, Marian Smith was her name. She came up with the idea of starting the Nokomis Club, and she asked my mother and Josephine Doud to join her. And what they did was, they made mittens and scarves for the schoolchildren who didn't have it. A lot of them, you know, didn't have mittens. Either they had them or lost them or something, but they needed it. There also was a dance drum here for the young people. And the ladies used to make the outfits for them to wear and give them to those who didn't have it. Yeah, they did a lot of things, and they thought that they were going to have an elderly building where, when they came out of the hospital they would be taken care of there. That's what they worked on there, and very hard, because they used to stand out in front of the post office there and sell baked goods. They did a lot of things but anyhow. . . .

I think it folded up [the nursing home project] because Marian passed away, and then there were other people that came into this club, this society, and then finally Dorothy Poupart came in and she became their spokesman, I guess. And handled the money. So they were quite thankful for that.

And my mother could speak, too, when she would get started you couldn't stop her from talking! [laughs] Did I say that Dad was a carpenter, and self-taught? Because nobody taught him how to do anything. As a matter of fact he only went to third grade. So when I would come home

---

[5] Artley Skenandore, who passed away in 2000, was Georgian's sister Betty's husband. He was a member of the Oneida Nation and was born on the Oneida reservation near Green Bay.

The Nokomis Club
Back row left to right: Dorothy Poupart, Dorothy Wayman, Celia Defoe
Front row left to right: Reva Chapman, Edna Williams, Josephine Doud
(Not pictured: Marian Smith and Georgian Kinstedt)

from school he would ask me, what did you learn in school today? And he would ask about problems in arithmetic and stuff like that. And so he was very interested in our education, I know that. He stressed it all the time: "You have to go to school and learn something, and your life would be a heck of a lot better."

Now when I went to school there were some Indian children who went to the public school. And why we were sent there I'll never know, but it was the choice of the parents. Because they had the government school there, which we probably could have attended. And then we went to, we were into this public school to start. Well there were a number—Jimmy St. Germaine was one of my friends there from the community, Wanda Brown, Andre St. Germain, Jesse Chapman, and John St. Germain. And Dad built a lot of homes and vacation homes on the other end of Pokegama Lake.

And he didn't have an electric saw or any of these fancy things. He had to use his strength, and the hammer, and the regular saw to cut those big logs and so forth. And he also built the Fireside,[6] and you know those big beams they have in there? He put those in there. He was [a wonderful carpenter], he was, there's no doubt about it.

At one time he made caskets here. And he even lined them. And that building was behind the one where I was born. It was my father who did all that, beautiful caskets. He built homes, and the vacation homes—there was a lot of vacationers who came up here all the time, and then later of course they decided to stay. But there still are quite a few on the lake. As you're going down [Highway] 47 by the fish hatchery, you can't go this way, so you have to go this way [gestures to the right], at the south end of the lake.

Someone had given him a dictionary. It was a used one of course, and worn—and he built this stand. Similar to the one you'd put the Bible on. He built this stand and opened the dictionary, and it was always there for us. We didn't have to go looking in the corner or whatever. This book was one of the main items in our home. He used to tell us, when you're reading, or you come across a word that you don't know, jot it down and afterward when you have time just go and look it up. And we used that dictionary so often, all of us.

In the summer we walked to the Agency because the Agency was giving away milk. So I was sent up there a few times at summer to collect it. We had a pail with us, and we went down to where the museum is, went down there—they call that the hot pond, did anybody mention that?[7] And we went through there, through the swamp. It was frightening to a little kid. They had a few boards here and there, and we used to jump, you know, from one to the other. And we'd come up by the Community Presbyterian Church there and walk on to the Agency. And they had a big pail of milk there that they would dish out into your kettle, your little container. And then we had to walk home with it, you know, and I think today—well, I'm not a milk drinker, I never was, you know. But I guess maybe that since we had to go through the swamp and all that stuff it was scary. That's why I never did care for milk, it kind of turned me off.

*   *   *

My brother Bill was the oldest and then me. And then Hiram and then my sister Doris. Then my brother Corky, Carlton was his name. My sister Betty and Leon and Joe, he was the last one. We were all about two years apart except for my brother Joe and Leon, there was about twelve

---

[6] The Fireside is a restaurant in downtown Lac du Flambeau that is still in operation.

[7] The Hot Pond was where logs were floated in the bay of Long Interlaken Lake at the base of the lumber mill, the current site of the museum and Indian Bowl.

Waswagon St. homes

years in between them. We lost my brother Corky in the Korean War. Otherwise they're all here [in Flambeau]. I know my brothers Bill, Hiram, Leon, Joe, and Corky were all in the service.

*   *   *

It was so poor here, you know. I remember that old mill, I was just a kid, little one, and they used to have the lumber mill here. That was where the [Indian] bowl is now. They had a railroad to this place, and it went out to other rails around where Carufels lived. When that folded up, you know, I guess they took all the lumber they could here and they left. But in the meantime these workers for the mill, lumberjacks I guess, had built shelters for themselves. They lived here then, you know, they worked here, and they weren't used to wigwams. That's how people lived—there may have been a few buildings around but not many. So when these workers, mill workers, had left their homes there and they knew they weren't coming back, then the Indians moved in there, wherever they could. Whenever there was anything available, they moved in. And of course there was no insulation in those places, and they heated the house by wood, they cooked by wood. Of course I think most people did that anyways. But now this is a different story, they're inside a building. So they didn't know how to handle this. They did the best they could, and they lived through that, but some didn't even have flooring. They had packed-down dirt. That's one thing I remember they had then.

I went into the Woodman Hall, did I tell you about that? I remember going in there. It was just a long building, like a longhouse, but they called it the Woodman Hall, and that's where the Indians would come in and meet. And they'd have their drum, and they'd sing and drum. And they smoked the pipe, east, south, west, and north, you know, they'd turn like that and everyone around them. Most people had mats that were woven, and that's how they'd come to places like that. There was no chairs to sit on. So they would sit on these mats, and then they'd roll them up when they were through. Well,

I went in there a few times, I don't know whether the thing burned down or what, but they did have that Woodman Hall and I was in there. It was wood on the inside. To tell you the truth, I don't know [why they named it Woodman Hall], I never questioned that, but that is a good question.

They would have the drum, and everybody would come. At one time though, there were people living at the village, members of the tribe. I don't know whether it's once or twice a week, they would walk in. Nobody owned cars, and they used to walk in from the village and bring their blankets, and they'd lay it down on the ground near the stores up there, near Oldenburg's store. And they would, different ones, their families and so forth would come to visit and they would stay all day. And they'd be eating and drinking—not drinking booze, but pop or coffee. And they'd visit there, but then they'd have to walk all the way back to the village after that! And it seemed like such a long way—to me it did anyway.

Homes were being built then, and we didn't have running water or toilets then, but eventually that came too. But I think the people got together more, it seems like we always had people in our house. And if we had started to eat, my dad would always say, "Sit down and have something to eat." And they would! And even though we had very little, not counting on company, he'd always invite them to our table.

We had a number of businesses here. There was a barber shop, and there was three gas stations, I believe. There was an ice cream parlor, you could go in and sit down on these wire chairs. There was a fresh fruit stand, a building, but it was only operated when the weather was OK. And they visited too. That was it, you always had somebody stop in and say hello. At Christmastime, they'd come in, and I remember the moccasins they wore in that snow, et cetera, and they would be going through to say Merry Christmas or Happy New Year. Then they'd go around in the living room like that, my dad and mother would give doughnuts. That was the Oneida way. They would give out doughnuts and then maybe an apple or so, whatever they had. Then they would go on. And the ground was so packed down, you know, from different ones going through there. And they'd go from house to house. It was just so nice to see that.

People shared a lot more then. I don't know what it is, they've forgotten. But there are some in the community who really care and are constantly giving of themselves.

You could only make [a living] in the summer, really. We cleaned cottages, and we worked at resorts. We worked in the kitchens and did washing, which was another hard job. That's just what my mother did, as a matter of fact, doing some of that work. My dad obtained a piano somewhere along the way, and my mother could play a little bit, but nothing that she could teach. So they decided that I was to learn how to play the piano. I think I was about ten years old. So she made a deal with a family not too far from us. This gal was from the east. And the Indian that married her was an attorney, a lawyer. And he brought her back here. She was an accomplished pianist. You could hear, you know when the doors were open, and you'd go by there, you could hear this beautiful piano play. So in exchange for lessons for me, my mother took in their wash. It must have been once a week, I don't know. At least I learned enough to play hymns [laughs], not too much after that, because how much washing can you do?

. . . . Dad said he had to get enough in for the winter for all of us to eat, et cetera. We had to do all that, the rice and berries and whatever. He would work, oh God, in the spring all the way through the fall, and then he'd have enough. I found a book where he kept track of his expenses. In there—it was so pitiful—he paid two dollars a month for a washing machine. Now how long would it have taken him? But we owned it. He had different expenses there, what it cost him to drive to work, to his building. . . . It was enough to keep you humble because every cent was accounted for. He did a fantastic job, and one thing about my father was that he was known as being an honest person and hardworking. He was.

People loved my mother also, because she did so many things for others. She lived here practically all her life. Went to school here as a matter of fact, in a little school near the post office, where that is now. There was a little school there, a grade school where she went. And she knew a lot of the kids then, growing up like that.

She would wash [the bodies of those who died] and put different clothes on them and fix them up. And they used to take a door off somewhere in the house there, and they would lay it on, like sawhorses, and they would put the body on there for viewing. So she was instrumental in that too. I remember there was a lady that died not too far from where we lived, maybe two doors down. And that was my first experience with a deceased. I know she went in and handled that. It was a friend of hers, a beautiful lady. . . .

As I kid we didn't notice the Depression at all because we used to be in the same boat. And I hear some of my gals now telling about: "Oh you guys were wealthy, you weren't poor like we were." Well it was just because of hard work and perseverance that we got through.

It must have been [during the Depression] because he usually had food, we had food to eat all the time, plus the berries we picked and canned. And then in the fall he would get like a bushel of apples and put the apples in a root cellar he built. Of course we always ran in there when there was a major storm, too, we would go down in the root cellar. [He stored] fruit, potatoes, and stuff down there where it kept very cool.

I'll tell you, the people were more friendly then. They got together more, and I think it might have been the American Legion here that got together, like amateur shows, musicals. Well one time they put on this program and I remember Ollie Vetterneck used to sing. She sang "Climb upon my knee, sonny boy. You are only three, sonny boy." And then my brother Hiram was the one sitting on my lap that she was singing to, oh gosh, I remember that. And then they used to have those that could play instruments of any kind or piano recitals they would have, different things like that.

They would come; they would bring maybe a cake they made or cookies or something, and they would have coffee afterward. And that was in the old Agency building, and you'd have to go upstairs, you know.

*   *   *

The American Legion used to fix [Christmas] stockings to give to different ones. That winter that my mother was away is when in the morning we found our stockings. And it had [a] harmonica, [an] apple, and an orange and nuts and hard candy. Oh, it was a wonderful treat that we found. But we didn't have a tree that year. And then my father had friends all over, you know, and he would go into town, and he would buy cigars, and then he'd go around to his friends. Maybe he'd get a bottle of wine, and he'd stop at his friends' just for a short while, and he'd give them the cigar. And then they'd have a glass of wine together. And then we were usually home, with seven kids you don't go too far way. Those were good memories.

He always taught us to give, that's better than taking, receiving.

At Easter we were usually home, and you know, Thanksgivings we never had turkeys. I didn't know what a turkey was. We had chickens, which we had all the time. Of course the men hunted. So we always ate late, which didn't matter to any of us really.

He'd fix up a sled, a toboggan, rather, with all kinds of supplies, because he didn't know how long he'd be gone. And he walked across the lake and on and on, you know. He went way over to [Highway] 70 and on the other side, you know, pulling that toboggan and his gun. He'd stay overnight, he had like a little canvas—we didn't have a tent but he had canvas—he would dig out the snow, and he'd put the canvas to cover the whole thing, and he'd be warm in there. Because he took these old blankets, et cetera, with him. But he never complained, he'd come home with either rabbits or something like that. Some animal anyway.

I did want to tell about one of things when I was a child, and the Agency school was in session. In May they had a Maypole, and that fascinated me. We went to this place, and they had decorated this big pole like a flagpole and put all those beautiful colors on the side, like strips, like ribbon or something. And then they would go around, in and out, in and out, weaving. That was one thing that really struck me, and I remember that as a kid. After that we would have a picnic, and everybody would bring something. I loved those picnics, and we would go out, although we could've had it at home, but it didn't seem the same. We had to be out there with the rest of them.

*   *   *

One thing my father did stress also, we went to church. We used up the whole pew with the family! The Community Presbyterian Church, across from the Catholic church. I know that we played hymns, and we sang, and we loved to sing! It was mostly after supper, at night, and even before the dishes were done we'd move on into the living room, and we'd start singing hymns, and each one of us would have their own selection they wanted.

*   *   *

We knew that Strawberry Island was sacred. I knew that, I heard that from way back. We were out in the boat, and we walked on Strawberry Island, but I had a funny feeling that we shouldn't be there. You didn't see any people there. And the Medicine Rock, you've heard about that, over by the village on Flambeau Lake. We just knew it was there, that too was not to be stepped on or walked on, nothing happened to it. And the only thing I know about Powell Marsh was blueberry picking. Dad would leave us off in the morning, and we'd have a sandwich or a keg of water, and we'd be in that hot sun all day long. And after that, then we'd go home and take care of the berries and stuff. But they sure tasted wonderful in the winter with homemade bread! Makes me hungry just thinking about it!

I haven't been out to Powell Swamp for a long time. When I first came back even twenty years ago, that's the place we went to look [for blueberries], and of course there wasn't anything there. You have to go into the open spaces now, too, in the woods, in the wooded areas. Sometime you happen to hit a ripe patch of berries. But gosh we used to fill those containers in no time, there were so many! And of course the raspberries, you can't see that around too much either. Blackberries are very plentiful, we have a whole bunch along the road, but I wouldn't even bother to pick them.

We used to pick cranberries. My father would know just where to go to pick those cranberries, although we didn't need that much, you know. My mother would just make sauce and have them with chicken, or one of those dishes. Never with turkey! [laughs] We never had turkeys. I don't know how much it cost to buy one, to start with, and we used to have chickens in a little fenced-in area. That's what we would eat when we wanted fowl. They did have a few eggs. . . . He always looked ahead. Both of my folks were really interested in the kids, I know that. But Mom was a lady that wouldn't feel sorry for herself, even after my dad passed away, and she was alone at Elks Point. But she'd always make contacts. She'd get on the phone and she would talk to someone, and if they said they were going into town, "Oh pick me up," she would say, and they did.

She never owned an automobile. But she got around, and she got around this country on little or nothing. They all say [they loved her] . . . and I loved her too. When I got back here, I had the time to spend with her. And she used to come out here practically every weekend with her little overnight bag. And then she'd stay for three, four days, and I just loved it. Because we were able to talk together. I never questioned before how she had met Dad or anything. And I found out that he used to work for the Ford Motor Company in Detroit before they were married! They met here, but Dad was called by his family to come back and support them or something. Because they were both elderly. [They met] through my aunt, her name was Pansy, my mother's sister who was married to the farmer here. And of course my dad, he did all kinds of things for work. And he had stopped at the Agency, at the home where Bairds lived. And they were introduced by her sister and her husband, that's how they met.

I learned a lot through them. And we would laugh when she would come here! You know, private things. She had such interesting stories and experiences. I wouldn't trade that for anything, we had the time and we laughed and joked, it was just wonderful. My husband loved her too. He missed her when she left us. My parents were pretty good parents. They didn't let us go running through the reservation without being supervised. They did [take good care of us.]

*   *   *

We all have jobs to do. We aren't just put here to have people wait on us. And of course the more jobs that you do, you learn from. You learn, and your parents would say, "Your job is to go to school right now, and you'd have a better life if you had a better education."

I think by the time you're twelve you start to see things differently in your home, and all you want is out. "I don't like that" or "I don't like this" or "I don't want to do this." You start rebelling. And actually your parents are only trying to help you. And it doesn't hurt to take on little jobs here and there because you find out what you really want to do. And the more jobs you take on when you're young like that, the better it is for you because you finally know, and you feel more comfortable with that.

And listen to your parents! They've been here longer than you have, and they know. They're only trying to steer you in the right direction, to enhance your life someday. You learn from that.

Miigwich, and on my Oneida side, yah-wa-go.[8]

---

[8]*Miigwich* means "thank you" in Ojibwe. "Thank you" is *yah-wa-ga* in Oneida.

Delia Smith and Grace Artishon

Delia and Grace were the daughters of John J. Webster, from the Oneida reservation in Wisconsin, and Carrie Smith, a Chippewa from White Earth, Minnesota. Their parents met at the Carlisle Indian School. Delia was born January 21, 1910, and Grace was born on April 30, 1912, in White Earth. They grew up on a farm and attended government boarding schools, first in Red Lake, Minnesota, and later in Odanah, Wisconsin. Grace moved to Lac du Flambeau in 1953 after she married George Artishon, a Chippewa from Lac du Flambeau. She and George had eleven children. Delia married Alpheus Smith from Oneida, Wisconsin, and lived in Milwaukee for many years, where she and her husband were very active in the Native community. They sponsored cultural activities such as craft and beading classes, lacrosse teams, basketball and softball teams, drum groups, and singing groups for funerals. They also participated in pow-wows and other events. When her husband retired, he and Delia also moved to Lac du Flambeau.

After their husbands walked on, the two sisters lived together in the house Delia's husband built on Fence Lake. Delia was active in the Senior Companion Program, and Delia and Grace both made frequent visits to the elders in their homes. They were taken on trips with elders to Canada and elsewhere, including a trip to Janesville, Wisconsin, to see the white buffalo. They also made a trip to the National Archives in Washington, DC.

Grace was a teacher to her grandchildren as well as to the children in the Lac du Flambeau School. As a foster grandparent she taught Ojibwe language and told stories to them. She also enjoyed doing beadwork until her eyesight started failing. Both Grace and Delia loved to play bingo. They enjoyed spending time visiting with children, grandchildren, nieces, and nephews. They started having family reunions on Memorial or Labor Day weekends in 1988, when they held a large potluck with all of Grace's children and grandchildren, who traveled from Wisconsin, Illinois, California, and Minnesota. They were very happy to see everyone, and Grace made her favorite recipe for fry bread. Grace's daughter Rose recalls that at this gathering her brother had three large rump roasts on a spit roaster, and her cousin Jim cooked fifteen chickens on a spit.

In their interview they describe their childhood growing up on the farm, picking berries and doing their chores, and life at the boarding schools. They also tell stories about what Flambeau was like in the 1950s and 1960s, and how much it has changed.

Interview with Delia Smith and Grace Artishon

This interview was conducted by Mildred "Tinker" Schuman

Grace: Her name is Getabiikwe[1]. . . . I don't know what that means. My name is Niizhobikwe.[2] As far as I remember, my grandma gave that name to me because she said it's just like two ladies sitting together. Grandma Smith gave us those names. Our grandmother and grandfather had a little church in Redby, Minnesota. He was Reverend Fred W. Smith. Her name was Sophie. She talked Indian all the time, and I think that's why she gave us an Indian name.

Delia: My father's name was John J. Webster, and my mother's name was Carrie Smith. My father came from Oneida, Wisconsin. He's Oneida. And our mother's Chippewa, and she's from White Earth, Minnesota. They met in school, at Carlisle Indian School. Their children are Charlotte, Fred, Stella, Raymond, Delia, Grace, Julius, and Oliver. They're our two youngest brothers, Julius and Oliver. He'll be eighty-two. I was born in White Earth, at home on the reservation.

Grace: I've been living here in Flambeau on and off since 1931. But this has been my home here now since 1953. We moved all over after I met my husband. My husband had grandparents here. That's why we came here and bought this house. It was owned by a man that lived in Mole Lake. It was a real terrible-looking place, but it was a house anyway, and my husband worked hard on it, built it the way it is now. He practically had to tear it all down to fix it up. That must have been in 1953. I have a daughter that was born at Doctor Kate's hospital,[3] that's Vicky. . . . I had eleven children.

Delia: My husband [and] I bought a place on Fence Lake in 1966. When he retired we bought a place up here because they bought a place here. I was taken care of good by our mother and stepmother from Odanah, Wisconsin. When I was seventeen I moved to Milwaukee and worked in a family home.

Grace: I can remember when we lived on the farm with our dad and stepmother. We had gardens, horses; we had eighteen cows, chickens. We used to help with the work around, feeding the chickens and doing other things, before we went to school. We got up early in the morning to help with the milk. We had a separator right at home to separate the cream, and we had to turn that by hand. After we got done with that we had to wash it out good. It had many parts to it, and we had to do all this before we went to school. Plus walking four and a half miles to school.

---

[1] Getabiikwe could be a version of Getebiikwe, which according to Joe Chosa means "Old Metal Lady."

[2] Niizhobikwe means "Two Women," as she says. It could also mean "Twin Women," according to Joe.

[3] "Dr. Kate's" hospital refers to the first hospital in the area, the Lakeland Memorial Hospital, first opened by Dr. Kate Newcomb. "Dr. Kate" was well known in the area as "the snowshoe doctor" or "the angel on snowshoes" for her delivery of health care to local residents all year round even in the winter when she would snowshoe to their houses.

We thought our stepmother was mean, but she was teaching us to do different things. Making homemade bread, home cooking. . . .

Delia: Sewing, crocheting, and stitching. Making everything. She taught us how to do a lot of things. Then we went to school, we went to church all the time. We were just busy with her all the time, and we thought she was so mean. But after we got older we found out that she was really good. I was with her when she passed away, because she was really sick, and she wanted me to stay right with her. That's what happened.

We enjoyed living on the farm, because we had a lot of things to do. We helped with the garden; we helped with everything. We learned so many things; it was really good after we got older that we knew.

Grace: We had to help make hay. Get out there and shock the hay with a big pitchfork. I remember that.

Delia: That's what I did when I got here, did cooking for a family. I worked thirteen years for one family. I cooked for them, they lived over on Crawling Stone Lake. Mrs. Seifert.

Grace: I worked for them first. Then when I quit working she took the job.

Delia: Then I took the job, and I worked for them. I'd work for them when they'd come for Christmas. They stayed for Christmas and New Year's, and I worked for them then. I did the cooking all the time. I just enjoyed my cooking. I get a Christmas card from her every Christmas. She still sends both of us a Christmas card. She lives in Chicago.

Delia: My dad and my stepmother [were my biggest influences]. Because they were teaching us different things to do. When I was working, people taught me different things, too, because I went to work when I was seventeen. And she was. . .

Grace: Sixteen. I had to go to school in Milwaukee half a day and work half a day. I worked for Dr. Hyde—they had two children. We babysat, took care of the boys, did housework. Doing dishes, sweeping, taking care of the little ones. Like nannies.

I can remember before I came to Wisconsin I stayed in a government school in Red Lake, Minnesota. I used to help around doing different things. One thing I remember, I had to take the ashes out of the stove with a little shovel, and when I was taking that out, I remember I looked up, and my mother was standing there. She came to visit me. That's all I can remember about that.

Delia: I stayed at that school too. But I did sewing all the time. Knitting, crocheting, sewing stockings, all that. Then our dad and our mother used to come to see us.

Grace: Our older sister Stella. One thing I remember, we were in this one room, we each had a bed. We were sleeping, and it was real cold at night. So we pushed our beds together, and we covered up with each other's blankets, and that's how we got warm.

I was about nine years old when I met my stepmother in Duluth. Didn't know who she was. She must have known because I was the only one that got off the train that time at Duluth. And that's where we lived on the farm.

Delia: From Red Lake we went to the Odanah school.[4] It was real good, public school. We stayed there till we graduated from the eighth grade. We had to take our final exam in Ashland, in the courthouse there, in order to pass the eighth grade. We could not stick to the teacher, she was there. When you didn't understand a question, you could ask the teacher.

Grace: One thing I remember one time, my girlfriend, her name was Helen Scott, she had a lot of money. She was buying new clothes because she had the money, and I didn't have the money to buy my clothes. My sister, she did all the sewing, one time she made my dress. And everybody was saying how pretty that dress was. It was prettier than the one my girlfriend bought at the store. So we had our final exams, and I passed—I was an A student. I remember that plain.

The teacher would make hot cocoa for us, we would eat there every day. We did a lot of walking to school, when we were young. They didn't have buses like they have now.

Delia: Our parents did farm work and gardening. Sometimes they'd sell to people, and sometimes we just put it away. They had chickens too. It was located on the old Highway 2, about halfway between Ashland and Odanah. It was a gravel road, and it was dusty. We had a wagon, and a little buggy, a horse-drawn buggy, and they'd drive us to school, or to go to church.

Grace: We did a lot of berry picking. Our stepmother used to can the berries. We lived off of that. Years back, our field was filled with wild strawberries. I remember picking those.

Delia: And raspberries, and blueberries. You'd go in the woods to find the blueberries.

Grace: It [Lac du Flambeau] has changed a lot since I've been here. The new buildings, the new schools, the churches. It had old houses, tar-paper shacks they call them. The only place that looked real good was the Gauthier's resort there. They had some stores along there. They had a hardware store, they had Oldenberg's, right on the Main Street there, that's where he was located. They had a garage there where people dropped their boat motors and stuff to be fixed, I remember that real well. Then that restaurant, Rena Keene's restaurant, the Dew Drop Inn, where they could go get something to eat. That's about all I remember that was there on the main street. Where the post office is, there was old buildings there. So it's changed quite a bit.

That restaurant was real nice. You could go in there and get what you wanted, a sandwich or coffee or tea or whatever you wanted. They didn't have big meals, just sandwich-type food.

Woodman Hall was the dance hall. Years back, the big bands came there. . . . We just lived on the corner there near that dance hall after I was married. They had real good pow-wows then. They used to be in the tall pines where that hotel and casino is now. That used to be just beautiful pine trees there. It was sad to see them take them down. But that's where they used to have their pow-wows. I danced, I remember my dress. I never did all the new dances they have now. Just a regular dance.

Delia: In Milwaukee my husband was a member of the Oneida tribe there, they used to have dances all the time. He was the head one there, they'd have dances all the time, in the summertime,

---

[4] Odanah on the Bad River Reservation, about a hundred miles northeast of Lac du Flambeau.

in the winter, and I danced, too, and helped him take care of everything. It was real good—people enjoyed him because he was a good worker. . . .

We used to go around and sing Oneida songs, too. At the Veterans' Hall.

Grace: Where Mrs. Hrabik works up there, that used to be a doctor's office. You'd go up there to get your medication. I remember one doctor, a tall doctor, Dr. Sitcock.

Grace: When I first came around here, the summer people that come up have resorts around here. The people in Flambeau used to guide them, go fishing or hunting. Just like they do now. Some had gardens, they lived off what they grew. I tried to have a garden, my land here is real sandy. I planted some carrots and onions and potatoes. It was just a small garden, but I think it was too sandy. It was just like a miniature garden, everything was small. It didn't grow good at all, it's just too much sand. . .

My husband's cousin, old Ben Chosa, he was a guide. Guided the people from Illinois who'd come up here every year to fish. He was good at cooking for them, preparing the fish, they'd eat it right there. Years back that water was so clear, you could drink it. Now you can't. Even Lake Superior. When I lived in Red Cliff, over sixty years ago, we could drink that Lake Superior water, it was so clear. Nowadays you're afraid to drink that.

I think that's also why they're worried about Flambeau Lake, Strawberry Island. If they build on there, that'd be really polluted then. That's why we're having bingo every Monday, to get it back.[5]

Grace: At Christmas we used to make gifts for everyone. . . . I remember when we lived at Odanah, our dad used to put a lot of hay in the wagon, in the back, and on New Year's Eve we used to go to all the different homes, wish everybody a happy new year. We'd be given an apple or an orange, or sometimes they'd put a big feed out. If they lived way out they'd put a big feed out to feed us. My dad used his horses, they had the bells on the horses. It sounded real good going on the sleigh. . . . We had blankets to cover up with us. Those were the days, I think.

Delia: That was really fun. A lot of us traveled together. Went way out into the woods visiting people, because the places were way out. Wished everybody a happy new year, you know.

We used to make maple sugar every year too. And we'd get out of school and go with our parents into the woods and live there until we got through making maple syrup, maple sugar. They didn't get after us about going to school, they just let us do that. After we got out of there, then we went back to school. It was really good.

We lived in a regular little cabin. It was real long, because when you made the sugar, cooked the sap first, you'd make a place for boiling it in different kettles. And they'd boil it at night, and we'd sleep like that. It'd be open up on top. It was real nice. We didn't really freeze, because it was heated, you know, when they were cooking the syrup.

---

[5] Strawberry Island, site of the last battle between the Sioux and Ojibwe and considered a sacred place. At the time of these interviews the owner, Walter Mills, was planning to develop the island. The Monday nights bingos were part of a large fundraising drive to protect the island.

Delia Smith (left) and Grace Artishon dressed in traditional outfits

Delia: There's a lot of things we did years ago they don't do nowadays. Yesterday we had a Valentine party. In those days we didn't do that. They didn't have that holiday when we were younger. But we always used to have old-time square dances, like at Woodman Hall. Every time we'd see the boys and girls, they'd always say, "Well let's have a square dance!" Sometimes they'd come to our house, and we'd move everything away and have a big square dance. Then we'd move to somebody else's house, have a square dance. They'd play the violin. There was a lot of music— boys used to make a lot of violin and all different kinds of music.

One time when we were real young, we were going to go to a party, and our stepmother said, "You've got to finish that quilt, sewing it all up, before you can go." So she and I hurried up and sewed that quilt and got it finished, and when we got through with it, we did the edge of it. Finished the whole thing. And we decided to go to a party, and she said well, you can't go. We said we quit the quilt, finished it, you told us we can go now. So we went and had a good party. [laughs]

Different things she'd tell us. But it's real good that she taught us a lot of things. We really enjoy the things she taught us. We thought she was really mean to us, but she wasn't. She was just teaching us. Thinking about it now, we're so happy that we learned so many things.

Grace: I can remember [the Depression years] when my first daughter was born. No work. Our brother used to go out and get rabbits. The rabbits in those days were good, now they're not. He used to get them, and he used to prepare it. When my first daughter was born, I nursed her and didn't have hardly any milk to feed the baby. That's what he used to do, he used to go out and get wild stuff to cook so that we could have enough to eat. Then we had a minister that used to be living near there, and she brought food over that we could have, because there was no work. You'd just have to live off mother earth. Right up the hill by my house here, I have that wintergreen. I used to go get that, make tea with that, wintergreen tea. One of my daughters really loved that. She used to always make it, drink it.

Delia: We used to have little picnics. Near a lake or in the woods. When they had the pow-wow, they'd have a picnic then too. We'd go to the pow-wow a lot; we'd both dress up in an Indian outfit. It was real plain, then, it was really Indian, the pow-wows. Like the Big Drum.[6] My stepmother got us a dress to dress up in, and she'd take us to the pow-wows. They'd have them by her house too. She really liked it; she really was interested in pow-wows. And she'd cook a lot too. She'd make a lot of meals, and we'd help her.

It's really good because she just did everything. Everybody liked her. This was where we grew up in Odanah, where they had the pow-wows. But different ones from different reservations would go up.

Sometimes they danced real late at night.

Grace: I can remember laying there, and somebody was beating on the wall, singing, singing just loud. I was sleeping, it woke me up that pounding, like a drum. Singing. That's the friends of our stepmother used to come there.

Delia: The dances were different then. Instead of the way they do now, we used to just move our feet, instead of raising them up and dancing. They called that a squaw dance.[7] They wouldn't let us do any other kind of dance, for the ladies, and the men would do their dances. The men's dances were kind of different. Real old dancing. They were doing it really short, not the way they do now. We used to enjoy it though, when we'd go and dance.

Grace: The two-step is almost like what they do now. And the snake dance. We used to do that, but not the real fast dancing. Real slow dancing. For the two-step, the men asked the women to dance. The women never did go and ask [like they do now]. They just had the regular squaw dance, and all the ladies would be dancing. They changed the way they use their feet, since they have the bowl there. They used to ask the audience if anybody wants to go down and dance, which is nice now that they do that.

Delia: And the ladies didn't dance like the men did, years ago, but they do that now. They dance almost like the men dance. They didn't years ago. The women did wear jingles then.

Grace: I remember my jingle dress. It was all cotton material.

Delia: The ladies all wore buckskin. And I had a buckskin dress. I even had it up to some time ago, but I gave it to my niece Rose. She's got the buckskin dress now. We danced a lot.

---

[6] The Big Drum refers to a traditional religion. (See Introduction.)

[7] Squaw Dance, now called the Women's Dance, is an old traditional dance in which the women step to the side with small steps, hands on hips, while facing the center of the circle.

Grace Artishon (left) and Delia Smith dressed in ribbon shirts

Marie Spruce

Marie Spruce was born on February 8, 1919, to William Henry Carufel, Sr., and Alice (Headflyer) Carufel. She grew up with her five sisters and six brothers in the home of her parents in the town of Lac du Flambeau in their house near the railroad depot where they would move in the springtime. Her father ran the Headflyer Store at the depot, a popular spot with visiting tourists and local Indian families, who would come to trade their wild rice, maple sugar, and other traditional foods for flour, sugar, lard, and canned goods. In her interview Marie shares many vivid memories of her childhood, both of her home near the depot, and of the Lac du Flambeau boarding school, which she attended until the eighth grade. She attended high school at Haskell Institute in Lawrence, Kansas. After graduating from there she returned to Flambeau, and in 1940, she accepted a position as the assistant girls' advisor at a school for Jicarilla Apaches in New Mexico.

There she met and married Thurman Bear, a Shawnee from Oklahoma, and together they opened a boarding school in Dulce, New Mexico. Thurman went to serve in the Army during World War II, when Marie returned to Flambeau and gave birth to their son Thurman Junior ("Bear"). She later married Robert Spruce, a Chippewa from L'Anse, Michigan. The couple adopted two of her niece's children, Alicia and Darryl. In 1972 the Spruces moved back to Lac du Flambeau and built the house near the old depot where Marie lived the rest of her life.

According to all who knew her, Marie was a kind woman with a ready smile and a dry sense of humor. She was a devout Catholic and always helped out at St. Anthony's Church in Lac du Flambeau, including cooking for the summer school catechism classes. Marie was very active both in the church and the tribe and served on the Tribal Elections Board for many years. She was also a talented seamstress and outfitted many in the community. As her interview shows, she was also a wonderful storyteller with a remarkable memory of her childhood. Marie passed away on October 13, 2002, in the house where she lived the last thirty years of her life, close to the site of her childhood home across from the railroad depot.

Interview with Marie Spruce

Donald Carufel, Marie's nephew, conducted this interview.

My father's name was William Henry Carufel, Senior, my mother was Alice Bimaasinokwe,[1] also known as Headflyer, Carufel. My grandfather on my father's side was Urgell Carufel. Charles Headflyer was her adopted grandfather, because her real father was a white man, and they never wanted to, he didn't want to acknowledge my mother, so she just took the name. Julia Bimaasinokwe [was my grandmother on my mother's side]. . . . I never knew them.

My dad was originally from LCO and I believe . . . his mother, Mary Carufel, LCO, but his father [Urgell] was originally from somewhere in Canada. He [Charles Headflyer] was originally from Red Cliff, but he lived here most of his life—by Trout River. He used to have like a berry farm. I remember him when I was little; he'd come in like a couple times a week with a little team of horses and a little wagon. And they'd bring milk, and they'd send the milk on the train to Green Bay. I remember that: Fairmont Creamery. I guess that's how [Headflyer Lake] was named.

Grandpa—my dad—came over here for some reason, and he had a little store, it used to be across the tracks.[2] Where—this is the old, across the track, when we were kids [points to a house in an old photograph]. And the house used to be right in here [waves towards the north], this house that's next door. Then in 1926 they moved it over across the track to where it is now [on the south side of the track]. And then later they added on this wing on this side which ended up as a kitchen, and the room upstairs—we always called it the dormitory because that's where the boys used to sleep. Your dad and Uncle Billy and Pudge [George] and all of them. See this here used to be, that's the barn and tool shed. And then this back here is a chicken coop, chicken house. That house that's over there now is right across the road from this. We lived there part of the time when we were growing up. And we also lived in the white house, it was on the other side. I was about ten or twelve when they moved it over. They moved it over in '26 . . . for more business. Because the depot used to be over there, right across. And my dad had the store. See this? That was the storefront. We used to have a big sign across it. It said "Carufel Candy Store" or something like that. But originally he had just basic flour, sugar, and stuff like that. Because there were a lot of people living around here, but they didn't always have time to go all the way into town. But there was a lot of Indian families that lived in this area. Down by where [County Highway] H is, and then over where Camp Wipigaki is, over in that direction, that's where Jack Patterson used to live.

---

[1] Bimaasinokwe means "Wind Blowing Along Woman." The name Headflyer could be a rough translation of this name.

[2] Charles Headflyer owned a general store across from the Chicago and Northwestern Railroad depot, about three miles from downtown Flambeau. The railroad brought many visitors and fisherman to Lac du Flambeau, as well as the mail train. From the depot buggies would take visitors to town and to the resorts, or guides would take them to their favorite fishing spot. The Headflyer Store served not only out-of-town visitors, but many of the Indian families who lived nearby, as Marie relates.

Charles Headflyer

Lac du Flambeau railroad depot

And Evelyn and Bob McArthur, Genevieve's grandma. And then right up here where Bill Ackley lives, that was where his mom and dad lived. A long time ago. Right up here.

And Kiboniki Point, that's where Jack Edwards and Helen Corn and Elizabeth—it used to be Kiboniki, but then she remarried, and her name was Pine. There was quite a settlement over on that point over there. And a lot of those people came over here to our . . . because I remember when I was little, maybe about—before I went to school, a lot of times different ones would come in, just get a few things, then they'd all sit around in the store part, the front part. And my dad had a wooden chest. And there was always enamelware, plates and bowls and cups. . . .

And he had this big old coffeepot, he'd put water down there in the morning, and they'd make tea from that. And then they'd have, like maybe old man Kiboniki, he'd say, "Let's have some tomatoes!" They'd usually buy those big cans like that [holds her hands to show a number ten can]. My dad always had a can opener there. He'd open it for them, and then they'd portion it out. And then just sit and visit and eat tomatoes with a little bit of sugar or a little bit of salt and pepper. Just like social hour. And then sometimes my ma wasn't too busy because of the kids, she'd bring in fresh bread. She was always baking. She baked almost every other day. Because we were a large family, when we were all home. When the older ones went away to school, we were still young yet. Like his dad [Donny's] and Billy and I and Pudge. But see this allotment in here is originally my mother's allotment.[3] And that's why we're trying to keep it in the family. Because we're supposed to partition it off, each one is supposed to get ten acres. That's in the process of being settled. But my portion here, when I moved this over where it is now, it used to be just right where the garage is now. That's where the house used to be. You'd come out on the front step; you'd walk right on the road.

And they used to live here before we moved up. See, my husband and I came up here in '72 from Detroit, because he was sick. Wouldn't be working anymore, so.

See, this house was built in '26, the same year that they moved this one over, the white one. It was built by Wilson Lumber Company. There used to be a lumber shed right across. That used to be a side track here, and over there. And then the lumber yard was right across from this house, right over here. The train would come right along back of the building, they'd unload all the lumber and supplies into the lumber shed. It was a great big building, kind of like a barn, and the front part was like a hardware store. But all this other lumber was like in, he had racks and everything.

But they built this house as a model. Before I had it redone, every room in the house had different woodwork. To give an example to people who want to be building. Because at that time there was a lot of people moving up here and building. Resorts and stuff like that. And then instead of plaster board, it was like rough, like slivery stuff. Rougher than that [particle board].

But anyway, each room had different woodwork. And then there was no bathroom on here, where you're sitting. That was the end of the house right here. You know when I moved up here in

---

[3] After the Allotment Act of 1887 was passed, formerly communal tribal lands were divided into forty-acre parcels and these "allotments" were signed over to the families who lived there. (See Introduction.)

'72, his [Donny's] dad did part of the work before we got here, but he couldn't get reliable help to get it all done, so we finished it up, his dad and I. We did get some help, but not what we really wanted. This was the kitchen right here, and the back door right there, and there was like a little porch, a closed-in porch. And then before they moved here, they made a little small bathroom on the end of the porch—a toilet and a shower. And then the front porch is where I have my sewing room now. That was two little rooms, and you'd come in like from that way, and there was a little hallway, there was about three or four doors. It was a porch to begin with, but then they divided it up and made two little small bedrooms. . . . Donny helped his dad put in my new well on the corner of the house. That was in '80.

I got this stuff [old photographs] from Pat[4] if I sell my house. If I sell I only want to sell to someone in my family. Because I don't want to give it up to anybody, just anybody. But if I do sell, whoever I sell to, I would just give them the land. I'm not charging for the land, I'm just charging for the house. But if nobody comes up with the money then I'll just stay here. I was going to go to Elks Point. I got my application in, they call every now and then. "No, I'm not ready yet!"

*   *   *

I had six brothers and five sisters. There's six of us left, four girls and two boys. My brother George ["Pudge"] lives over across there, and Bill lives out on Fence Lake. My oldest sister's in a nursing home in Rhinelander. My kid sister lives in Lake Tomahawk, and my sister next to me is living in Wausau. We're the only ones left now. Sophie is ninety-one. We went down for her birthday, she's doing real good. I mean physically she looks good. But she's very confused at times. Almost every time we go she asks, "How's Ma? How's Pa?" And I say, "Well, they're gone." "Well I didn't know they died!" and stuff like that. You know she just has so much time to think about things that she gets kind of mixed up. But physically she's in pretty good shape for her age.

[I was born] February 8, 1919. I'm seventy-seven, I'm now an elder. Big deal. I was born uptown, where Leon Valliere [Senior] lives. There used to be a house there; that's where I was born. Because doctor wasn't sure that he could get out here to deliver me, so at that time my dad was postmaster. He rented this little house in town, and we lived there all winter. And we came back here in the spring, after the roads got open. But that's actually where I was born. I think George was the only one that was born in the hospital, and that was in Rhinelander. The rest of us were all born at home. We used to have doctors that, if we were lucky enough, they would come to the house. But we didn't have . . . we used to have field nurse, they call them. Like Nancy is now.[5] I don't know if she makes home visits, but that's what they used to do. Because see they had like a

[4] Pat Hrabik-Sebby, who was the director of the Lac du Flambeau Historic Preservation Office at the time. She had since retired, though her friendship with Marie continued.

[5] Nancy DiCristina, now retired, was a community health nurse at the time, and visited many elders in the community, including Marie.

small clinic up where the BIA building is. Even when I first moved back, where the BIA building is, that big two-story. That used to be the boys' dormitory during boarding school days. And then in the middle was this great big water tower. And then another big building is sort of H-shaped. And that was the girls' building and kitchen and dining room. And upstairs on the dining room side was the gym.

*   *   *

We moved up here in '72. Before that I lived in Detroit, Michigan. Taylor, it's a suburb of Detroit, we bought a home there. My husband used to work at Cadillac Motors, then he got sick and they said he wouldn't be able to work anymore. We stayed there a couple years after he was diagnosed. We were up here that summer, I talked to my ma, and I said, "If we move up here, will you give me some land?" "Anywhere you want," she said. I wanted to be in the woods over there, but it just didn't work out. Anyway, we moved up here in '72, in June. So we've been up here—twenty-four years? My god. You see they [Dave's family] used to live here, and they moved in January, they moved out on Wayman Lane, out where his mom lives. And then when we came up, we stayed in that little house across the road all summer. Then we built this house, and we moved in here around Halloween. I said, if I have to sleep on the floor, I said, I'm not staying over there any more. It was so cold, we had a real cold fall. So we just moved in and made that extra room that we added on, we made a nice bedroom for my husband. I slept out in the, what used to be the porch, where the sewing room is. Then Alisha was in this, my bedroom now. See Bob and I didn't have any children of our own. I was married before. Then I have one son, lives in Dearborn. But we adopted a couple of my niece's kids when we were back in Michigan. Then Alicia came up with us because she was just starting high school. She and Donny are the same age, two weeks apart, something like that.

I don't know if [my second husband Bob] has a real Indian name—he was supposed to have gotten an Indian name, but I don't know if he did or not. [My first husband Bear] we just call him Bear. Makwa. My first husband was from Oklahoma. He was Shawnee and something else. We used to always say Cherokee, but he wasn't Cherokee. He was from Oklahoma. Then Bob was from L'Anse, Keweenaw Bay.[6]

*   *   *

Bad memories [of boarding school].[7] Oh well. I know we went up in the fall, we'd have to go. My ma would take us up there, you'd register us or whatever. We stayed in dormitories, it was

[6] L'Anse is a town on L'Anse Bay in the Upper Peninsula of Michigan, the home of the L'Anse Band of Lake Superior Chippewa Indians.

[7] She is describing the government boarding school in Lac du Flambeau.

like—it wasn't too much military style when we were there, but before that everything was very military style. But then next to the girls' dormitory was the schoolhouse, a big two-story. They used part of that building they added onto, but the main part of it was the power plant.

And then those buildings around there were all connected with the boarding school. Like where Beverly Bauman's house is, that used to be the farmer's house. And then those other buildings closer to the bridge, that used to be the dairy part and the warehouse or whatever. It was quite a bunch of stuff back in there. Then over across the other way, there was a great big two-story building, they called it the club. That's where the teachers lived. Because most of the time they were all single people. Mostly women. Then there was the doctor's home and probably the principal or somebody. And then where Don Smith's house is, they built there, but before that there was a big house, I think the superintendent's house. And there was some other houses, I don't know who lives there now but—all that part of the outfit was boarding school. And then where the, like deer registration place is, that used to be a big warehouse. That's where they got our supplies, I suppose. Clothing and whatever. And then across from the BIA building there was another two-story building. Upstairs was the sewing room. . . . There was quite a complex there, a lot of buildings.

[It was] not too bad at times, but then I don't have a lot of good memories either. Because we had to go there no matter what, you know. Then they generously let us come home in the spring [smiles ironically]. And then, well the older girls, we had to do the work in the kitchen, in the bakery and the dining room, clean up the dormitory rooms and whatever. And then upstairs on that one side was a great big dormitory, a girls' dormitory. . . . We didn't have steam heat there at the time, it was just a big stove. And they just put the beds in rows like big army style beds, I guess, metal, they'd stand about that high [puts her hand two feet above the ground].

We used to freak out the matron and hide. Pull the blankets down and hide under there. And then one corner, there was a little small bathroom. Didn't always work, and we'd have to go all the way downstairs. And then on the bottom part of that part of the building was, when you come in the main door, there was the washroom, the shower, there's showers on one end, and then there was the clothing room and sewing room. And then way on the end was, oh they tried to call it a library for a while, but—if you were real good then you could go in there and sit and play checkers.

And then in between there was what they call a playroom. Just a big room with a ladder. You just go back and forth on it, it would—metal. Then there was steel beams like that all through the building. I remember there was one in the playroom, and we used to get up on the ladder and slide down on it. You know, try to do tricks on it. At one time, I think I was probably in the sixth grade, I was—I got on there and I was going to imitate what one of the other girls had done, turn over like. And I slipped and fell, knocked a tooth out. And that night I was on the program. Teacher made me get up there anyway, and I was lisping, you know? I was so conscious of it, one of my front teeth.

And then that middle part of the building was like H-shaped, the front part was a kitchen. And then upstairs was the matron's quarter's. And then there was a hallway like that down to the

The H-building Marie describes, the girls' dormitory

dining room, and a big stairway up to the dormitory upstairs. And then this part here there was like the cook's room, and then there was a little small bathroom on the end. She used that bathroom, and the dining room matron was on this other side, and there was a stairway here in the middle from the front going up to the gym. That's where we'd have basketball games and stuff like that. Then on the other side was the dormitory.

I think I did one time [try to run away]. I didn't get very far.

*   *   *

Each teacher had like fifth grade or fourth grade. During the day you'd have English or Arithmetic or whatever. And then in later years we used to go to the sewing room for, supposed to be home ec. All we did was sew on buttons and help hem clothes. But we used to wear sort of like uniforms, we always called them "hickory." You know what these, they're like blue and white striped, like mattress ticking? That texture. But anyway that's what we used to wear as uniforms, like that. And then for Sundays we had like navy blue serge, long sleeves, and the only color on it was, we had a strip of buttons down here [points down below her left shoulder], and they were covered with red. And then like a piping on the side. And that was the only color. And no belt.

And then in the spring that one year, oh in that sewing room we thought it was so great, we got new uniforms for spring. White. With like, that strip was all like, we used to do hand embroidery on it. Mrs. Gurnoe would sit, snap you on the fingers if you didn't, if you didn't get the stitch just right. Snap you and make you take it out and do it over.

She was a Indian woman from Bayfield. They always question that she was Indian, but she was. They had one girl, Dolly. "Precious." We had to take care of her. She'd always make up stories you know. [In a whiny voice] "Marie didn't take me to the bathroom when I wanted to go." Then she'd say, haul me out for that. I'd have to take her in her quarters and help her get her bath and get ready for bed and stuff like that. And then the head matron was Clara Lee [sighs]. She was a widow, and her mother lived with her. She had a room upstairs, second floor. And then old lady

Lee, she was kind of chubby. And she'd get all upset about somebody or something, you know. She'd come down the hall and she'd be just literally bouncing, and her face would be red as. . . .

And that one time we went to the movie at the auditorium, on Friday night. I think it was something like King Kong. And on the way home, after the movie we were coming back to the dorm. Somebody said something like "Here comes King Kong!" and some of the boys started chasing us. Everybody screaming and hollering, you know. The next day we were all punished. We went to the movie that night, we were all punished. In the playroom we had to march, round and round, just—march. Not really military style, just march. We marched for *two hours*. And I can still remember that. My legs were just like trembling from being—no excuses. You'd tell her you want to go to the bathroom. "You can wait. You can wait." I mean in a lot of ways, they were kind of bad.

I'm trying to think who [my classmates were]. Maxine Decota. Celia Defoe, she was there part of the time, I think she came down from Bayfield. . . . And then Marcella Beson. I don't remember if she was here for boarding school, but she was here for what they call day school. See in 1932, that was the year Delores [Marie's daughter] was born, '32, all of a sudden they said boarding school was abolished, and they were going to start having day school. No more boarding school. They had all the stuff up there yet, but you just didn't live there anymore. Well see we lived out here, and they didn't have time to make arrangements for us for, you know, taking us to school, because there wasn't buses.

So that fall his dad, Dave, and my brother Bill and I, we went to Mount Pleasant, Michigan, to boarding school over there. And then there was another family, Devines, they used to live out by Winchester. They were in school, but I don't think they're living now either, none of those kids. And then Blanche Wayman—what was her name? She's dead now anyway. I can't think of anybody else besides me. . . . I know I'm one of the elders, elder elders. Because I'm seventy-seven.

After I finished, got home from Mount Pleasant, we just went one year, and then we came back here, and they had what they call day school. We used to ride with the mailman, because there was a train come in about 9:00. We were always late, but that didn't count. It was Dave and Bill and I and I think George for a while. They'd take us, drop the mail off and then take us to school and then come and get us after school and bring us home.

And I remember one time we had a real bad storm, a real blizzard. I remember my dad came in, walked in town, across the lake. We used to cross the lake there, where the Indian bowl is? Right across to about where Pat Hrabik's house is, somewhere in there. There was a regular trail. You know, be built up after several weeks, about that wide. I know my dad came over to the school to get us, and he talked to somebody, I don't know, in the office. And we knew there was, we used to call them "horse blankets." There was like khaki, wool capes. They had brought in a shipment but nobody would wear them. But he knew they were in that warehouse. So he got one for each of us. And we put them around us.

And then he brought a piece of rope. And he'd tie it to his waist, and he tied Bill and Dave, and then I was on the end. And then we came back across the lake. You could hardly see! I mean that's how bad it was. And then a lot of those kids followed us. But I mean, he made that sort of arrangement to make sure we wouldn't, you know, if we'd fall or anything. And then we got back here, back to town, and the mailman brought us most of the way home because the road was still not fully drifted over yet. But he brought us, yeah, just about all the way home. And then we didn't go to school at all the next day. It was just real terrible, real bad.

Then after, when I finished the ninth grade up here, then I went to Haskell to school. I finished Haskell, and I went back. Then after, I went back to Haskell for one year of post-grad work. I wanted to take nursing but my health was such that I couldn't, you know. They wouldn't accept me. So I came home that fall. I was debating about maybe going to Chicago to work.

Then I got a letter from—somewhere. New Mexico. No, from Haskell, asking me if I wanted this job. It was to go to Jicarilla Apaches to be the assistant girls' advisor. So I took it. And the big salary! $720 a year, 60 bucks a month. But in those days that was real good money. And everybody—"Did you hear Marie's going? She's going out West. She's going to some reservation to work in the school!" Big deal. Well I went, went by myself. I think they sent me some money from Ashland for my ticket. I'm not sure, but I think that's what it was.

I went out there in October. October 1, 1940. And I got married out there to Bear, he was working as—we opened a boarding school. And prior to that, the mission, Dutch Reform mission, had a boarding school, but they had worked something out for the federal government to have a school for the kids. So we went out there, it was a brand new buildings, dormitories, but we went—they bused the kids "downtown" they called it, to the school. There was a school there already, and that's where they bused the kids. But that's the way I got out of Flambeau. During the war, I came home and stayed here for awhile, and then he came off furlough, and then he was discharged. I was still living here. I lived over in that little house over there for a while. In the summer. And then I moved to Rhinelander. I was living in Rhinelander when I was pregnant, and that's where Bear [Thurman] was born.

When his dad came back, we had a chance to go to California or somewhere in Arizona. You know, for a job. We went back to New Mexico after the war and still stayed there awhile. And then when Bear was old enough for high school, we moved to Riverside, California, and he'd go right across the campus, across the road to parochial grade school. And then he graduated. And then for high school, he could've just gone out the main gate, across Magnolia, go into Corona to a boys' school. And of course there was all kinds of schools and colleges and everything. But Bear just couldn't stand the city. So we moved back to Fort Apache. We were there a couple years, and then I pulled up stakes. Divorced and came back home. Went to Michigan.

I loved it [New Mexico]. It was really nice. It was up in the foothills of the Rockies. You could look out of our kitchen window . . . there was what they called Archuleta mountains, that was the foothills of the Rockies. A certain time of the day, you could look up there, you could see the reflection, it was a certain metal pole. And that was the state line. Colorado was just on the other side. I liked it because . . . the altitude was just a little over a mile high. I really liked it out there, it was pretty country. We really had it made as far as our living.

So then we got the idea to go to California. I'd liked to have stayed there, but he wouldn't stay. We went to Fort Apache and then White River, just down the road a couple miles. Then he quit working at the school and transferred to the hospital, as cook. Anyway, that's what happened.

When I went away to work, I mean I just, it was what I wanted to do because I just wanted to get away from here and see how the rest of the world lived. And boy did I find out! It's OK.

* * *

Grandpa had the store, and like I said he was postmaster during the time when I was born. And then my ma used to just housewife. And then she worked as, she was like supervisor of the WPA sewing school. That was in that BIA building, upstairs. They made clothes, dresses, and clothing for the kids, you know, on the reservation. Not in boarding school. The boarding school was no longer. That was like when it was the Depression, it was kind of hard times. My dad stayed and took care of the kids. Because my dad only had one arm. He would take care of the kids, and then my sister Rose came and stayed part of the winter with them and help take care of the house and kids. But then she went back to Chicago, because she was working down there. And that was, she was up there about three years I think.

* * *

[Dave] was in the Marines, Bill was in the Navy, Pudge was in the Navy. Ray was, he never was in the service because he had TB when he was quite young. He had to leave school. But those—then I had one brother that died when he was an infant. He had meningitis, he died when he was an infant. Thurman [my husband], he was in the Army. My son, he was in the Marines.

* * *

During boarding school [for recreation] we used to have basketball teams, baseball in the summer and stuff like that. There used to be Indian dancing over, what do they call it—by Little Pines, back in there, sometimes they'd have dances back then. But a lot of it is where Bear River is now. That was developed after I came back up here. They had started it before I moved back up. Bear River is the only pow-wow stuff that I remember.

We used to, in boarding school days, we were lucky if we could get home, even for the day. Like maybe Christmas or Easter. At the time we only had Mass one Sunday a month. I remember I told Sister and Father about it, and they laughed because they had to haul a sleigh in. He always had at least a team of horses and cows and chickens and stuff. But he'd always come in on church day. My ma and them would be in, he'd have the kids in the back wrapped up in blankets, and they'd have hay in the back. And then they'd come up to church, and then they'd, we'd walk from the boarding school to church.

And I know Al Kobe told his version, that if you walked on the left side of the road you went to the Catholic church, and if you over here you went to the Protestant church.[8] But I don't remember that part of it. But he's older than me anyway. But anyway we'd come up to church one Sunday a month, and then after church my dad would put us all in the back of the sleigh. And a couple times, instead of going right back to school, he came like towards town and then come across on the lake and old lady Lee had a conniption: [in a high squeaky voice] "Oh Mr. Carufel, you shouldn't do that!" He said, "Well I did it." Right away. You know, just trying to give us a little bit of a sleigh ride, nothing wrong with that. She was a character!

[At Christmas] we always had a tree. I remember we used to have little clip on things that you clip on the branch. And then they had a little candle like that, then there was a little reflector behind it. We'd have that at night, and then in the morning you'd get up and get your gifts. Never a lot, never anything real fancy, usually clothes, or if ma saved enough coupons I'd get a doll, or saved bread wrappers or whatever. They did the best they could, we were never considered well off or anything like that. Like I said, they did the best they could.

*   *   *

There was quite a bit of activity here with all the trains because we used to have at least four every day except Sunday. But in the summer there was always six trains. That one special for the summer they called the fish train. It would leave Chicago at night and get up here about seven in the morning, and that's when a lot of the people coming up as tourists, or maybe they had homes up here, they would come on that train. Then it would go back south about seven at night.

The other train would come early in the morning, like six o'clock, and they always called that the mail train because they always had somebody here from the post office—they had a regular driver, he'd pick up all the mail and then take it in. And then about ten o'clock there would be a train going south, it went just as far as Antigo, and that was also a mail train. And then the afternoon train would come in about four, and the night train going south would be about eight o'clock.

So there would be quite a bit of activity, in the summer especially, with all the extra trains and all the extra people coming up here. There were several camps, like for the YMCA and Adventure's Camp over here on Fence Lake, and they would come in on one of these trains, maybe the early morning train. And there'd be people out here to meet them, like in little trucks. And

[8] Al Kobe, also a Lac du Flambeau tribal member, wrote an autobiography, *Great Spirit*, in which he describes his boarding school experience.

there'd be one baggage car with nothing but baggage for the kids, because they did a lot of the camping, actual camping, not staying in a cabin or something.

Then they'd go around to all the different like, supposed to be points of interest, like the fish hatchery, I suppose, and they'd take them on hikes. Go up here to the Fire Tower, used to be over here. You could see it from here, but they took it down several years ago. But the YMCA camp was all men, and there was a couple, they had one little, one daughter. They were in charge of the camp for at least ten years that I remember. And they were probably here longer than that, but that's what I remember.

They'd come up and meet passengers, like the men from Chicago, from the Y, would be coming up maybe. They'd stay two weeks at a time. It was like their vacation. But they had a lot of activities out there, canoeing and whatever. Then once a summer they'd always have like a field day, and they'd have people come in from other camps around here. They'd have like a competition with swimming and baseball and whatever. And then a lot of times they would take my brothers and I out there to spend the day with them, you know. Supposed to give it local color, I guess.

*   *   *

There was some people lived down towards Fence Lake, out by Sand Lake, both ends. I guess you'd call it the south end of Sand Lake, and then over here on the other side. And then back up in here by Pokegama, back in the woods anyway. But I mean they had their own little plots of land, and they didn't really care about living in town. But they would come in here when we had the store, and my dad would get special things for them. They'd tell him one time, "Get me a pair of shoes," and they'd pick it out from the catalogue, like Sears or Montgomery Ward. Then he'd make out the order and send it in, and when they'd come back, they'd have it.

And then a lot of these older people, they'd come in maybe every other week and they would just take their time about shopping. I mean it was more of a social thing besides just going through your groceries. But they'd sit around the store part and just sit and visit.

My mom had a wooden chest in the store, and she had extra enamelware dishes and silverware in there, a couple can openers. My dad would always put a teakettle on the heater. He always had hot water, and they could make tea. So when a lot of people would come in, he'd fix a big kettle of tea for them. And then they would decide—they'd sit and visit, and they'd decide they wanted some fruit or something, and they'd get a big can of peaches or tomatoes or pears, I guess, and he'd open it for them, and then they'd just dole it out. Just sit and eat and enjoy it, and you know, talk about what was happening, what they'd heard about if somebody was sick somewhere else, or in town. It was just sort of a gathering place for these people.

And then they'd pick out whatever they wanted from the shelves, and they'd tell them, you know, like they'd get their flour or salt or sugar. And they used to have big barrels of sauerkraut and pickles way in the back, in the shed. And when they'd say they wanted some sauerkraut or whatever, one of us, or my mom, we'd have to go back and dole it out. A lot of them carried those little lard pails with the covers. Then they'd take so much, they'd say they wanted half full of sauerkraut or whatever.

Then sometimes if they were kind of short on money they'd trade, because they'd bring in rice or maple syrup or maple sugar, and sometimes sugar cakes. And then they'd sort of, you know, trade back and forth. That was one of the things I remember—listening to all these old people talking. They always talked Ojibwe, they didn't, very seldom, talk in English. But then they'd sit and talk and laugh about, you know, tell stories I suppose, and laugh and just have a good time. It was just a way of, you know, part of their social life.

And then some of them would have a pony, maybe they'd come in on a pony, or else they'd maybe have a wagon. If they'd do that, then usually they'd get a big bag of flour to take back to their camp or whatever. But it was all, I mean that's part of it that I remember. And then some of them would ask my ma if she could spare some milk, because we always had at least two cows, and we always had horses and chickens and pigs. But they'd ask her if she could spare some fresh milk, and then they'd have a little pail, and she'd give it to them.

And then in exchange they'd maybe give her rice, or whatever. Not always cash, you know. Because a lot of the people, they didn't have regular jobs and a lot of it was trading back and forth. That's just the way they did it. Some of them would bring in fish, especially in the spring, you know, they'd go spearing or put out their nets, and they'd bring in whatever they had. Or they'd bring in maybe a hindquarter or something, and they'd want to trade.

My dad always used to go hunting too, and he was a pretty good shot even though he only had one arm. He had a spot back in there where he always went in the evening, and he had put the casing of the bullet, he had a tree that he pushed them in. I don't remember where the last time how many they counted, but the boys used to go with him sometimes. They'd say, "Well Pa's got so many by this time," or whatever.

And then I remember one time, my nephew used to live with us. But he went away to Flandreau that one year. He was about sixteen I guess. He got off the train that night, coming for like vacation. He had a nice little white shirt on and everything. Kind of dressed up. Came over to the house and he—"Where's Grandpa?" And I said, "Well he's out in the woods." His usual place at night.

And he took off and went across the fields and out in the woods, where my dad was, and my dad had just shot a deer. And that crazy kid, he helped him clean it out, because they'd always bury the things back in the woods. And he picks up the deer and puts it around his shoulder. White shirt or not, he didn't care! He was so glad to see everybody. He come home and says, "Grandpa shot this just for me!" He was just so happy. Because whenever you went away to school, I mean it was always kind of sad, but . . . you knew you were going to come home eventually, but . . . it was still sad. Even yet I think about it, different times. Even going up here to the boarding school, because we couldn't come home all the time, just maybe once a month, if we were lucky.

But sometimes folks'd come up to visit us. And then like during the winter, a lot of times, my mom and dad would go to church with the wagon. And then after church we'd all pile on the sleigh or the wagon, and then dad would take us back up to school.

*   *   *

Over on Sand Lake there was Salts, and old man Corn and his wife, Waashkwoshinokwe,[9] they called her. And then there's another family back in here [gestures north of her house], I can't think of what their Indian name was, but they were Martens. And then over across on the other end of Sand Lake there was Jack and Mary Patterson. And later Evelyn and Bob McArthur. That's Genevieve's grandma, Genevieve—she works at the Elderly [Center]—Rangell . . . and Kenoshas.

My dad used to have a sugar camp, down, you go down the track by Sugarbush Lake, back in there. That road that goes around there now is close to where his camp was.

He'd go out early in the morning, and I went out there a lot of times with him. Even after I was grown, married, and everything, I was home and couple winters and I went with him and helped him pack sap. It's really a lot of work. We just came in all the time, we never—he would usually cook until dark a lot of times, and then he'd just come home. Walking on the track. I told you he only had one arm, and he'd fixed himself sort of a yoke thing that he could carry two buckets.

He used that a lot here like when the pump would give out by the barn, he'd carry it from the house over there to the barn for the trough for the horses or cows. And then he'd use that same yoke thing to carry the syrup in at night. And I know a couple times he was so tired he was just all in, he cut across from the track to a neighbor down here, close to where you are [on Pokegama Lake Trail]. He asked him if he would bring him home because he just couldn't walk any more.

And then when you're in the sugar camp, usually you have a set trail. You know, and they have all these spiles on the trees and the cans hanging on them. Because I helped Dave a couple times, too, when he had his sugarbush over on [Highway] 47 there. You make like a circle, you go around, and you hit all these trees. You go way to the back first and walk this way with your buckets, you know. You empty the little—usually we use like gallon cans like coffee cans or number ten cans from the—we always had a whole bunch of them. You just poke a hole in the, put a nail and nail it to the tree, then fix this spile so that it comes right into the can.

We'd have to go and empty that sap into the buckets, and then you bring the buckets in and try to walk with, with two buckets! [laughs] Then certain times when, you know it's getting time

---

9 According to Joe Chosa this may be a variant pronunciation of Wishkoshinokwe, "Whistling Wind Woman."

to quit, then the snow gets kind of honeycombed. You'd be walking along and down you go—it's funny, but yet it's hard work too. That's the way they always did it, so . . . and I think a lot of people still do.

I know Dave had that sugarcamp over there, it was closer, in a way, but we did it just the same as my Dad had always done.

A long time ago the men would cut them [the spiles] from wood, you know they would carve them, you know like that. But they got them now so that they're metal. I suppose aluminum. Anyway they have a little hook on them like that, you put it, you put the spile in the tree, and it drips down like that and drips into the bucket, or the can.

Usually Dad would boil it down to syrup and then bring it in, and my ma would make sugar or sugar cakes. But sometimes you know like when we were younger, we'd stay out there all day. And my mom would even be with us a lot of times. And then just for a treat, he'd take one small pot and cook it down faster and get it to a certain stage, and you just make, you take a bunch of snow and build it like that tight [forms a cone with her hands], and then you kind of hollow out little round places, and you pour that syrup in there and it hardens. And then a lot of times if it isn't cooked enough, it ends up kind of like taffy. But when she'd make it here, she always used little fancy muffin tins. I've got one of her tins yet, a little round one. But now they make real fancy ones, I've seen a lot of people that are selling maple syrup candy, and they're like stars, maple leaves, stuff like that, the more modern ones.

Lac Du Flambeau Oral History Project Interview Questions

1. Background history: (first and last names)

    a. Do you have an Indian name?
        What does it mean?
        Do you know who gave it to you?
        Why were you given this name?

    b. What is your father's name?
        What is your mother's name?

    c. What is your grandfather's name of your father's side?
        What is your grandmother's name on your father's side?

    d. What is your grandfather's name on your mother's side?
        What is your grandmother's name on your father's side?

    e. Do you remember any of your great grandparents?

    f. Where did your family originally come from?

    g. Do you know how your parents met?

    h. Who are your brothers and sisters?

2. When were you born? Where?

3. How long did you live where you are now?
        a. Where did you move from?
        b. Why did you move?

4. Name your immediate family members (children).

5. What do you remember about your childhood?

6. Who had the most influence on your life while growing up? Aunts, uncles, parents, or other?

7. What school did you attend? Dates? Locations?

8. What kind of classes did you take?

9. Do you remember your classmates? Who were they?

10. What kind of work did your parents do?

11. Were any of your family members in the military?

12. Has Lac du Flambeau changed? How has it changed? Describe the changes.

13. What changes have you seen in your lifetime on the reservation?

14. How did people make their living?

15. How were holidays celebrated?

16. What celebrations or ceremonies do you remember? Do you remember any that no longer continue?

17. What do you remember about the Depression years?

18. What kinds of songs did they sing when you were a teenager?

19. What did families do for recreation?

20. What do you remember hearing about Strawberry Island, or any other places of sacred, historical or cultural significance on the reservation?

21. What advice would you give to a young person who wants to live a good life?

Bibliography

Bieder, Robert E. *Native American Communities in Wisconsin 1600–1960* (Madison: The University of Wisconsin Press, 1995).

Bokern, James. "History and the Primary Canoe Routes of the Six Bands of Chippewa from the Lac du Flambeau District." Master's thesis, University of Wisconsin–Stevens Point, 1987.

Bresette, Walt and Rick Whaley. *Walleye Warriors: The Chippewa Treaty Rights Story* (Warner, NH: Tongues of Green Fires Press, 1994)

Danziger, Edmund J. *The Chippewas of Lake Superior* (Norman: University of Oklahoma Press, 1978).

Densmore, Frances. *Chippewa Customs*. Reprint ed. (St. Paul: Minnesota Historical Society, 1979).

Great Lakes Indian Fish and Wildlife Commission GLIFWC, PO Box 9 Odanah, WI 54861
"Annual Treaty Fishing Statistics"
"1989 Chippewa Spearing Season-Separating Myth from Fact"
"1991 Guide to Understanding Chippewa Treaty Rights,"
Masinaigan (newspaper) January/February 1990

Goc, Michael J., ed., *Reflections of Lac du Flambeau, Wisconsin 1745–1995* (Friendship, WI: New Past Press, 1995).

Hickerson, Harold. *The Chippewa and their Neighbors: A Study in Ethnohistory* (Prospect Heights, IL: Waveland Press, Inc., 1988).

Lac du Flambeau Band of Lake Superior Chippewa Indians, Waaswaaganing Ojibwemowin, Lac du Flambeau Ojibwe Language Department

Waaswaaganing Ojibwemowin: Ojibwe Language Manual (1992).

Iskigamizigeyaang geyaabi omaa Waaswaaganing [We still boil down here at Lac du Flambeau] Videotape (2002).

Manoominikewin omaa Waaswaaganing [Wild Rice Making here at Lac du Flambeau] Videotape (2002).

Akwaawaawin omaa Waaswaaganing [Spearing Through the Ice here at Lac du Flambeau] Videotape (2003).

Nesper, Larry. *The Walleye War: The Struggle for Ojibwe Spearfishing and Treaty Rights* (Lincoln: University of Nebraska Press, 2002).

Nichols, John, ed., *Statement Made by the Indians: A Bilingual Petition of the Chippewa of Lake Superior, 1864* (London, ON: Centre for Research & Teaching, 1988).

Styles, Cindy M. *National Register of Historic Places Registration Form: Lac du Flambeau Bureau of Indian Affairs Boarding School* (Lac du Flambeau: Lac du Flambeau Historic Preservation Office, 2002).

Vennum, Thomas Jr. *American Indian Lacrosse: Little Brother of War* (Washington, DC: Smithsonian Institution Press, 1994).

_____. *Ojibwa Dance Drum: Its History and Construction* (Washington, DC: Smithsonian Institution Press, 1983).

Warren, William W. *History of the Ojibwe People*. Reprint ed. (St. Paul: Minnesota Historical Society Press, 1984).

Wrone, David R, and Nelson, Russell S. *Who's the Savage: The Documentary History of the Mistreatment of the Native Americans*. Rev. ed. (Malabar, FL: Krieger Publishing Company, 1982).